A VISUAL CRUISING
GUIDE TO THE
SOUTHERN
NEW ENGLAND COAST

A VISUAL CRUISING GUIDE TO THE

SOUTHERN NEW ENGLAND COAST

New London, CT, to Portsmouth, NH

JAMES L. BILDNER

International Marine / McGraw-Hill

CAMDEN, MAINE ▪ NEW YORK ▪ CHICAGO ▪ SAN FRANCISCO ▪ LISBON ▪ LONDON
MADRID ▪ MEXICO CITY ▪ MILAN ▪ NEW DELHI ▪ SAN JUAN ▪ SEOUL
SINGAPORE ▪ SYDNEY ▪ TORONTO

Fishers Island East Harbor (page 37).

The McGraw·Hill Companies

Published by International Marine

1 2 3 4 5 6 7 8 9 QPD QPD 3 2 1 0 9

© 2010 James L. Bildner

Library of Congress Cataloging-in-Publication Data
may be obtained from the Library of Congress

Questions regarding the content of this book should
be addressed to:
www.internationalmarine.com

ISBN 978-0-07-148919-5
MHID 0-07-148919-3

Questions regarding the ordering of this book should
be addressed to:
The McGraw-Hill Companies
Customer Service Department
P.O. Box 547
Blacklick, OH 43004
Retail customers: 1-800-262-4729
Bookstores: 1-800-722-4726

Photographs by Jim Bildner and Roger Brul.

NOTICE: The information, charts, and illustrations contained in this book are not for navigational purposes. None of the material in this book is intended to replace any government-issued navigational charts or other government publications (including Notices to Mariners) for up-to-date information regarding changes, additions, and deletions to existing navigational materials. All material in this book is subject to change at any time. The author and publisher do not guarantee nor warrant that the information in this book is complete, correct, or current. The author and publisher shall not be liable to any user of the book for any loss or injury allegedly caused, in whole or in part, by relying on information contained in this book.

Great Point Lighthouse on Nantucket (see page 154).

To Nancy and Lizzie, who, more than ever, continue to fill my life with joy, happiness, and love and remind me what really matters.

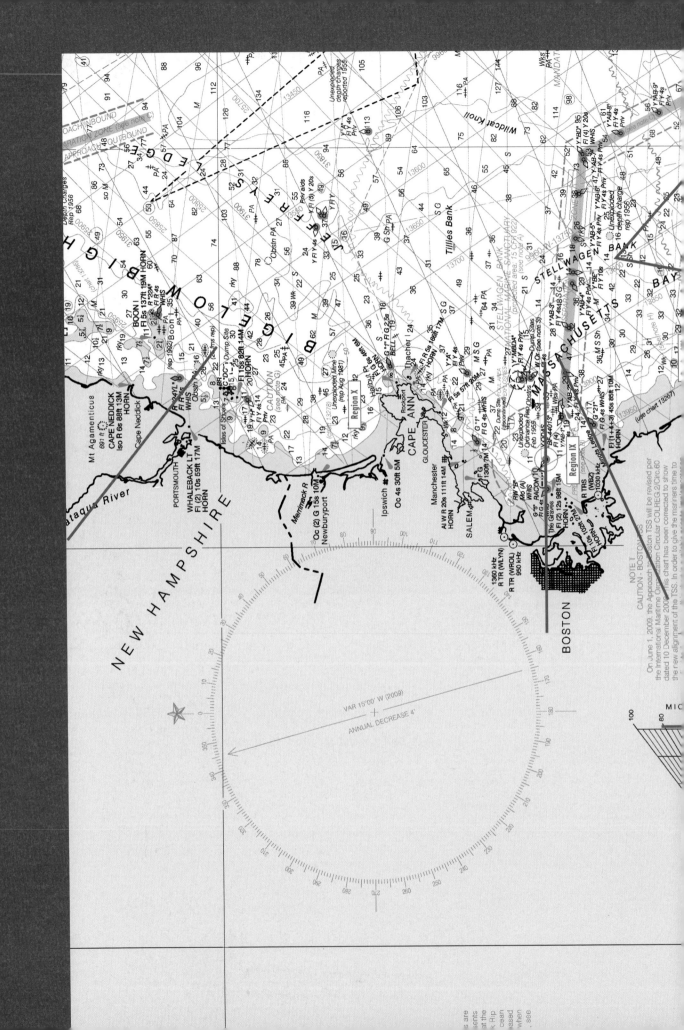

CONTENTS

INTRODUCTION

As I write this in June 2009, it has been less than a week since we made our last flight over the coast of New England to shoot photos for this book. Lifting off from Massachusetts' North Shore on a beautiful day, we made our way first to the rugged, offshore Isles of Shoals, then down the coasts of New Hampshire and Plum Island Sound. After flying over Cape Ann and historic Marblehead, we headed for Boston. From 30 nautical miles out and 700 feet above sea level, Boston stands like a latterday city of Oz, its downtown high-rise buildings framed by surrounding water. Continuing south, we passed over Plymouth, where the Pilgrims landed in 1620, then overflew the Cape Cod Canal and Cape Cod itself, with its endless nooks and harbors. Then we headed offshore to reconnoiter with majestic Martha's Vineyard, remote Nantucket, and the storied Elizabeth Islands.

From there we crossed over Buzzards Bay and flew south over New Bedford and South Dartmouth, Massachusetts, to the Sakonnet River, Narragansett Bay, Newport, and Point Judith—being struck yet again by Rhode Island's multitude of inland passages that afford a cruiser unlimited opportunity to explore and to find shelter.

As a last hurrah we headed offshore again to fly over Block Island, circling over the Great Salt Pond, with Montauk, Long Island, spread out just a few miles to the south. Then we flew shoreward once more to touch the Connecticut coast along the eastern end of Long Island Sound—shooting photos of Mystic, New London, Stonington, and Fishers Island—before returning home.

To see the New England coast close up is the dream of any cruiser, a dream we share and have been fortunate to realize countless times over the decades from the deck of our boat. To see it from a few hundred feet in the air is equally inspiring, and I feel lucky indeed to have been able to do so many times while researching and writing this book.

Putting together our previous book, *A Visual Cruising Guide to the Maine Coast*, was an act of pure joy despite the work it entailed, and compiling this new book has been no less so. The sheer size of the coast and islands of southern New England exceeds what any one book like this can cover, so we have included the ports, harbors, and islands that best represent the flavor of this remarkable region, together with a selection of lesser-known and less crowded gems. We've focused above all on those harbors and passages that called the loudest for an aerial photographic treatment. In each harbor, one or more photos depict the recommended approach and the navigation aids that will help you relate your position to the photographic angle and view. Next to the photograph is a segment of the corresponding navigation chart for convenient reference and orientation. Last, we provide pilotage notes based on our own observations. We mention the presence or absence of marine and shoreside facilities but do not provide detail, as this book is intended to augment—not replace—the fine cruising guides that exist for this region.

Our hope is that this book will encourage you to explore New England's varied coastline and perhaps to discover new harbors, anchorages, and passages to which you'll return again and again. One thing is sure: There is no lack of inviting destinations on the New England coast.

After more than three decades of sailing and exploring these waters, each cruise still feels as new and adventurous to us as the first one, and each season gives us new stories to share with friends and fellow cruisers during the cold New England winter. People often ask what has changed over thirty years, and our answer is always the same—nothing and everything. At 55, I see these waters through a different lens, but the water, if anything, seems bluer, the anchorages more stunning, and the stars at night closer. And when it comes to sailing and navigation, these waters still provide excitement—sometimes too much for Nancy's taste—and great peace.

As with our previous book, this project would not have come to fruition without the countless hours of painstaking work that my fantastic assistant, Abby Crocker, contributed over the better part of a year. She was pregnant while working on our Maine guide, and that was tough, but now her twins have turned four—and that might be even tougher. But the kids are now out on the water during the summer, and I have no doubt that they will someday be sailing with this book in hand.

My thanks and appreciation go out as well to my friend and fellow pilot, Roger Brul, who has traveled with me on this voyage as he did on the Maine one. And my sincere thanks and gratitude go to my editor, Jonathan Eaton, whose great talent and attention to detail are ever present throughout this book, and to Molly Mulhern, the book's artistic designer, who made sure the photographs came to life and all the pieces work together. Finally, my thanks go to the "kitchen cabinet" of reviewers we consulted along the way.

Use this book to find your own special anchorages, whether during the long winter, when daydreams guide the finest passages, or during the summer when the deck moves beneath you and the salty tang of the surrounding ocean makes your senses come alive.

We'll see you out there.

Looking south down the Sakonnet River toward Sakonnet Harbor (page 94).

A Few Notes on Using This Guide

This book is intended to supplement a set of up-to-date charts, tide tables, and other navigation aids. It is by no means intended to replace them. This book is also intended to be used in conjunction with—not instead of—any of the existing New England cruising guides. The photos within this book do, however, provide a perspective of the New England coast that is not available from any other printed resource or navigation tool.

Here's how the book works: One or more arrowhead icons have been added to most charts within this book. The arrows (and their numbers if more than one on a chart) correspond to the location the photo was shot from, looking in the direction of the arrowhead. The icons are intended to give the reader a quick understanding of how each photo relates to the chart, and how both the photos and charts relate to what you're seeing from the helm. Again, the placement of the icons is approximate.

For your further guidance, we've overprinted key buoys on several aerial photos, often with a recommended track to follow. (There are many buoys that we did not add to the photos; we chose only the most useful approach buoys.) These buoy and track locations are likewise approximate. Be sure to use your own navigation tools and wits to determine your position, course, and intended destination. Nothing replaces good common sense.

The text provides further clues and instructions on how to enter each harbor and navigate the passageways. Please note that steering directions within the text are *general* directions—mostly cardinal and intercardinal compass points. They are not intended as actual courses to steer. They are expressed for the most part with reference to the *true* compass rose, and with no regard to magnetic variation.

It's also important to note that the waters covered by this book include many thoroughfares, narrows, and passages. As such, it is possible for a navigator to enter a waterway from two directions, *both* of which seem to be coming from sea, or at least open water. Obviously the buoys cannot be arranged to follow the "red-right-returning" maxim from both directions. The rule of thumb for intracoastal passageways is that as you move clockwise around the continental United States, red is to starboard. But given the complexity of some of these passages, even this doesn't cover all situations. The book proceeds generally from southwest to northeast, moving "up" the coast as would a navigator approaching from the south. From this approach, many of the thoroughfares will be entered with green to starboard. Pay close attention to your charts.

These waters of New England are constantly changing—just ask anyone who has sailed off the coast of Martha's Vineyard or Nantucket—and so are navigational aids that mark them. Be sure to use the most up-to-date NOAA charts (and/or their digital counterparts) when underway. Remember, too, that tides and currents play a critical role in navigating these waters. The range of the tides generally increases as you cruise farther east, but tidal currents depend on local geography and are a lot more variable. Finally, weather and astronomical conditions can quickly make a seemingly easy daysail seem like the Sydney–Hobart race. Know your tides and currents well.

This book couldn't possibly cover every harbor or anchorage along New England's variegated coastline. We have included most of the ones that are considered the core jewels of these waters, but there are many more within your reach. Take the time to explore the land and waters around you—they won't disappoint.

Finally, a note on the chart segments in these pages: We've labeled each one with chart number, edition, and scale to make it easier for you to select appropriate charts. But in adapting the chart segments to these pages, we've often had to enlarge or reduce them. Thus, the scale shown is the scale of the original NOAA chart but not necessarily the scale of the chart segment in this book.

Bristol Harbor (page 86).

REGION I

13205
38th ed., Feb. 07
NAD 83
Soundings in feet
1:80,000

New London is less than 30 nautical miles west of Point Judith, but any passage between the two is complicated by the lack of an anchorage along the 14-mile coast between Fishers Island Sound and Point Judith, and by the strong tidal currents and treacherous shoals and rocks that separate Long Island Sound from Block Island Sound. Some 110 miles long and 21 miles wide at its widest, Long Island Sound communicates with the Atlantic Ocean through the East River and New York Harbor at its western end and through Plum (Island) Gut, The Race, and Fishers Island Sound at its eastern end. Through these constricted openings must pour enough seawater to fill the sound on every rising tide and empty it on every falling tide.

The results are dramatic. The flood through Plum Gut—the southwestern-most of the sound's eastern openings—averages 3.5 knots, while the ebb averages 4 knots, strong enough to set up standing waves when opposed by the wind. Between Little Gull Island (off Plum Island) and Race Point on Fishers Island to the northeast is the noto-

Eastern Long Island and Fishers Island Sound
—New London, CT, to Point Judith, RI, including Block Island—

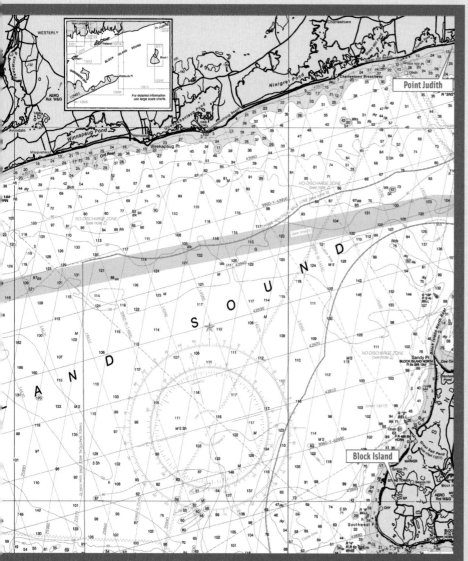

angle across rather than flowing through the passes. Of the five passes, only Watch Hill Passage, Sugar Reef Passage, and Lords Passage are recommended to boaters lacking local knowledge.

Navigation between New London and Point Judith is further complicated by the busy traffic that characterizes these waters. Cruising sailors and powerboaters, racers, picnickers, anglers working the rips for bluefish and stripers (The Race is famous for its rich sportfisheries), tug-and-barge traffic between Boston and New York, ferries crossing the sound or plying between New London and Block Island, lobsterboats, commercial fishing vessels, and Navy and Coast Guard vessels operating out of New London and Groton all converge along this coast. It is not unusual to see a submarine heading to or from the submarine base located in Groton.

Still, these waters offer a magical feel and a unique combination of delights, including Mystic Seaport; the commodious, breakwater-protected harbor of Stonington; the dunes and beaches of Napatree Point; the sheltered shoal-draft waterways of Little Narragansett Bay, the Pawcatuck River, and Point Judith Pond; and offshore, the legendary yachtsman's destination of Block Island. If you are eastbound, this is a chance to breathe deeply of sweet, cool air from the Atlantic and to enjoy the transition from the urban bustle of New York and the harbors of central and western Long Island Sound to the more open waters ahead. You will also enjoy more dependable breezes—a welcome relief from the often windless summer days of the western sound.

rious 4-mile-wide main opening, The Race, with currents that range from 2.5 to 6 knots on ebb and flood and are characterized by strong rips, boiling eddies, and—when the current sets through a strongly opposing wind or sea—steep seas. The half-hour slacks at high and low water are the best times to transit The Race.

The third opening, at the eastern extreme of Fishers Island Sound, offers a choice of five passes through the rocks east of Fishers Island. Tidal currents average about 2 knots through all five passes and, unhelpfully, tend to

However you choose to spend your time in this area, make sure you allow enough time to experience the full range, diversity, and beauty of its offerings.

■ NEW LONDON ■

FACING its sister town of Groton across the mouth of the Thames River, New London commands the northeastern corner of Long Island Sound. This is one of the primary yachting sites between New York and Boston. If you are approaching from the west or south, shape your course to leave Bartlett Reef and the 35-foot light on its southern end, Little Goshen Reef, Goshen Ledge, and green-and-red can "R" marking Rapid Rock to port, then carry a northerly heading between flashing green "1" and flashing red "2" at the mouth of the New London Harbor Channel. Be sure to account for the strong tidal currents that sweep this area, especially if you are navigating at night.

When approaching from Fishers Island Sound to the east, you have the option of following Pine Island Channel to the north of Black Ledge, then entering the harbor channel north of its mouth.

The Thames River is a bustling commercial and military port. Ferries run to and from Long Island, and there is always activity around the Coast Guard Academy, on the New London shore of the river, and the naval submarine base on the Groton shore. Your chart will show you the locations of anchorage areas reserved for Navy and Coast Guard vessels and also the security perimeter around the sub base, which you must stay outside. But the channel is deep, well marked, and well maintained,

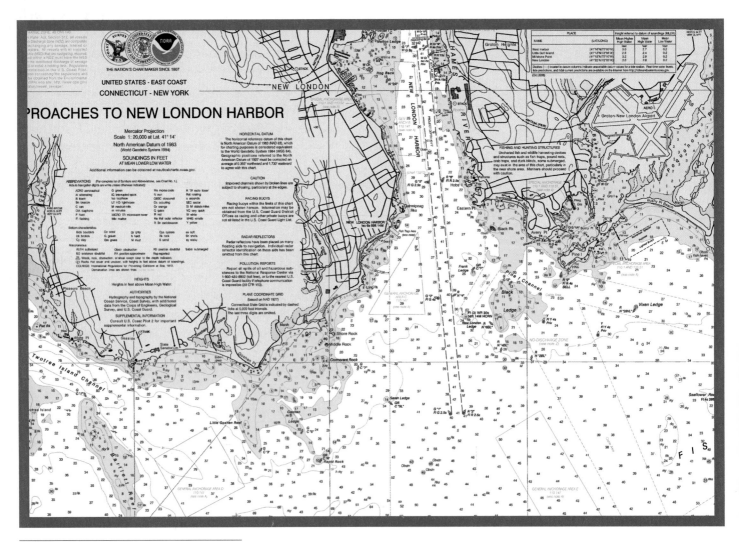

13212 , 38th ed., Nov. 08, NAD 83, Soundings in feet, 1:20,000

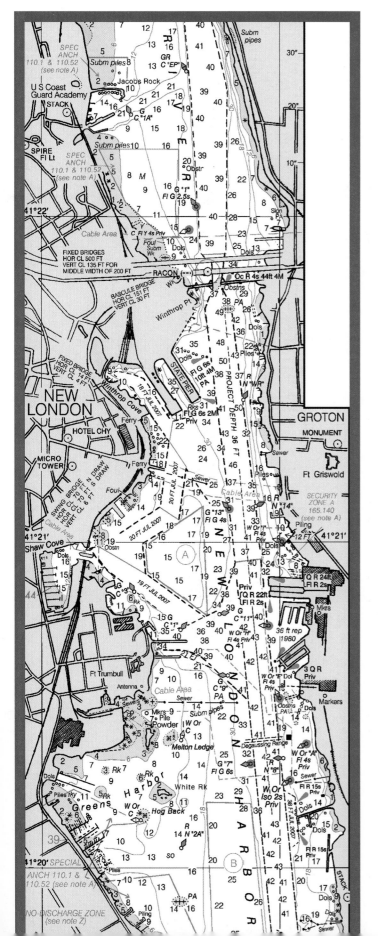

and there is ample depth west of the dredged fairway for small craft intent on avoiding close encounters with ships.

Greens Harbor (see photo page 19) provides the seawardmost and also the best Thames River anchorage and mooring access, though it can be crowded with boats in midsummer. Marina dockage is available in Shaw Cove as well as Greens Harbor. Indeed, marinas abound, and every conceivable yachting need can be satisfied in New London. This old industrial city has restored its attractive waterfront.

As home to the USS *Nautilus* Memorial/Submarine Force Library and Museum, the U.S. Coast Guard Academy, Connecticut College with its surrounding 750-acre arboretum, numerous parks, public beaches, and a wide range of shops, museums, and ethnic restaurants, New London and Groton provide an almost unlimited number of things to do, making a visit well worthwhile. If you're lucky you might see the square-rigged training vessel *Eagle* arriving or departing, perhaps even with middies standing at attention on its yardarms.

Cruisers wishing to avoid the intense traffic of New London Harbor or looking for a transient spot near the coastwise route may find an attractive alternative in the cove east of Avery Point and north of Pine Island (see chart page 18), at the combined mouth of Baker Cove and the Poquonock River (both of which are too shallow for cruisers). The cove provides moorings and some limited anchorage possibilities, though the holding is poor. The presence of the Groton–New London Airport's main runway on the shore nearby may mean that your night's stay is not a quiet one.

12372
38th ed., Nov. 06
NAD 83
Soundings in feet
1:40,000

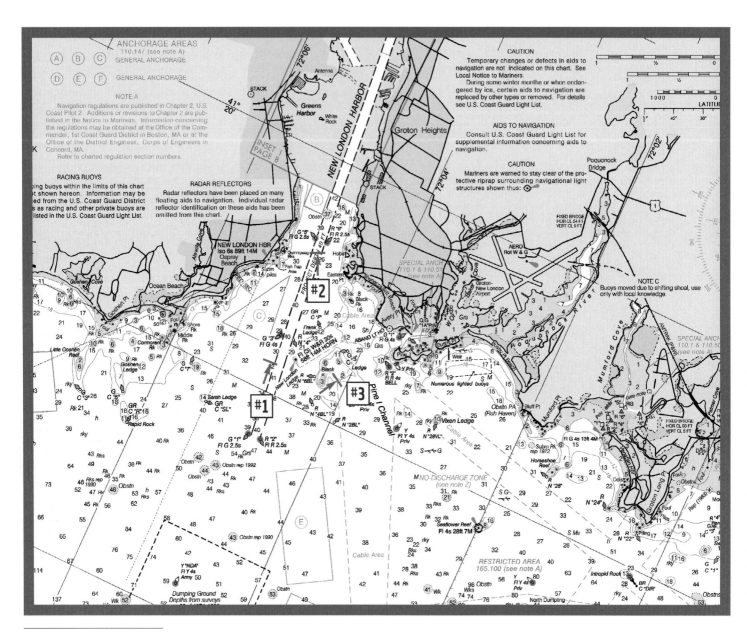

12372
38th ed., Nov. 06
NAD 83
Soundings in feet
1:40,000

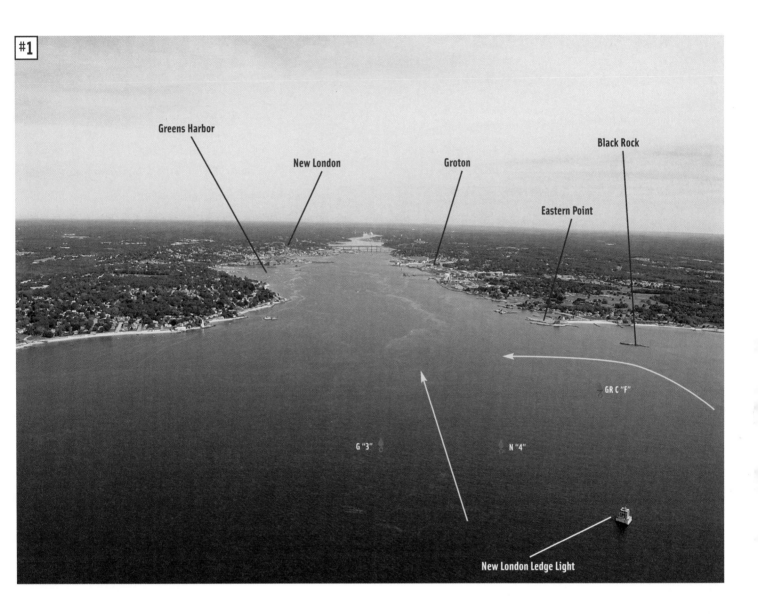

#1

Greens Harbor

New London

Groton

Black Rock

Eastern Point

GR C "F"

G "3"

N "4"

New London Ledge Light

#3

Avery Point

Baker Cove

Poquonock River

Pine Island

R "2" BELL

C "3"

■ THE MYSTIC REGION ■

A BOATER turning east after leaving the Thames River immediately approaches the western end of Fishers Island Sound. Seaflower Reef stands guard over the western approach, and a half-mile to its southeast are the islets of North Dumpling, South Dumpling, and Flat Hammock. Behind them lies the entrance to West Har-

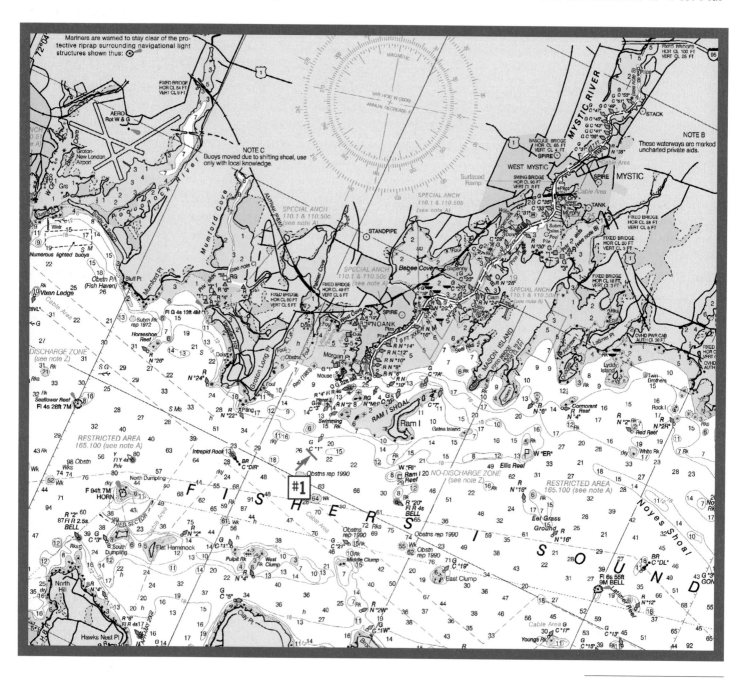

12372
38th ed., Nov. 06
NAD 83
Soundings in feet
1:40,000

bor on Fishers Island. The U.S. Coast Pilot describes Fishers Island Sound as "exceedingly treacherous, characterized by boulder patches which rise abruptly from deep water." In *The Thousand Dollar Yacht,* a delightful memoir of sailing out of Stonington in the 1960s in a decked-over sailing dory, Anthony Bailey acknowledges that the currents "are fierce, especially for a section that does not have a great rise and fall of tide, and lobster pot buoys are now and then dragged under." He goes on to say that the Coast Pilot "is perhaps right in proclaiming the dangers of the sound, but it remains a glorious place to sail." Fishers Island Sound belongs more to Block Island Sound than Long Island Sound, he asserts, for it "partakes of the swell and the open sea.... In Fishers the summer breezes are salty. Even on calm July afternoons one can successfully whistle for a wind."

The 94-foot-high lighthouse on North Dumpling (a square house with light tower) is the most obvious marker in the western sound, and some 2½ miles northeast of it lies the Mystic River entrance. Defined by Ram Island to the south, Mason Island to the east, and the Noank peninsula to the west, the Greater Mystic Har-

bor area is a must stop, home to countless marinas, moorings, restaurants, and stores and the much-loved Mystic Seaport Museum, the largest maritime museum in the country, which reserves a dock for visiting mariners.

From North Dumpling, a northeasterly course will take you to black-and-red can buoy "DIR" (Danger Intrepid Rock—see chart page 24), marking the 13-foot spot of Intrepid Rock. From there, continue northeast to green can "1," leaving it to port, then turn north to pass between green can "3" and red nun "2" off Swimming Rock, to the west of Ram Island Shoal. Proceed north to lighted red buoy "4" (flashing red 4 seconds) marking Whale Rock, leaving it close aboard to starboard. (It's important to follow the channel closely as you make your way past Ram Island, as numerous hazards sit just inside these markers.) Turn northeast to leave red-and-green nun "MH" to starboard, then turn northwest to enter the final approach channel east of Morgan Point, between nun "6" to starboard and quick-flashing green mark "5" to port. Follow the series of nuns marking the channel along the Noank shore into

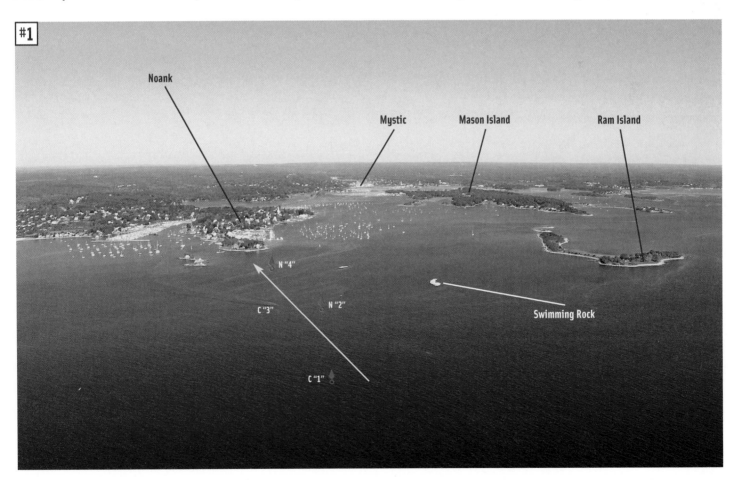

the inner parts of Mystic Harbor. As of this writing, the channel depths are greater than 10 feet.

Thanks to an abundance of marina slips and moorings, it is surprisingly easy to get an overnight berth here, especially nearer the mouth of the river. Room to anchor is harder to come by.

Though it will seem as though the channel winds and twists endlessly, a trip up the full navigable extent of Mystic River to see the many sights along the way is well worthwhile. As the channel continues along the west side of Mason Island, past Sixpenny Island and then Willow Point on the western shore, Mystic's bustling downtown comes into view. Unless your boat can squeeze under an 8- to 10-foot vertical clearance (depending on the tide), you'll have to wait for the Am-

trak railroad bridge here to swing open. The bridge tender monitors VHF Channel 13.

Mystic Seaport Museum is a mile or so above the railroad bridge, tucked along the eastern shore of the river near the head of navigation. Occupying more than 40 acres and 100 buildings, the Seaport maintains the square-rigged whaling vessel *Charles W. Morgan*, the square-rigged *Joseph Conrad*, the Grand Banks fishing schooner *L.A. Dunton*, the schooner *Brilliant*, and other wooden boats large and small as well as a planetarium, boatbuilding programs, art collections, and a marine library. Just north of the Seaport is the Mystic Marine Life Aquarium, displaying over 6,000 specimens of marine life in over 40 exhibits.

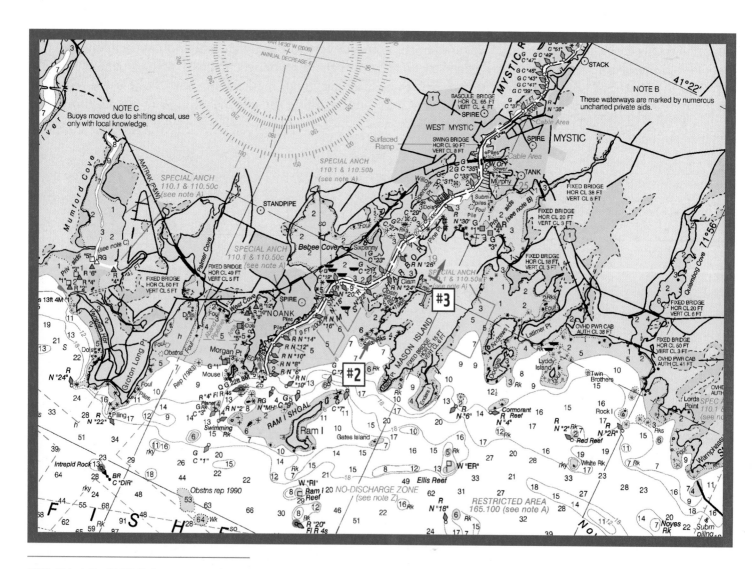

12372 , 38th ed., Nov. 06, NAD 83, Soundings in feet, 1:40,000

#2

Sixpenny Island

Mason Island

C "21"

C "23"

N "24"

N "22"

#3

Mystic Shipyard

Swing Bridge

Mystic Seaport Museum

Governor Marina

Mystic River Marina

Masons Island Marina

■ APPROACHES TO STONINGTON AND LITTLE NARRAGANSETT BAY ■

FROM the eastern end of Fishers Island Sound, the best approach to Stonington (or the entrance to Little Narragansett Bay), leaves 46-foot-tall flashing red light "4" on the western end of the outer (Middle Ground) breakwater to starboard. From there, a due northerly course will take you into Stonington Harbor, leaving 31-foot flashing green light "5" at the eastern end of the west (Wamphassuc Point) breakwater to port. Alternatively, to head into the circuitous entrance of Little Narragansett Bay, you can follow a northeasterly course from the Middle Ground breakwater, leaving flashing red buoy "2" (Academy Rock) and red nun "4" to starboard (keeping west of the 4-foot spot between nuns "2" and "4"). (See additional chart on page 28.)

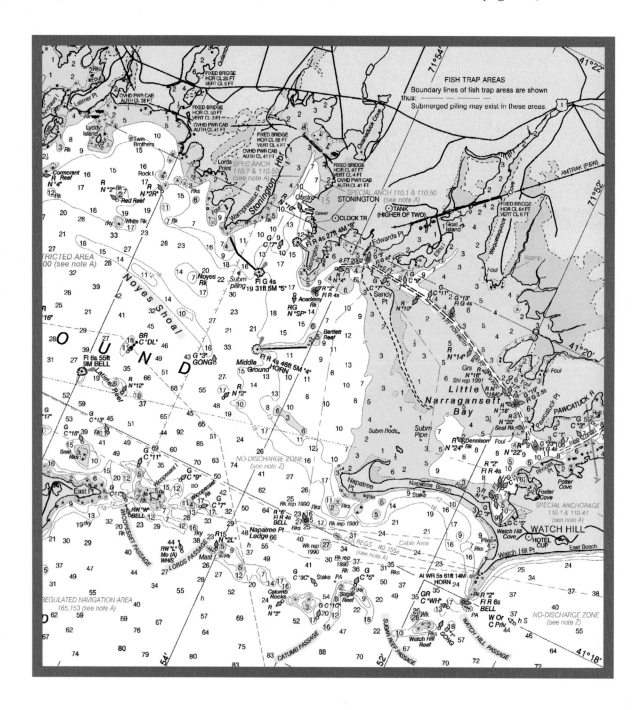

#1 (See page 28.)

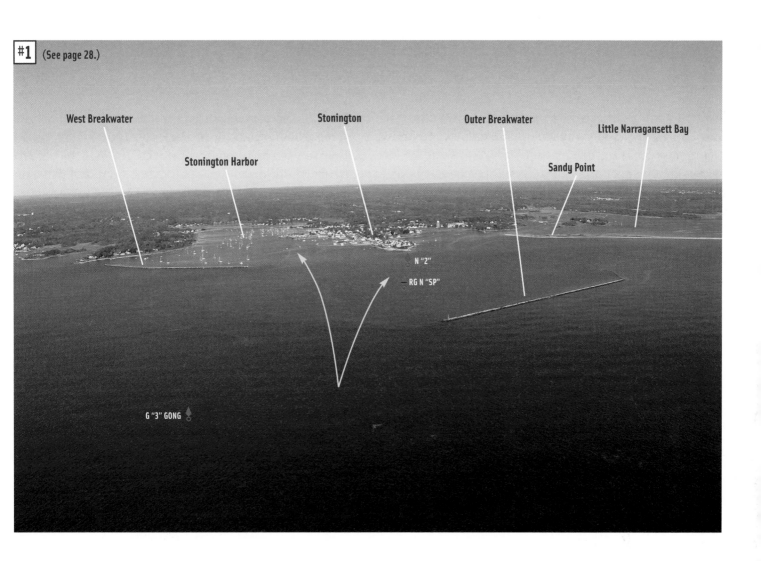

West Breakwater

Stonington Harbor

Stonington

Outer Breakwater

Little Narragansett Bay

Sandy Point

N "2"

RG N "SP"

G "3" GONG

12372
38th ed., Nov. 06
NAD 83
Soundings in feet
1:40,000

■ STONINGTON ■

DUE to the charms of the picturesque town, the harbor's easy entry and room for anchoring, its proximity to popular cruising destinations, as well as the breakwaters that protect it, Stonington has become a favorite stopover for cruisers. As the photo indicates, there is ample anchorage both inside the west breakwater—though this area is exposed to easterlies—and in the anchorage areas designated on the chart. The anchorage at the harbor's northeast corner is likely to be crowded with local boats, however. You may be able to get a berth on this shore at Dodson's Boatyard. Also on the eastern shore, nearer the mouth of the harbor, is the Wadawanuck Yacht Club with its active members and launch service.

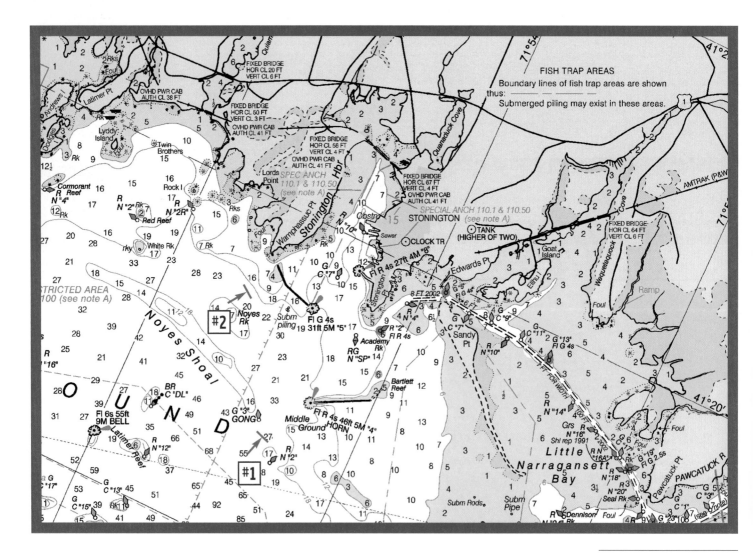

12372
38th ed., Nov. 06
NAD 83
Soundings in feet
1:40,000

#2

Wamphassuc Point   Stonington   Little Narragansett Bay

■ LITTLE NARRAGANSETT BAY ■

THOUGH often skipped by cruisers who judge it a shallow backwater distraction from the deeper waters just to its south, Little Narragansett Bay is a hidden gem for shoal-draft boats. Make the approach east of Stonington Point as described above, arriving at the western end of the dredged channel around Sandy Point, which has a controlling depth of 7 feet as of this writing. From the northern edge of Sandy Point, the channel continues southeasterly to the tip of Pawcatuck Point and the mouth of the Pawcatuck River. As our photos suggest, Little Narragansett Bay is prone to shoaling, and it's easy to miss the buoys and encounter the hazards. This excursion, though delightful, should only be attempted with up-to-date local knowledge and good weather.

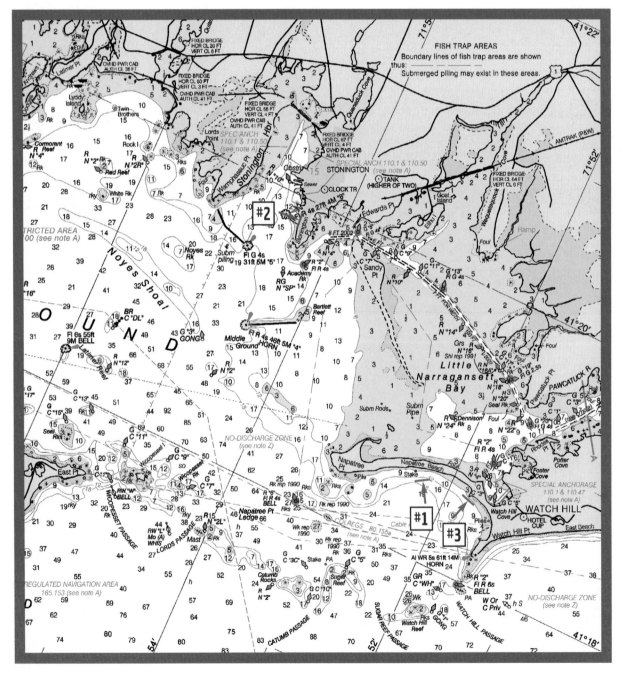

12372
38th ed., Nov. 06
NAD 83
Soundings in feet
1:40,000

#1

Napatree Point

Mystic

Stonington

Sandy Point

Little Narragansett Bay

#2

Little Narragansett Bay

Sandy Point

C "7"

G "5"

N "4"

Stonington Point

#3

Pawcatuck Point — Pawcatuck River — Colonel Willie Cove

C "3"
C "1"
N "20" — N "22" — G "23"
R "2" — C "1"
N "4" — C "3"

Napatree Beach — Watch Hill Cove

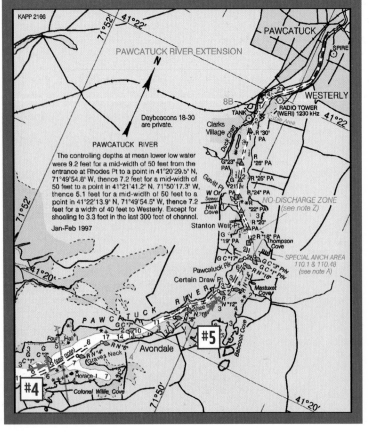

KAPP 2166

PAWCATUCK

71°52' 41°22'

PAWCATUCK RIVER EXTENSION

SPIRE

WESTERLY 41°22'

8B

Daybeacons 18-30
are private.

RADIO TOWER
(WERI) 1230 kHz
Cable Area

TANK

Clarks
Village

Duck Chan

R "30"
PA

PAWCATUCK RIVER

The controlling depths at mean lower low water
were 9.2 feet for a mid-width of 50 feet from the
entrance at Rhodes Pt to a point in 41°20'29.5" N,
71°49'54.8" W, thence 7.2 feet for a mid-width of
50 feet to a point in 41°21'41.2" N, 71°50'17.3" W,
thence 5.1 feet for a mid-width of 50 feet to a
point in 41°22'13.9" N, 71°49'54.5" W, thence 7.2
feet for a width of 40 feet to Westerly. Except for
shoaling to 3.3 feet in the last 300 feet of channel.

Jan-Feb 1997

G "23"
"28" PA
R "26" PA
Gavitt Pt
W Or
Hall
Cove
R "24" PA
"22" PA
Stanton Weir Pt
G
"19" PA
U 2 R "18" PA
Thompson
Cove
G C "17"
C G C "13"
RN "16"
SPECIAL ANCH AREA
110.1 & 110.48
(see note A)
NO-DISCHARGE ZONE
(see note Z)

Pawcatuck Riv
Certain Draw Pt
RN "12"
Mastuxet
Cove
Babcock Cove

#5

P A W C A T U C K   R I V E R

Avondale

Four Mile
Hall
Graves Neck
RN "6"
Horace I
C "3"
Colonel Willie Cove

#4

71°52'
41°20'
71°50'
41°20'

Once having arrived at Pawcatuck Point, you have two or three choices. The first is to leave flashing green buoy "23" to port and head northeasterly up the Pawcatuck River. In a shoal-draft boat you might find a snug anchorage in Colonel Willie Cove, Thompson Cove, or one of the smaller coves along the river, or a berth for the night at one of the river's marinas. The nominal channel depth remains 7 feet at least to Clarks Village, though shoaling may reduce that. Continue upriver to Westerly only with shoal draft and caution, keeping in mind that the river narrows considerably. The hospitable Westerly Yacht Club, in Thompson Cove, may well mark the upriver extent of your voyage.

The second alternative from Pawcatuck Point is to turn south into protected Watch Hill Cove (photo #3 above), which is tucked inside the landward end of

---

12372
38th ed., Nov. 06
NAD 83
Soundings in feet
1:40,000

#4

Pawcatuck River

Graves Neck

Colonel Willie Cove

N "6"

N "4"

C "3"

Napatree Point at the extreme southern end of Little Narragansett Bay. We love this simple and protected spot, which offers warm saltwater swimming on Napatree Beach and is overlooked by the Watch Hill Yacht Club. You may be able to rent a mooring from the club for the night. More adventurous cruisers can run southwest from Pawcatuck Point to find a picnic or overnight anchorage in the lee of Napatree Beach when the wind is from the south. This anchorage becomes hazardous in a northerly, however.

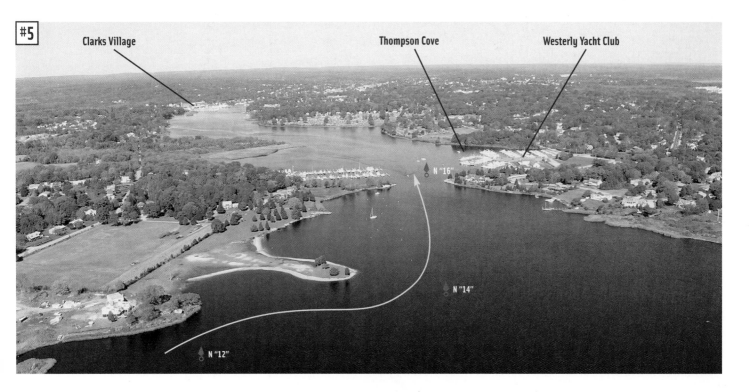

#5

Clarks Village

Thompson Cove

Westerly Yacht Club

N "16"

N "14"

N "12"

■ FISHERS ISLAND HARBORS AND THE EASTERN APPROACHES TO FISHERS ISLAND SOUND ■

DEPARTING or entering the eastern end of Fishers Island Sound, cruisers have a choice of five passages into or from Block Island Sound. When approaching from the east, we usually navigate through Watch Hill Passage or Sugar Reef Passage, though Lords Passage is probably a little more straightforward than Sugar Reef Passage and may also be more convenient if you're approaching from or heading toward Block Island. Any of these is preferable to the other two alternatives, Catumb and Wicopessett Passages, both of which are trickier and less clearly marked. (Wicopessett Passage is sometimes subject to breakers.) The Fishers Island Sound passages provide a more direct approach to Fishers Island from the east than the remaining alternative,

through The Race—and the Fishers Island Sound passages can also be safer when a wind opposes the tide. The Race, however, is easier to navigate at night or in poor visibility due to its relative lack of hazards and its excellent buoys and lights.

After transiting one of the passes from the east, we like to shape our approach to Fishers Island from just south of red flashing bell "6" off Napatree Point. From there we coast along the northern shore of Fishers Island, leaving the green cans off Wicopesset Island, Seal Rocks, and Youngs Rock to port. From there, easy passage can be made into any of Fishers Island's three harbors—East, West, or Hay.

12372, 38th ed., Nov. 06, NAD 83, Soundings in feet, 1:40,000

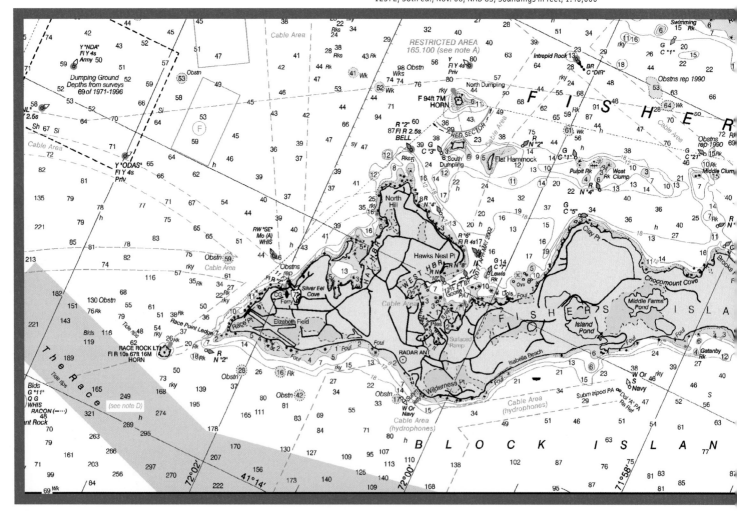

#1

East Harbor

West Harbor

East Point

Latimer Reef Light

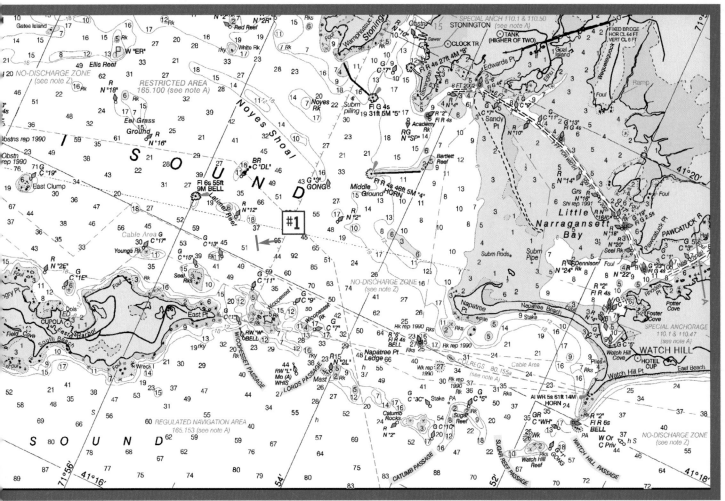

EAST HARBOR

FROM green can "17" off Youngs Rock, a southwest-erly course will take you down the centerline between red nun "2E" and green can "1E." From there, an easterly turn will take you into the deepest water along the southern edge of the harbor. We have found reasonable holding ground over the 10- and 11-foot charted sound-ings there. East Harbor is home to the Fishers Island Club.

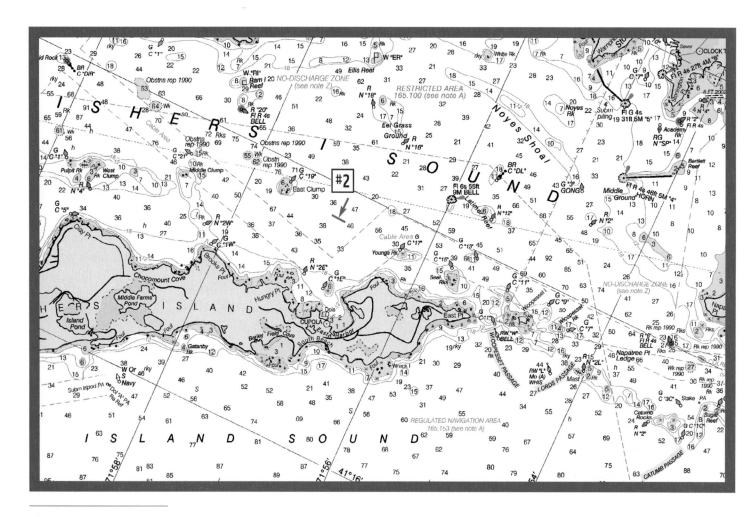

12372
38th ed., Nov. 06
NAD 83
Soundings in feet
1:40,000

#2

East Harbor

Hungry Point

WEST HARBOR

THIS is by far the most popular harbor on Fishers Island, and we include two photos for it. The inner harbor photo shows the shoaling on both sides of the entrance. If approaching from the east, leave can "5" to port and lay your course for flashing red buoy "6" off Hawks Nest Point. From the north, approach between red nun "2" off Flat Hammock and green can "1" off Pulpit Rock. From the west, approach between flashing red bell "2" and can "3" south of South Dumpling. From flashing red buoy "6," nuns mark the dredged channel into the harbor.

Because the harbor is so popular in the summer, space may be limited. The Fishers Island Yacht Club provides launch service and will help as many yachts as possible. If you desire to anchor for the night and space is hard to find, you can anchor in the area south of Goose Island. Most boats will choose instead to anchor outside the dredged channel.

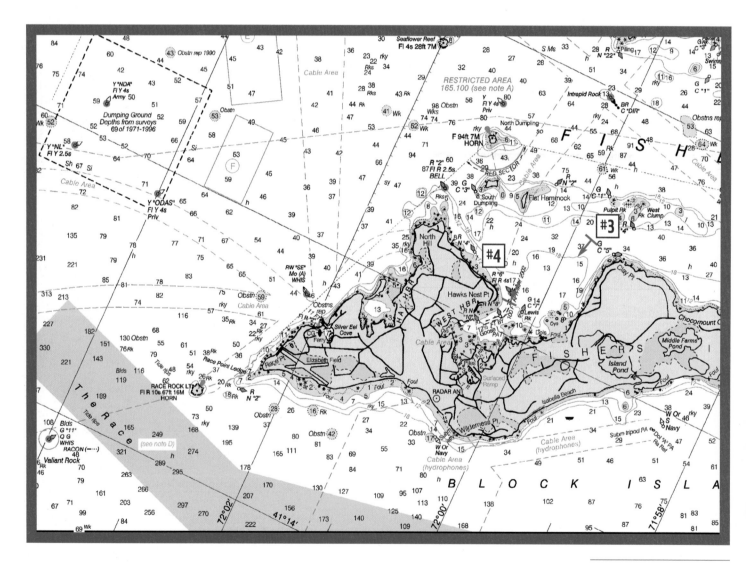

12372
38th ed., Nov. 06
NAD 83
Soundings in feet
1:40,000

#3

West Harbor

Hawks Nest Point

#4

Goose Island

N "10"

HAY HARBOR AND SILVER EEL COVE

GIVEN its limited space and inhospitable approach, Hay Harbor should not be attempted except in shoal-draft boats whose skippers know the local waters. Once inside, you'll find deep water in the center of the harbor.

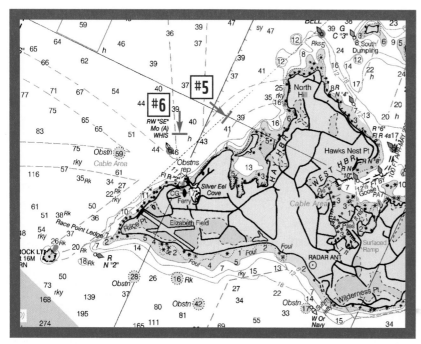

12372
38th ed., Nov. 06
NAD 83
Soundings in feet
1:40,000

West Harbor

Hay Harbor

#6

Silver Eel Cove

Race Point

RW "SE"

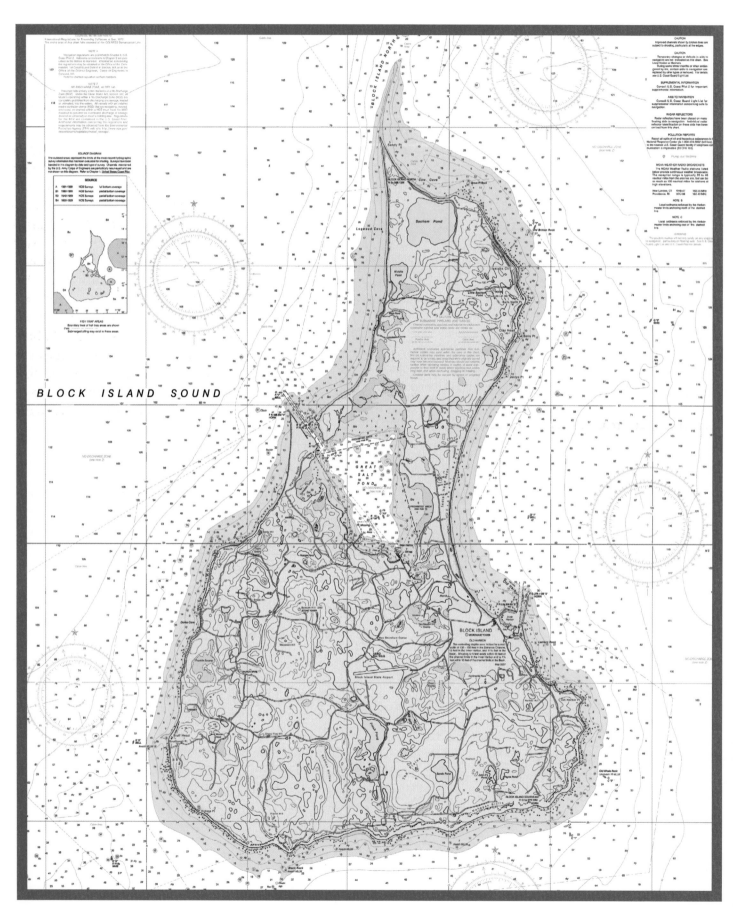

■ BLOCK ISLAND APPROACHES ■

FROM a distance or in hard weather, Block Island seems a brooding, solitary offshore sentinel. Sixteen miles southeast of Fishers Island and nearly 25 miles southwest of Newport, it is far enough seaward to be cloaked with mysterious allure. Yet it is just 9 miles offshore from Point Judith and 10 miles east-northeast of Montauk, making it a practical weekend destination for southern New England boaters and a favorite destination for Narragansett Bay and Connecticut and Long Island cruisers.

The island takes its name from Adriaen Block, the Dutch explorer who sailed this coast in 1614. It is small—about 7 miles long by 3½ miles wide—and does not afford to the big, open waters of Block Island Sound the sort of shelter that boaters sometimes praise and sometimes curse on Long Island Sound. A significant sea can build quickly on Block Island Sound in a strong summer breeze, or a fog can set in with little warning over the cool offshore waters. Occasionally wind and fog will accompany one another over the sound—a rare occurrence on the New England coast.

North Light on Sandy Point, Block Island's northern terminus, stands 58 feet above the water, flashes white every 5 seconds, and has a nominal range of 13 miles. When approaching from Fishers Island Sound in clear weather, you will have North Light and the island's clay bluffs in view well before you lose sight of Watch Hill Light (61 feet; nominal range 14 miles) behind you.

When approaching from Point Judith or Narragansett Bay, be sure to stay clear of North Reef, a spit projecting more than a half-mile north from the island's northern tip. Keep north of green flashing bell "1BI" even though there is deep water between the bell and North Reef. There are strong tide rips off the island's north end, and this is not a place for a shortcut. (There will often be small sportfishing boats working the rips in this area.) The distance from bell "1BI" to the Great Salt Pond entrance is just over 3 miles. If making this journey toward the end of a long summer day, you're likely to have plenty of company.

13217
15th ed., Nov 06
NAD 83
Soundings in feet
1:15,000

GREAT SALT POND

WE'VE had some great times on Block Island, and Great Salt Pond is one of our favorite places to spend the night. The low-lying entrance can be visually indistinct, but the 49-foot flashing red light at the end of the jetty marking the entrance's starboard hand is hard to miss in clear weather, and its horn is distinctive in fog. Make your final entrance approach from red bell "2" marking the seaward end of the dredged channel. Proceed cautiously, leaving green can "5" to port, passing between flashing green "7" and flashing red "8," and leaving red nun "10" close to starboard at the channel's inner end, which favors the starboard side of the cut. The channel is usually busy, and shifting sand can cause shoaling along its edges. From here, moorings and anchorages will be readily apparent.

Though the harbor is as busy in the summer as you would expect, the town does a reasonable job handling the heavy traffic, and town- and marina-owned guest moorings are generally available for a fee. If you wish to anchor, pay particular attention to the weather and depth, and make sure the anchor is well set in what is generally a poor holding ground of soft mud and sand. We know from experience that more than a few boats will drag their anchors at night even in light winds, and overnight squalls of wind and rain are not unusual, often causing a great midnight spectacle of fouled anchors and bumping boats.

The southeastern side of the pond generally provides more room for error and gets some protection from the surrounding topography. Anchoring is prohibited in the northern reaches of the pond, one southeastern pocket, and also in the area of the mooring field and shorefront facilities at the pond's southern end.

Size and ease of access make Great Salt Pond by far the preferred harbor on Block Island, despite the fact that many of Block Island's attractions are in the town of New Shoreham (the island's only town), a taxi or bike ride (or an easy ½-mile walk) away.

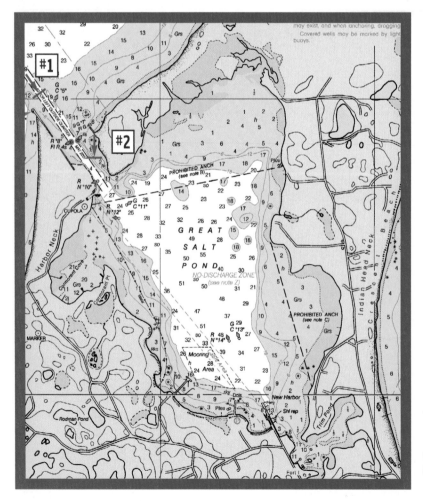

13217
15th ed., Nov. 06
NAD 83
Soundings in feet
1:15,000

#1

Great Salt Pond

Harbor Neck

#2

Old Harbor

New Harbor

Cormorant Cove

Harbor Neck

OLD HARBOR (EAST HARBOR)

THOUGH tempting because of its proximity to more of the island's shops and restaurants, Old Harbor is also home to the ferries from Point Judith and Providence. Though well protected by its breakwaters, it will be extremely crowded, and as of this writing, no anchoring is permitted. In an emergency or for a limited time, there is a town dock available, though this is tightly controlled by the harbormaster. The approach into Old Harbor leaves green can "5" off the breakwater's outer end to port. From there, simply follow a southerly course down the channel's centerline.

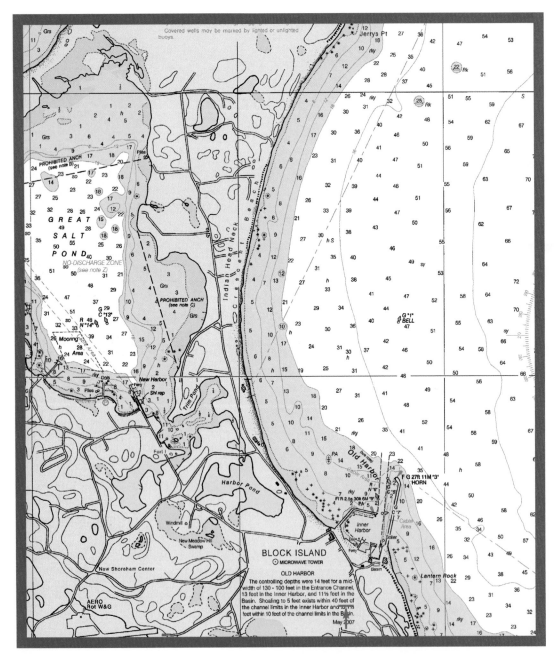

13217
15th ed., Nov 06
NAD 83
Soundings in feet
1:15,000

Old Harbor

Red Light at Jetty

Green Light at Jetty

■ POINT JUDITH HARBOR ■

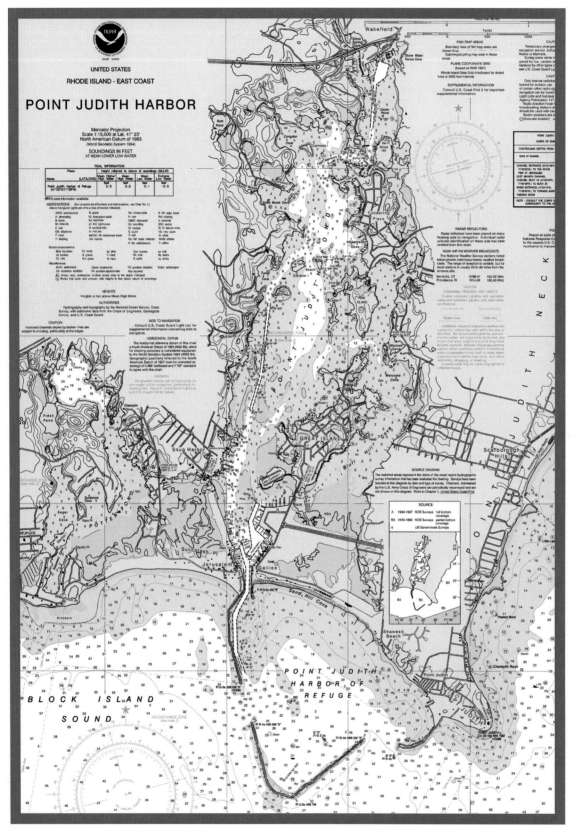

POINT Judith Harbor is NOAA's collective name for the Point Judith Harbor of Refuge and Point Judith Pond, which is accessed through a narrow dredged channel from the Harbor of Refuge's northwest corner. Point Judith itself is prominently marked by 65-foot Point Judith Light, its occulting light having a nominal range of 16 miles.

13219
12th ed., Oct. 01
NAD 83
Soundings in feet
1:15,000

THE HARBOR OF REFUGE

ENCLOSED by breakwaters on its west, south, and east sides and by land to the north, Point Judith's Harbor of Refuge is a sheltered deepwater anchorage. Surge and swell make their way through the entrances, however, and there is little to see or do on the breakwaters, so this is not so much a destination as a place to rest or to escape fog, heavy weather, or impending darkness.

The two entrances through the breakwaters, known as West Gap and East Gap, are both well

13219 , 12th ed., Oct. 01, NAD 83, Soundings in feet, 1:15,000

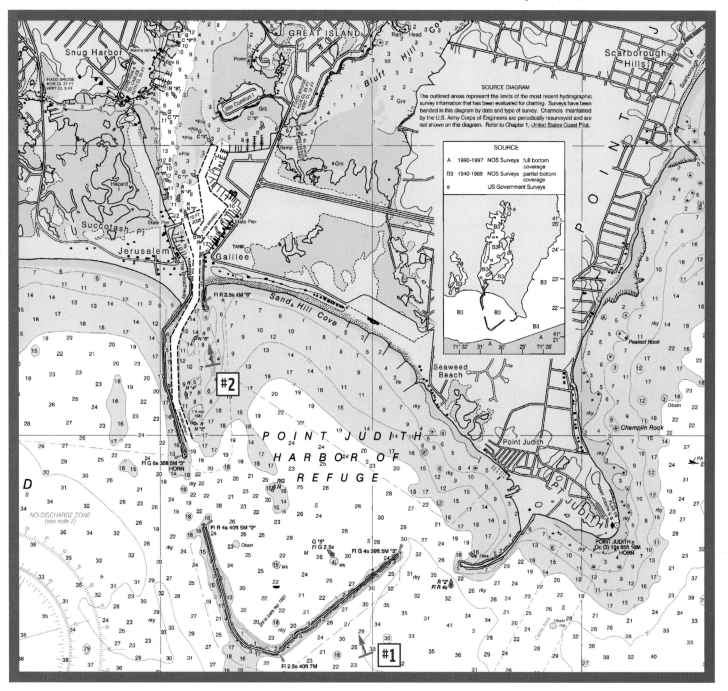

marked. Five hundred yards wide, the West Gap is marked by 35-foot flashing green light "3" (which also has a horn) on the end of the port breakwater and 40-foot flashing red light "2" on the breakwater to starboard. The 400-yard-wide East Gap, which opens northward, is bounded by 39-foot-tall flashing green light "3" to port and by flashing red buoy "2" off the landward breakwater to starboard.

We have never chosen to anchor here, preferring instead to head into Point Judith Pond, but if you do anchor, you will find your best shelter from the prevailing southerlies near the southern edge of the harbor, inside the V-shaped outer breakwater. The holding is said to be good there. Sand has shoaled the tip of the outer breakwater's apex, so resist the temptation to get too near the breakwater. Swell can make the middle reaches of the harbor uncomfortable, and anchoring near the approach channel for Point Judith Pond would expose you to constant jostling from passing traffic. You can find temporary anchorage at the harbor's north end to use Sand Hill Cove Beach (an excellent swimming beach) or visit the village of Galilee.

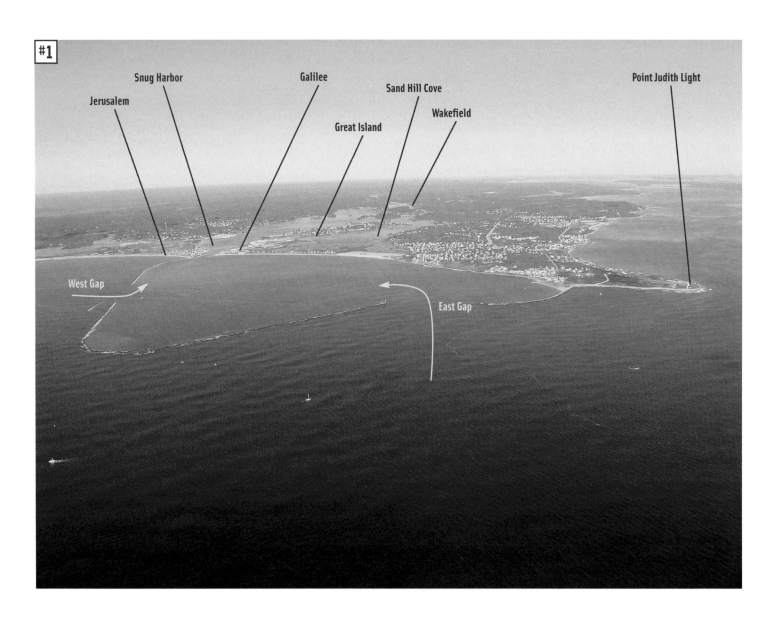

#2

Jerusalem

Snug Harbor

The Breachway

Galilee

Great Island

N "6"

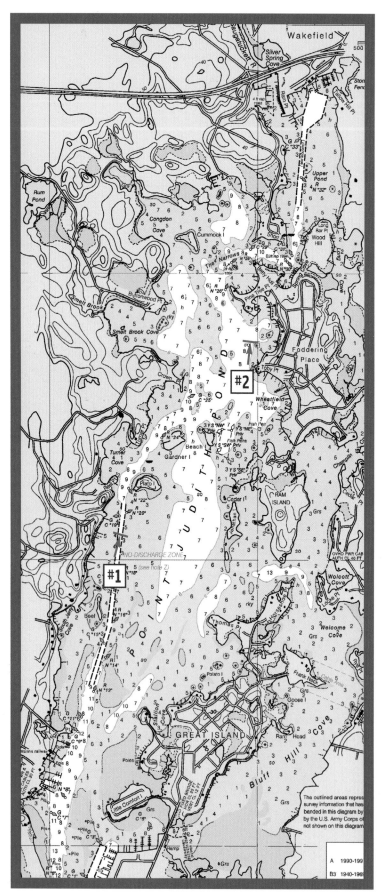

POINT JUDITH POND

TO ENTER Point Judith Pond from the Harbor of Refuge, follow the channel that runs just inside the western breakwater, beginning at nun "2." The channel's northern end brings you to The Breachway, the cut between the hamlet of Jerusalem (to port) and the village of Galilee (to starboard). We have found the 150-foot-wide channel to be well-marked all the way to the pond, and the dredged depth was 11.8 feet to the Jerusalem state pier as of May 2007. But traffic is heavy in The Breachway, and the current is reported to run at 4 to 5 knots on flood and ebb; choose your tides accordingly.

Once inside you can tie up for a short time in Galilee, but this is a major commercial fishing port (one of the most productive on the East Coast) and does not cater to yachtsmen, so an overnight berth is unlikely. You might have better luck on the Jerusalem side, and you can then dinghy across to Galilee to enjoy its fresh seafood markets and seafood restaurants. With an active sportfishing community as well as a commercial fishing fleet, the waterfront is extremely busy in summer.

If you choose instead to continue into the pond, the channel leads you just off the Jerusalem state pier and northward past Snug Harbor, favoring the western shore. The shoal areas are close on either hand, so stay inside the buoys and be wary of uncharted shoaling. We have found this excursion fascinating and enjoyable. You'll find room to anchor in the pond's middle and upper reaches amid peaceful surroundings that include marshes, waterfowl in great variety and abundance, and woodlands. Point Judith Pond is a welcome break from the busy coastal waters.

If you're feeling especially adventurous, you can transit The Narrows at the pond's upper end (beginning at nun "26") to reach the town of Wakefield, where there are several marinas and room for sheltered anchorage in 3 to 6 feet of water.

13219
12th ed., Oct 01
NAD 83
Soundings in feet
1:15,000

#1

The Narrows

Wakefield

Upper Pond

Point Judith Pond

Narragansett Bay

Turner Cove

Plato Island

#2

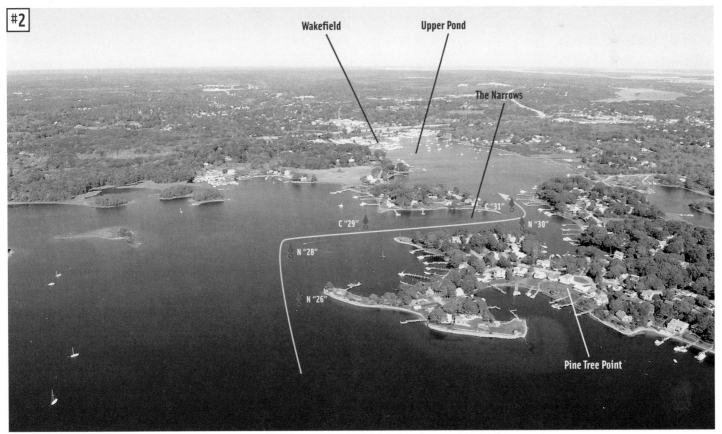

Wakefield

Upper Pond

The Narrows

C "31"

C "29"

N "30"

N "28"

N "26"

Pine Tree Point

REGION II

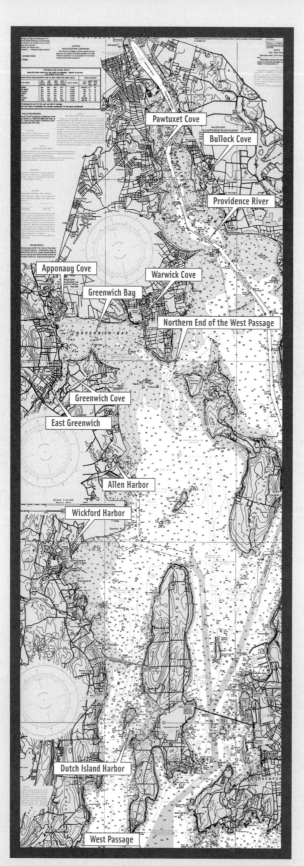

Pawtuxet Cove

Bullock Cove

Providence River

Apponaug Cove

Warwick Cove

Greenwich Bay

Northern End of the West Passage

Greenwich Cove

East Greenwich

Allen Harbor

Wickford Harbor

Dutch Island Harbor

West Passage

13221
57th ed., Feb. 08
NAD 83
Soundings in feet
1:40,000

NARRAGANSETT BAY
—THE WEST PASSAGE AND PROVIDENCE RIVER—

Narragansett Bay in Rhode Island is one of the most popular boating destinations on the East Coast. Its many interesting and sheltered harbors, its numerous marine facilities, and its proximity to population centers and transportation routes mean that there is always a lot of on-the-water activity. There are more anchorages and highlights than we can hope to cover here, but this and the next two chapters will provide the flavor and a good sampling of what the bay has to offer.

From the south and Rhode Island Sound, there are several deep and well-marked entrances to Narragansett Bay. The westernmost channel is called, appropriately, the West Passage, while the middle channel is the East Passage. Farther to the east, an approach can be made via the Sakonnet River. All three routes are popular, with the East Passage being possibly the most used due to the presence of Newport and the main shipping channel leading north to Providence.

Tidal currents in Narragansett Bay are generally moderate, but they increase in several narrower passages. For example, currents can reach approximately 1.5 knots in the approaches to Newport (Region III) and exceed 2.2 knots in the constricted waters between Tiverton and Portsmouth (Region IV). Between the pylons of the Newport (East Passage) and Jamestown (West Passage) bridges, one will often encounter stronger currents than in nearby areas. At all times, sailors using the wind for power will find it advantageous to seek a favorable current, particularly if sailing to windward.

A strong ebb blasting gale-driven sea can create extra-rough or even dangerous seas in the bay's outer approaches. The *Eldridge Tide and Pilot Book* includes a very good set of tide and current tables, as well as some tide charts, covering these waters.

If you are approaching from the southwest, from Block Island and Pt. Judith, the first possible landmarks will be the towers on the Newport/Pell Bridge, located well up the East Passage past Newport (see photo on page 79). The bridge provides 194 feet of vertical clearance, and the towers supporting the roadway are much taller. In fact, on a clear day, this structure can be seen from Buzzards Bay in the east and Block Island in the south.

■ WEST PASSAGE ■

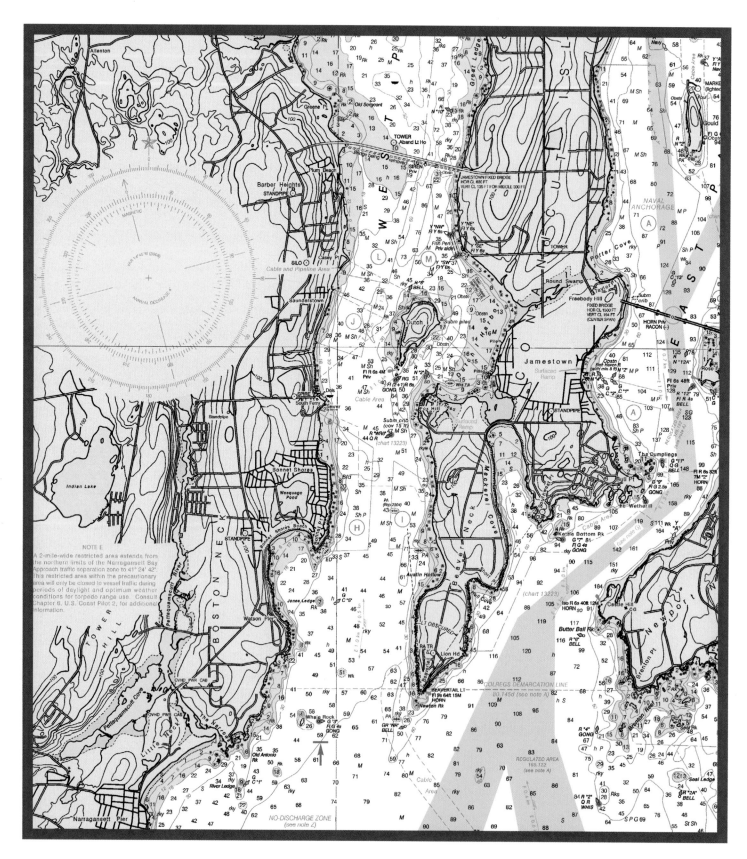

THE West Passage provides direct access to Dutch Island Harbor and Jamestown, Wickford, and East Greenwich and Warwick in Greenwich Bay. It is also possible to connect with the East Passage south or north of Prudence Island.

In your approach to the West Passage, it is best to leave flashing green gong "3" (east of Whale Rock) to port and green-and-red bell "NR" (south of Newton Rock) to starboard. The 64-foot lighthouse on Beaver-tail Point is obvious in clear weather. From this southern approach, follow a northerly course up the middle of the bay, paralleling the shore of Beaver Neck to starboard. Flashing red-and-green gong "DI," south of Dutch Island, marks the approach to Dutch Island Harbor. A recently restored light tower with a privately maintained light, flashing red at 6-second intervals, is just north of the gong.

13221
57th ed., Feb. 08
NAD 83
Soundings in feet
1:40,000

■ DUTCH ISLAND HARBOR ■

POPULAR because of its ease of access and relative protection as well as its proximity to Jamestown, Dutch Island Harbor is a must for anyone navigating these waters. Given its size, the harbor can accommodate a large number of boats on moorings, and there is anchoring room, too. The harbor can be relied on to provide a comfortable space for a night or two, even during the height of the season. The general anchorage areas are

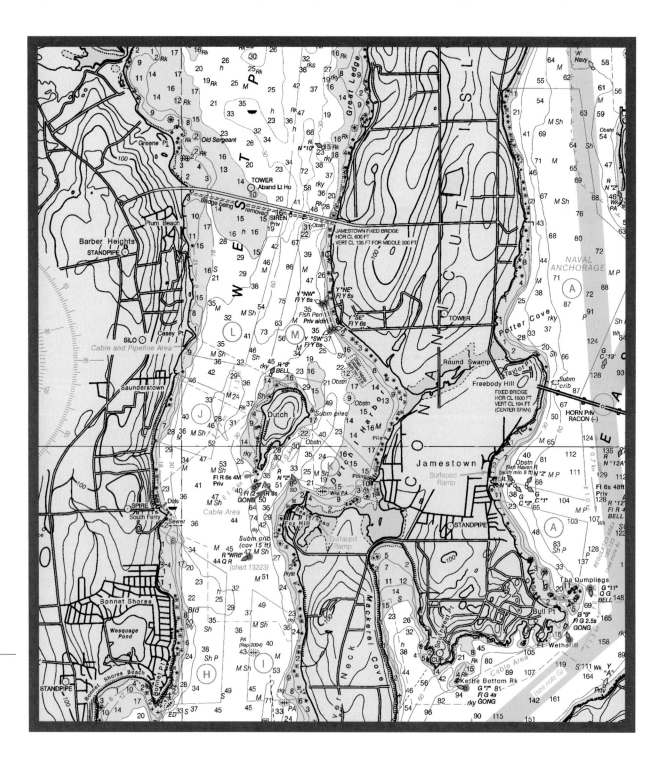

13221
57th ed., Feb. 08
NAD 83
Soundings in feet
1:40,000

well indicated on the chart and lie just north and east of Beaverhead, but there are lots of other spots to choose from as well.

The approach is simple. Steer east from flashing red-and-green gong "DI," leaving red nun "2" to starboard. From there, the anchorage and mooring areas will be self-evident. The boatyard offers rental moorings and full services. It is a short walk over the hill into the town of Jamestown (Region III), where there are nice shops and restaurants.

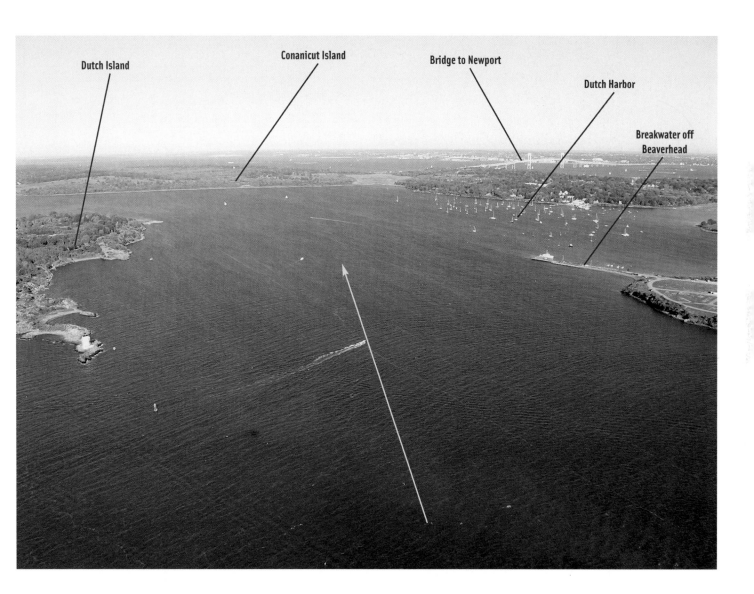

Dutch Island   Conanicut Island   Bridge to Newport   Dutch Harbor   Breakwater off Beaverhead

■ WICKFORD HARBOR ■

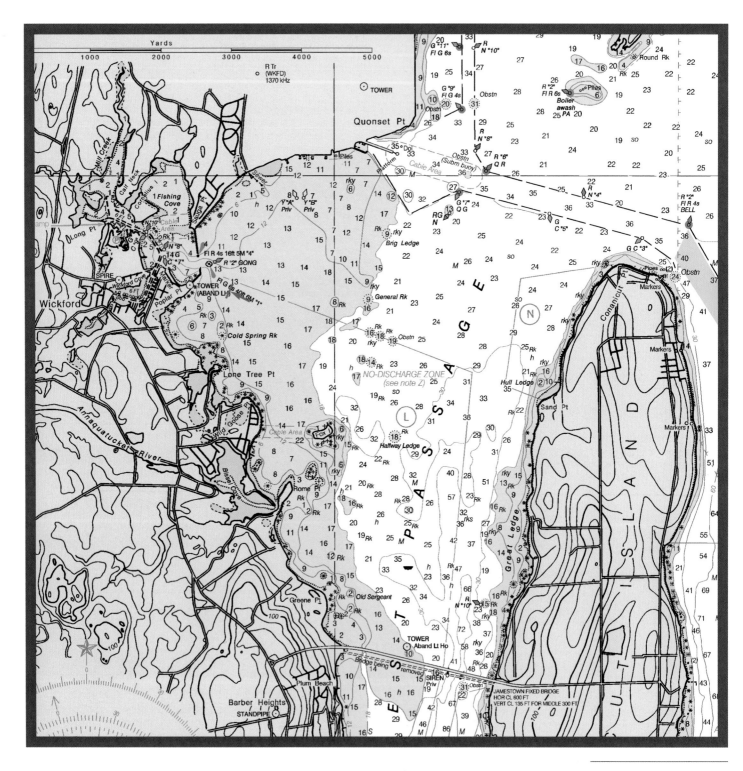

13221
57th ed., Feb. 08
NAD 83
Soundings in feet
1:40,000

BEARING almost due west from the northern tip of Conanicut Island, the approach to Wickford is easy. When northbound through the West Passage, you will see a privately maintained light tower to port immediately after passing beneath the new Jamestown Verrazzano Bridge. From there, a northerly course takes you past Fox Island, which sits to the east of Wild Goose Point. Continue northwesterly to flashing green light "1" off the northern end of the breakwater that angles northward from the abandoned lighthouse at Poplar Point. This is the southernmost of the pair of breakwaters that shelter the harbor entrance. Red "2" lies just outside the breakwaters, and red light "4" marks the southern end of the northern breakwater.

As the photo shows, there is plenty of anchorage just behind the breakwaters, but all services lie farther up in the inner harbor. Note shallow Charles Rock inside light "4" and the breakwater, and the rapid shoaling both north and south of the deep water. The inner harbor channels, which fork to the south and north, are well marked, and the available services are apparent along the shores. The small and very walkable town offers numerous shops and restaurants as well as most marine services. Though it's not on the harbor, there is a marine consignment shop a bit inland that offers lots of interesting gear at good prices.

■ ALLEN HARBOR ■

BOATERS who are looking for something slightly off the beaten track, and who are not deterred by the huge piers at the Davisville Depot to its south, will find Allen Harbor, north of Quonset Point, to be well protected. Allen Harbor can be approached from either the east or west side of Hope Island. Boats heading up the West Passage from Wickford can follow the shipping channel around Quonset Point and past the Davisville Depot. Once north of the depot, a northwesterly course will take you to green can "1" and flashing red "2" marking the entrance to the dredged channel that works its way between Spink Neck and Calf Pasture Point and into the main harbor. There is a marina to the left upon entry and a mooring area farther in.

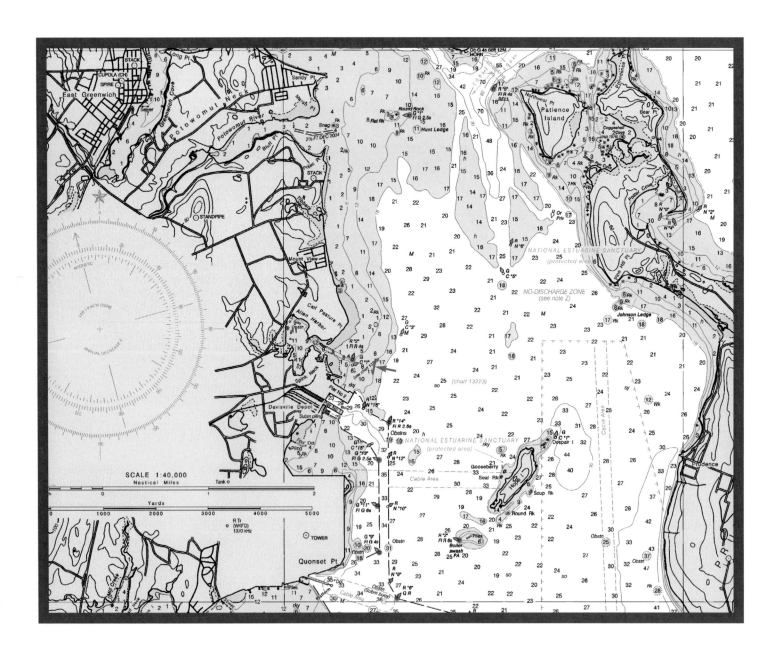

Pier No. 2

Spink Neck

Allen Harbor

Calf Pasture Point

C "1"   R "2"

13221
57th ed., Feb. 08
NAD 83
Soundings in feet
1:40,000

■ GREENWICH BAY APPROACHES ■

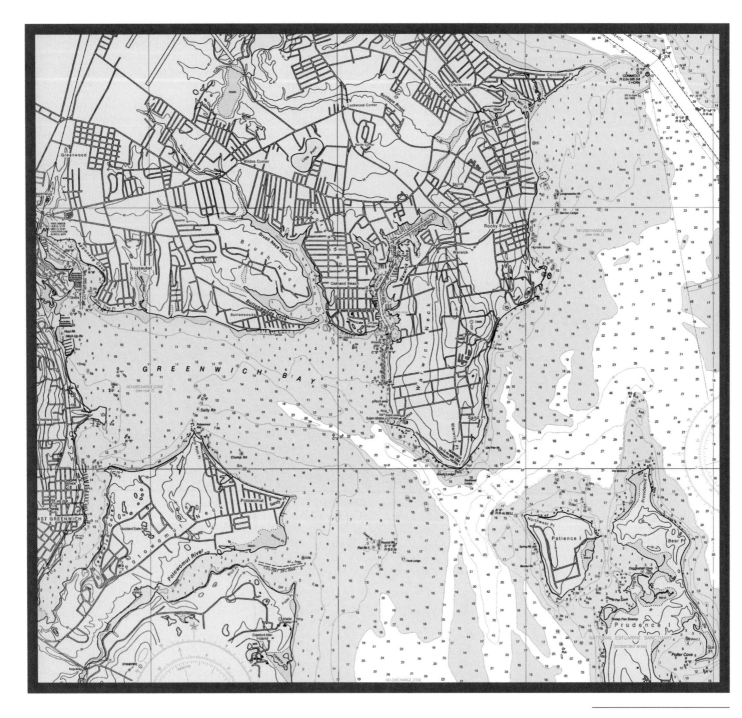

13224
38th ed., Nov. 06
NAD 83
Soundings in feet
1:20,000

GREENWICH Bay is home to three harbors with several marinas and mooring options: Greenwich Cove, Apponaug Cove, and Warwick Cove. The approach to all three begins with flashing green light "1" off Round Rock (note shallow Flat Rock just to the west; see chart on page 66). From there, a northerly course takes you to green can "3" west of Warwick Point and Warwick Neck.

#1 (See page 66.)

Potowomut Neck

Greenwich Cove

Apponaug Cove

Brush Neck Cove

Warwick Cove

■ GREENWICH COVE/EAST GREENWICH ■

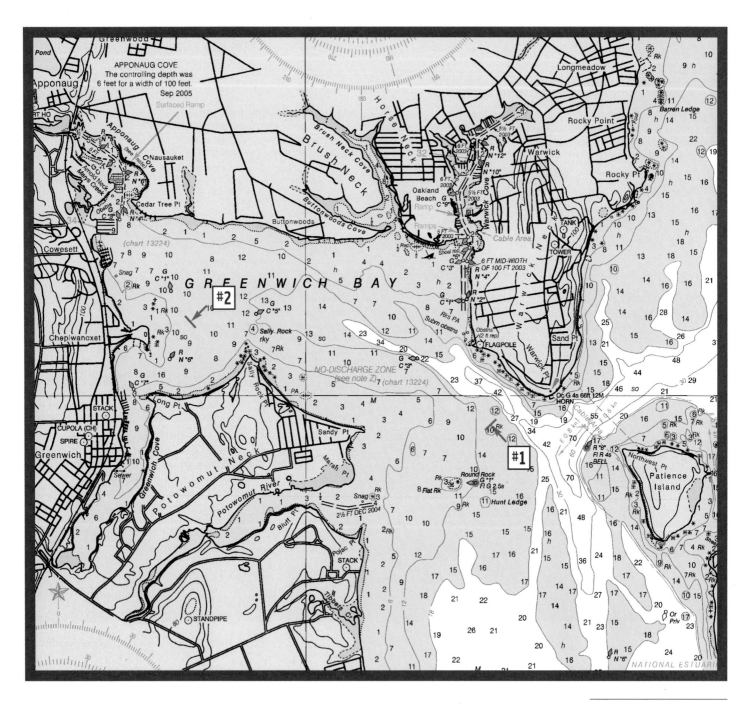

13224
38th ed., Nov. 06
NAD 83
Soundings in feet
1:20,000

EAST Greenwich, home of the East Greenwich Yacht Club, is a cozy and attractive harbor. To enter it, follow a west-northwesterly approach from green can "3" to reach green can "5" north of Sally Rock. From there, turn to port and pick up red nun "6" off the spit of land just east of Chepiwanoxet. Leaving the nun to starboard, continue southwesterly. Leave green can "7," west of Long Point, to port, then head south into the middle of Greenwich Cove. Ashore you will find almost anything you'd like to eat and drink, and a short but energetic walk up the hill takes you to some shopping areas with larger markets and a West Marine store. In typical Rhode Island fashion, most marine services can be found here or nearby.

#2

Potowomut Neck

Greenwich Cove

East Greenwich

Long Point

■ APPONAUG COVE ■

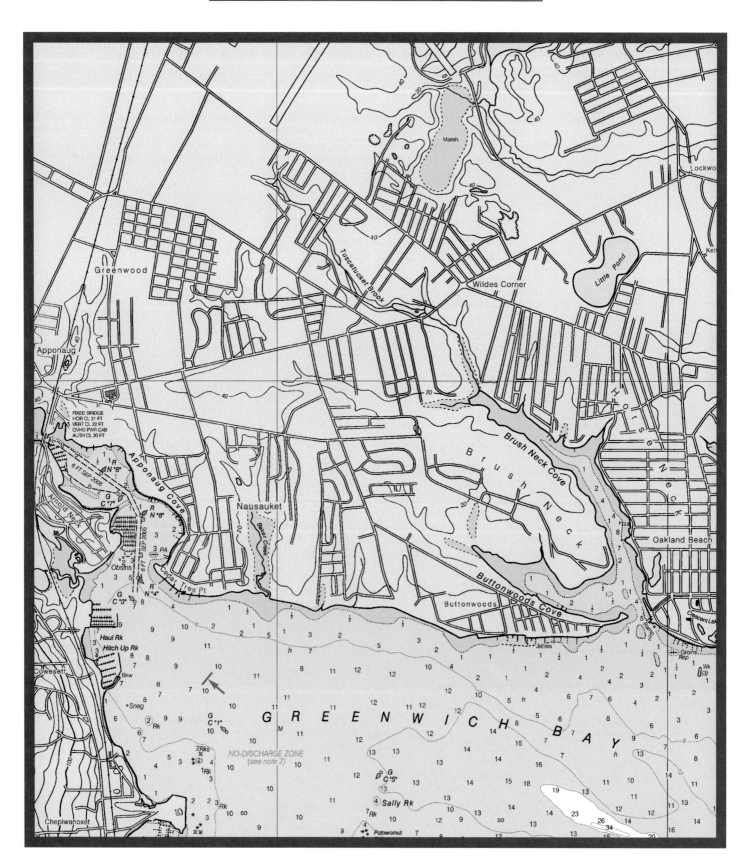

Arnold Neck

Apponaug Cove

Cedar Tree Point

C "3"   N "4"

APPONAUG Cove lies north of Greenwich Cove, in the northwest corner of Greenwich Bay. It is clearly marked by the large marinas on the west side of its entrance. From green can "5" at Sally Rock, proceed north-westerly, passing green can "1" to reach green can "3" and red nun "4" west of Cedar Tree Point. From there the channel continues to wind around into the center of the cove.

13224
38th ed., Nov. 06
NAD 83
Soundings in feet
1:20,000

■ WARWICK COVE ■

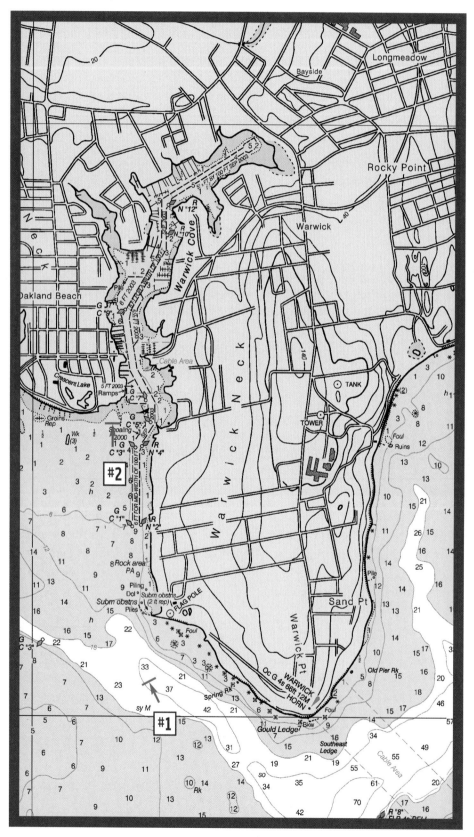

ON the eastern edge of Greenwich Bay, skirting the western shore of Warwick Neck, is the dredged channel that leads into Warwick Cove. Enter the channel from the south between red nun "2" and green can "1," lying north of the prominent flagpole at the end of Warwick Point. Farther in, the charted channel shoals to 6 feet or less at low tide. Warwick Cove offers a number of marinas, services, and restaurants, and boaters with a little time to spare will find it a hospitable place to spend the night. A bit up the road from the marinas is a busy road with the best Ace Hardware Store we've ever seen—featuring dinghies, motors, marine supplies of all sorts, and a very helpful staff. There are engine shops, battery stores, canvas workers, and even marine welders nearby.

13224
38th ed., Nov. 06
NAD 83
Soundings in feet
1:20,000

#1

C "5" N "6"

C "3" N "4"

C "1"

N "2"

#2

Warwick Cove   Providence River   Warwick Neck

■ NORTHERN END OF THE WEST PASSAGE ■

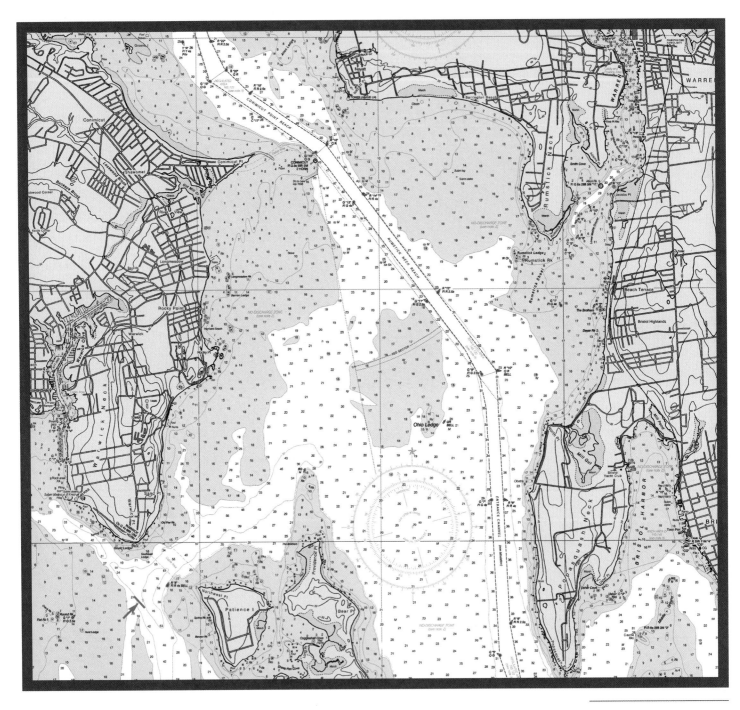

13224
38th ed., Nov. 06
NAD 83
Soundings in feet
1:20,000

THE narrow passage between Patience Island and Warwick Point, just outside Greenwich Bay, forms the northern end of the West Passage. There are no real difficulties making this passage, which is well marked by a 66-foot flashing green lighthouse on Warwick Point and flashing red bell "8" to the northwest of Patience Island.

Once through the passage you will find yourself in the approaches to the Providence River, where you merge with boats northbound through the East Passage. To your north and east lies the well-buoyed shipping channel leading up the river to Providence.

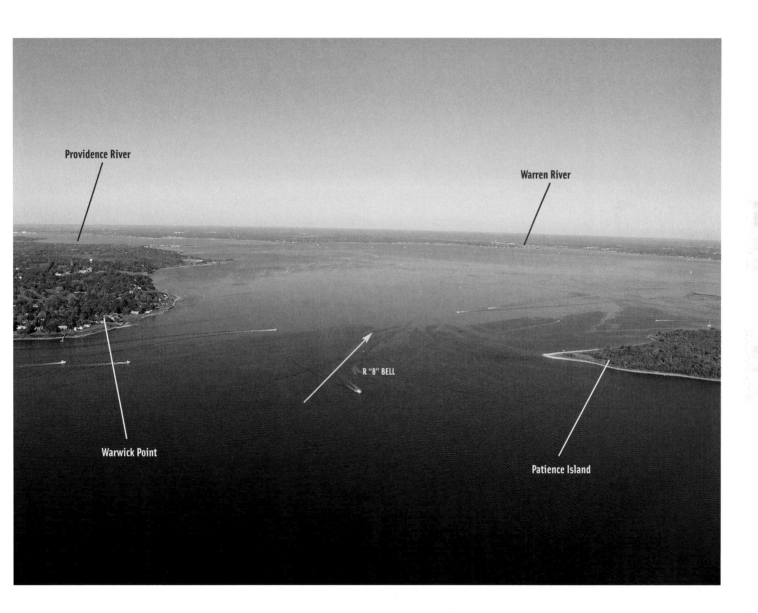

Providence River

Warren River

R "8" BELL

Warwick Point

Patience Island

■ PROVIDENCE RIVER/BULLOCK COVE ■

13224
38th ed., Nov. 06
NAD 83
Soundings in feet
1:20,000

IF you proceed upriver between the prominent 58-foot lighthouse off Conimicut Point to the west and Nayatt Point with its abandoned tower to the east, you will see on the eastern shore, approximately 1.5 miles north, the entrance to a wonderfully protected, often overlooked harbor called Bullock Cove, which is home to the Narragansett Terrace Yacht Club and several marinas. Surrounded by homes, the harbor has a well-marked though shoaling approach channel leading to the narrow entrance between Bullock Point and West Barrington. As of 2008 there was perhaps 6 feet of water in the channel at low tide, but deeper-draft boats could traverse it safely on a favorable tide (and do, routinely), and it was due to be dredged in 2009.

From the lighthouse off Conimicut Point, head west of north to pick up lighted green buoy "1" and red nun "2" at the southerly end of the Bullock Cove approach channel. The marina to the right inside the entrance offers gasoline only, but the marina farther in on the right provides both gas and diesel. Among the three marinas you can get almost anything done from wooden boat repair to a blister job on a fiberglass hull. The largest marina has been known to work on America's Cup yachts and around-the-world racers.

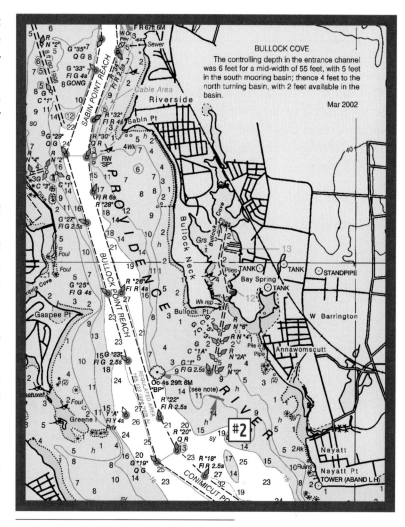

13221, 57th ed., Feb. 08, NAD 83, Soundings in feet, 1:40,000

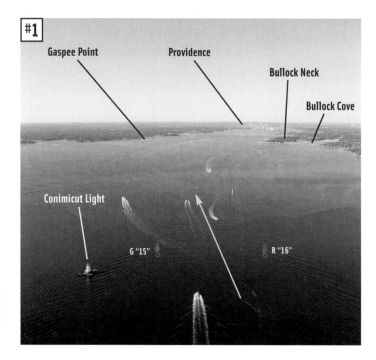

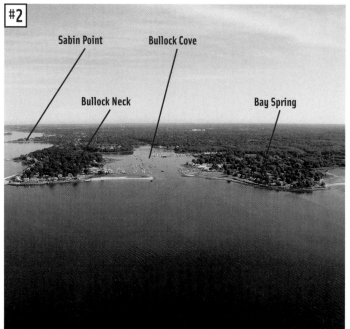

■ PAWTUXET COVE AND EDGEWOOD ■

JUST up the Providence River from Bullock Cove are two additional spots worth exploring if you have the time: Pawtuxet Cove and Edgewood. Both anchorages on the river's western shore are easily approached via dredged channels that branch off from the shipping channel. For Pawtuxet, continue north along Bullock Point Reach (the shipping channel) until flashing green "29." From there, a hard left turn will take you between red nuns and green cans through the narrow approach channel and inside the Pawtuxet Cove breakwater.

A good place to anchor on this stretch of the river is opposite Pawtuxet, south of Sabin Point, off the town of Riverside. You'll see some moored boats and possibly the East Providence Harbormaster, who is in charge of this area. The holding is good and the shelter decent unless it is blowing hard from the south. There's a public park, with possible dinghy landing at a launching ramp at charted Crescent Park. A short walk up the hill leads you to an historic carousel, a couple of small eateries, and a small grocery store.

To reach Edgewood, head northwesterly from flashing green "29" into a long side channel marked with green cans and red nuns. This leads eventually into the harbor. Edgewood is home to the Rhode Island Yacht Club as well as the Edgewood Yacht Club, both of which are known to be hospitable to visiting yachts.

Edgewood is just 2 miles downriver from downtown Providence, and though relatively few boaters venture all the way upriver to New England's second largest city, it is a worthwhile trip if for no other reason than to say you've done it. The river's shores become generally quite industrial above Edgewood, and the main ship channel (which is well marked) is the best place to travel given the numerous hazards and shoals outside the channel. Cruisers share this fairway with oceangoing freighters, tankers, barges, and tugboats.

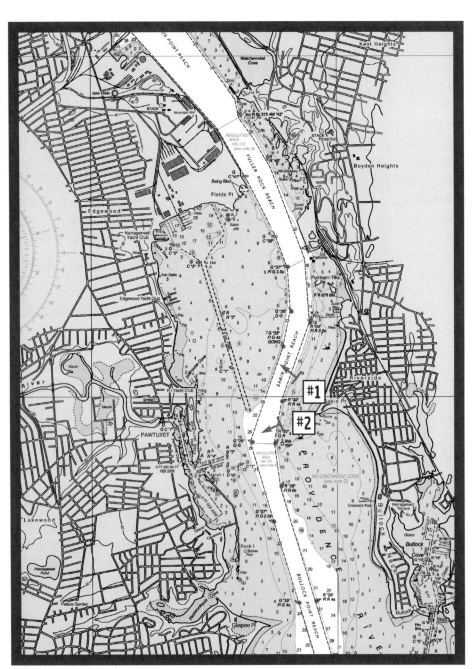

13224, 38th ed., Nov. 06, NAD 83, Soundings in feet, 1:20,000

#1 — Stillhouse Cove · Edgewood · Providence

Boats that can fit under the 21-foot vertical clearance at Providence's hurricane barrier (which is closed for storms) will find transient dockage at a marina within walking distance or a short cab ride of the downtown district with its many shops and restaurants. Providence has one of the most walkable downtowns anywhere. The neighborhood around Brown University is particularly interesting, with an eclectic mix of ethnic restaurants, bookstores, museums, and appealing shops. This is an excellent place to meet crew or guests arriving by car, bus, or train.

Boats unable to clear the hurricane barrier will find a marina at India Point on the Seekonk River, just downstream from the 40-foot bridge over the river.

#2 — Pawtuxet Cove

REGION III

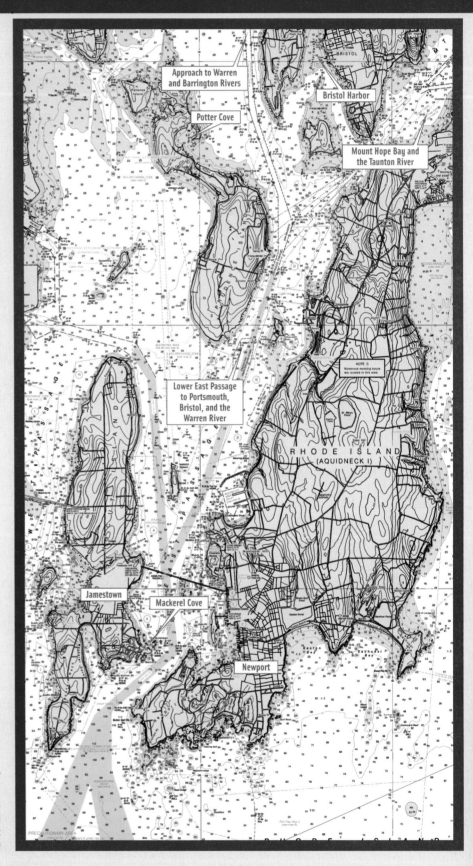

13221
57th ed., Feb. 08
NAD 83
Soundings in feet
1:40,000

For the approach from Rhode Island Sound to Narragansett Bay, see Region II. The waters leading to the East Passage are generally deep and obstruction free except for the occasional lobster float, but you should observe the marked traffic separation lanes for commercial traffic, especially in poor visibility. Due south of the entrance, and well offshore, is large red-and-white whistle buoy "NB," which is in the area where large ships will be picking up or dropping off their pilots. Approximately 2.65 miles northeast of "NB" is large red whistle "2," south of Brenton Reef. Red gong "4," immediately west of Brenton Reef, should be left to starboard by inbound boaters.

Staying west of the line between buoys "4" and "6" will get you safely past Brenton Point to your east. In clear weather you'll see prominent 64-foot Beavertail Light on the south end of Beaver Neck to the west. With Beaver Neck trending north to Conanicut Island to your port, and world-famous Newport Neck with its Castle Hill light and horn on a rocky promontory on your starboard hand, head northeast toward Fort Adams and the entrance to Newport Harbor. The water near Castle Hill is deep right in to the shore, and locals will be seen skimming along the edges of the channel.

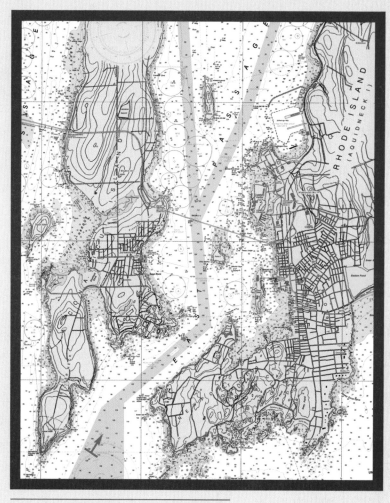

13223, 40th ed., June 08, NAD 83, Soundings in feet, 1:20,000

Conanicut Island — Mackerel Cove — Claiborne Pell (Newport) Bridge — East Passage — Castle Hill — Newport Neck — Beaver Neck

■ NEWPORT ■

TO enter Newport, round the flashing red horn "2" and light off Fort Adams and head east, leaving red nun "4" to starboard and green can "1" and bell "3" to port. These are among the busiest and most famous waters in New England. It is not unusual to arrive amidst one or more sailing fleets entering or leaving the harbor, historic 12-meters (former America's Cup boats) blasting along under full sail, harbormaster's boats moving to and fro, huge megayachts searching for berths, tour boats entering and leaving, and numerous other cruisers, like yourself, wondering where to go next.

The several major parts of Newport Harbor are divided by marked channels to facilitate the arrival and departure of large vessels. The main part of the harbor, full of moorings for locals and transients, is between Goat Island and the Newport waterfront to the east. Another huge mooring area is east and south of Fort Adams, in protected (except from the north) Brenton Cove. The Brenton Cove mooring area extends east past the Ida Lewis Yacht Club to red day marker "6" on Little Ida Lewis Rock. There is a marked (with small buoys)

anchorage area in a triangle with the peak located just off the yacht club dock. If you can't find the anchorage area, you need help locating a mooring, or you just need some advice, contact the Newport harbormaster on VHF channel 16, working channel 14.

Marinas are located along the Newport shore to the east and north and on the shore of Goat Island. The Newport Yacht Club is in a small basin in the northeast corner of the harbor. In order to secure reservations, it is wise to contact any of these places prior to arrival.

In addition to the above, there is another mooring area north of the small bridge (vertical clearance 14 feet) connecting Goat Island to the mainland. This area is mostly for local boaters on moorings, though you may be able to anchor north and west of the moored fleet (ask the harbormaster).

Depending on the time of year and your preferences, each of these areas has its advantages. The main mooring area is closest to town with its numerous restaurants and its tourist action, while Brenton Cove is generally somewhat quieter and more sheltered in the summer's prevailing southwest winds. Famous Ida Lewis Yacht Club and the New York Yacht Club's Newport Station are centers of world-class sailing competitions and equally glamorous parties and events, if you are a member or know someone. The Newport Jazz Festival, now dubbed George Wein's Jazz Festival 55, at Fort Adams, is a wonderful way to spend an August weekend on your boat, and there are many other festivals and events throughout the summer. You can join others anchored just offshore from the fort, well within hearing range of the music.

13223
40th ed., June 08
NAD 83
Soundings in feet
1:20,000

In addition, Newport is a pleasant town in which to walk around and see the sights. The mansions of famous Bellevue Avenue are as spectacular as the palaces of Europe, and a stroll along the Cliff Walk provides an oceanside view of these Gatsbiesque haunts. The "Point" section of Newport, north of the Goat Island Bridge, is an area of narrow streets and old restored homes. In fact, Newport, once the principal port city of Rhode Island, has one of the finest collections of old homes in New England. Other activities of particular interest to mariners include the Museum of Yachting, the area around Bowen's Wharf where yachties hang out both ashore and on fabulous boats of all persuasions, and Oldport Marine, which provides not only launch service all over the harbor but very interesting harbor tours.

#1 Ida Lewis Rock · Brenton Cove · Fort Adams

#2 Goat Island · Brenton Cove

#3 Ida Lewis Yacht Club · Brenton Cove · Fort Adams · Goat Island

■ JAMESTOWN AND MACKEREL COVE ■

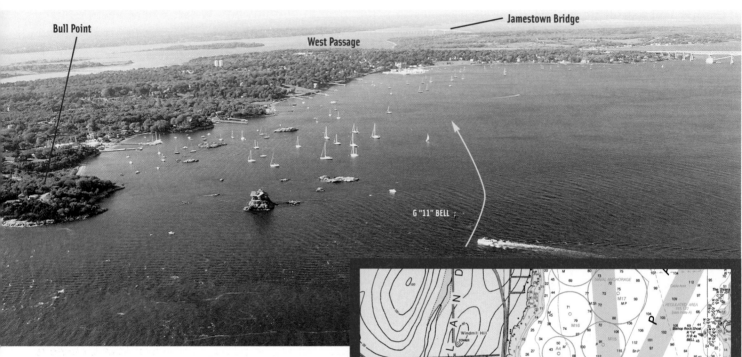

Bull Point

West Passage

Jamestown Bridge

G "11" BELL

JAMESTOWN is located on Conanicut Island to the west of Newport. The main harbor is somewhat protected by Bull Point to the south and Freebody Hill to the north, though it is usually roiled by wakes, and it's wide open to winds from northeast to southeast. It can be a great place to duck in and spend the night if you want to avoid much busier Newport. Whenever we've visited, we've moored off the Conanicut Yacht Club and, depending on the weather, had a very peaceful night. The small town offers several cozy eateries and interesting shops just a short stroll from most docks.

South of Jamestown, roughly opposite Castle Hill, is the entrance to Mackerel Cove, a deepwater slice between Beaver Neck and Conanicut Island. While there are no services there, it's a beautiful place and can be materially more protected than Jamestown in big winds from the north, though there is often a swell rolling in from offshore. If the winds are from the southwest, which is likely, your boat may lie sideways to the incoming swell. Holding is not the best in places.

13223, 40th ed., June 08, NAD 83, Soundings in feet, 1:20,000

■ LOWER EAST PASSAGE TO PORTSMOUTH, BRISTOL, AND THE WARREN RIVER ■

THE view north from Jamestown and Newport is dominated by the Newport/Pell Bridge, which, with 194 feet of clearance under its center span, is visible in clear weather from Buzzards Bay and Block Island. If you head north beneath the bridge and pass east of Gould Island, you will see the U.S. Navy base to your east. Gould Island was formerly the site of a naval torpedo range, and the area continues to be used for research into anti-subma-

Prudence Island Hog Island Arnold Point Dyer Island Melville

rine systems and other undersea warfare technologies. Don't be surprised to see various naval vessels on exercises in this area. The U.S. Naval War College is south of the base, north and east of the bridge.

A northeasterly heading will take you up the East Passage and to the east of Prudence Island, the passage narrowing between Dyer and Prudence Islands. East of Dyer Island are the large marinas and repair facilities of the East Passage Yachting Center and the Hinckley Company (charted as Melville), along with numerous ancillary businesses for every kind of boat from daysailers to megayachts. If you can't find the part or get it fixed in the Melville complex, you're in big trouble!

Red nun "22," near the southwestern end of Dyer Island, and red bell "24" off the island's northwestern end conduct you safely past. From there—in the middle of the channel and approximately midway along the eastern shore of Prudence Island—you have a direct shot to flashing red-and-green bell "SP," which puts you at a Y-shaped intersection. You can proceed northwest past the northern end of Prudence Island to Rumstick Neck Reach and the Providence River, or you can head northeast to the Mount Hope Bridge, Mount Hope Bay, and Fall River, Massachusetts.

13223, 40th ed., June 08, NAD 83, Soundings in feet, 1:20,000

■ POTTER COVE AND BRISTOL HARBOR ■

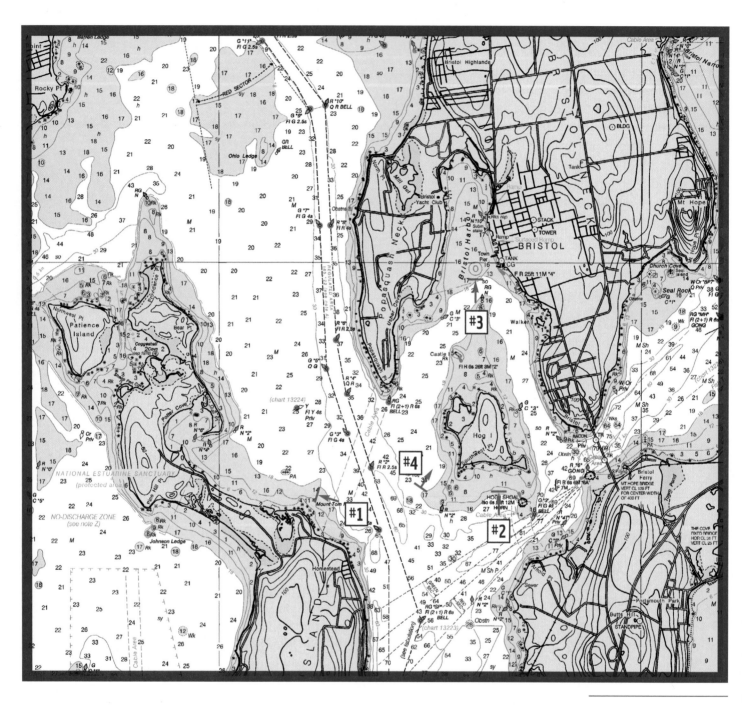

13221
57th ed., Feb. 08
NAD 83
Soundings in feet
1:40,000

THREE miles northwest of red-and-green bell "SP" lies the entrance to Potter Cove, inside a hook of land forming the northern point of Prudence Island. With many local moorings, a few free state moorings, and usually lots of anchoring room, the cove is well protected and has good holding.

To reach the cove, continue north from flashing red-green bell "SP" to flashing green "1," just off Homestead on Prudence Island. From there, a turn to port will lead you directly to Gull Point, at the entrance to Pot-

ter Cove. Give a wide berth to charted but unmarked Mount Tom Rock. Leave red nun "4" and red nun "6" to starboard as you enter the cove. The deepest anchoring area is northwest of nun "6," with depths dropping off close to shore and in the northeast portion of the harbor. The area surrounding the harbor is mostly public land, and you are welcome to roam ashore through old trails and overgrown roads. Beware of the deer ticks that are numerous in the summer, since they are vectors for Lyme disease.

#1

Prudence Island

Patience Island

Greenwich Bay

Warwick Neck

Potter Cove

Bear Point

Gull Point

■ BRISTOL HARBOR ■

(See chart page 84.)

THREE miles northeast of Potter Cove is Bristol Harbor, a great place to visit. If heading north through the East Passage, you can choose either the left-hand or right-hand channel from flashing red-green bell "SP" and still enter Bristol Harbor through one of its two entrances—one to the west of Hog Island, and one between the eastern shore of Hog Island and Bristol Point.

Bristol Harbor remains one of Rhode Island's classic harbors, with plenty of deep water access on either side. Steeped in history, Bristol is home to the Herreshoff Museum and a hospitable yacht club on the eastern shore of Popasquash Neck. There are a number of town and marine services on the harbor's eastern shore, as well as numerous shops and restaurants. Bristol's 4th of July parade is one of the largest and most spectacular in New England, and the town boasts several excellent chandleries and repair facilities.

For those choosing to enter from the west, the best approach is from the flashing red-and-green bell off Popasquash Point. From there, a northeasterly course takes you past light "2" on Castle Island Rock to starboard. Continue on the same course to the designated general anchorage (full of moorings) just to the west of the town pier and across the way from the U.S. Coast Guard Station on Bristol Neck. Be sure to leave the red-and-green nun, marking hazards to its south, to starboard.

For those coming from the east, the passage is equally unmistakable and begins with flashing green bell "3" to the south of the 54-foot lighthouse on Hog Island Shoal. Leave the bell to port, and once clear of it, begin a slow turn to port. Proceed up the middle of the fairway between Bristol Point and Hog Island Shoal, leaving green can "3" to port, and continue northerly past Walker Island until you make light "4" and the U.S. Coast Guard Station ahead. The only real hazard remaining is the red-and-green nun that sits midway between the two channels, just south of the harbor, marking hazards to its south. Keep this well to your port as you pass by.

#2

Popasquash Neck

Bristol Harbor

Walker Island

Bristol Point

Hog Island

#3

Bristol Yacht Club

Bristol Harbor

#4

Popasquash Neck

Bristol Harbor

Hog Island

■ APPROACH TO WARREN AND ■ BARRINGTON RIVERS

AROUND Popasquash Neck from Bristol Harbor, and 2 miles north, is the approach to the Warren and Barrington Rivers. We could as easily have covered these rivers in Region II, as these are the waters where cruisers inbound up the West and East Passages converge.

As the photos indicate, though generally deep, the approach to the Warren and Barrington Rivers requires careful attention. Strong currents and a large number of navigational aids, marking various obstructions, must be respected. The entry point begins between flashing green "1," east of Rumstick Shoal, and red nun "2" off Bristol Highlands. Follow a northeasterly heading from there, leaving green can "5," east of Rumstick Point, to port. From there, the channel curves closer to the point—leave the red nuns to starboard, favoring the starboard side as you navigate to the green light on Allen Rock. It is possible to anchor in Smith Cove to the northwest of Allen Rock, or you can leave the rock to port, squeezing between it and nun "12" to its east. Adams Point will then lie to port, and the formal entrance into the Warren River will be on your starboard bow. The river is full of moorings, and there are several marinas located along its shores.

A mile north of Adams Point the river channel forks, with the left, buoyed fork being the entrance to the Barrington River. The hospitable Barrington Yacht Club lies just before the low bridge spanning the river between Tyler Point on the east and the town of Barrington to the west. Like Bristol and many other towns on Narragansett Bay, this area offers mariners almost anything in the way of marine repairs and services. If they don't have what you need on site, you can usually order it up from some other nearby business.

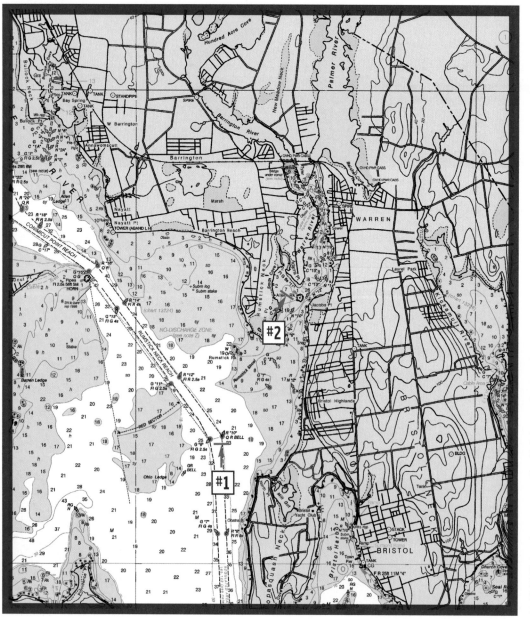

13221
57th ed., Feb. 08
NAD 83
Soundings in feet
1:40,000

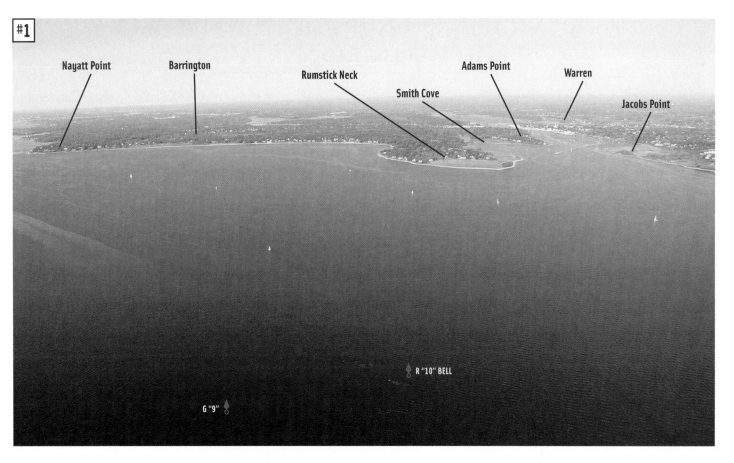

#1

Nayatt Point

Barrington

Rumstick Neck

Smith Cove

Adams Point

Warren

Jacobs Point

R "10" BELL

G "9"

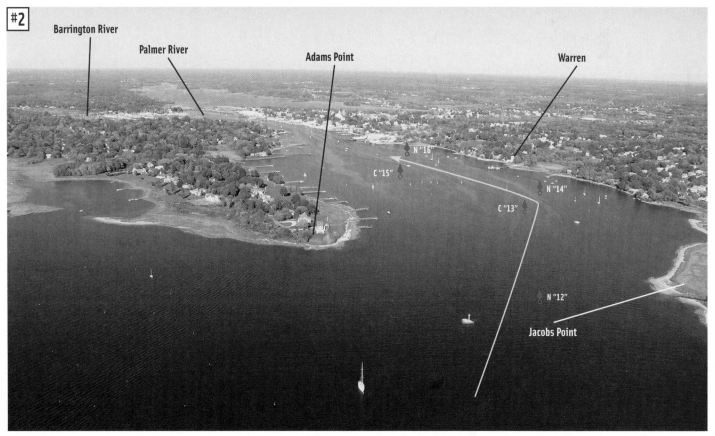

#2

Barrington River

Palmer River

Adams Point

Warren

N "16"

C "15"

N "14"

C "13"

N "12"

Jacobs Point

MOUNT HOPE BAY AND THE TAUNTON RIVER

ONE of the hidden jewels we found while researching this book is Bristol Narrows and the Kickamuit River just to its north. Bristol Narrows is in the northwest corner of Mount Hope Bay, and the standard approach is made from lighted green can "1" off Mount Hope Point. From there, a northerly heading following along the eastern shore of Bristol Neck affords sufficiently deep water to the entrance of the narrows, which is marked by green can "1" and red nun "2." After passing between these buoys, wind your way around the western shore of

Coggeshall just to the southeast of Touisset, observing the buoys and favoring the starboard side of the narrows. There is plenty of anchorage well into the river, and it's very well protected in almost every condition. This is a favorite local hurricane hole, but it has no marine facilities.

Continuing northeast to the head of Mount Hope Bay, one eventually reaches Fall River, Massachusetts, and the Taunton River. Downstream of the high-level bridges at Fall River, you'll see a large and inviting marina on the eastern shore. From there a short walk or cab ride will take you to Battleship Cove, featuring the USS *Massachusetts* and her 16-inch guns that were capable of hurling one-ton projectiles 20 miles. Other exhibits you can board include a submarine, a destroyer, and a Soviet-era missile corvette.

Adventurous boaters can explore farther up the Taunton River by passing through an opening bridge (with a high-level replacement bridge under construction). The river eventually narrows and becomes quite pastoral in parts. There are several good boatyards well upriver, including a friendly yacht club where gas and diesel are available. Just be careful to avoid shoals by staying in the marked channel.

13221
57th ed., Feb. 08
NAD 83
Soundings in feet
1:40,000

#1

Kickamuit River

Bristol Narrows

C "7"

N "6"

Coggeshall

N "4"

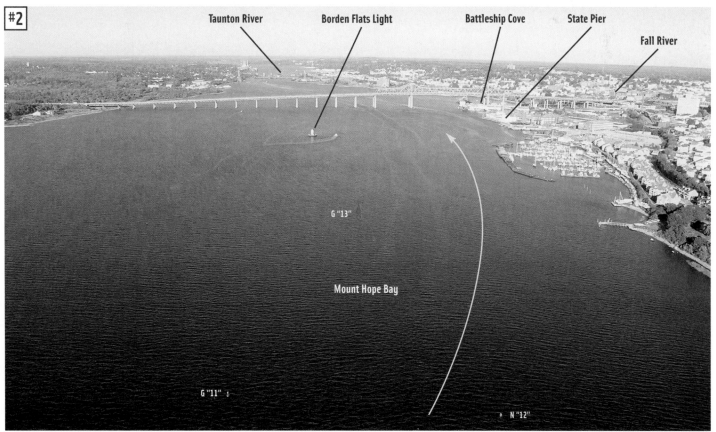

#2

Taunton River

Borden Flats Light

Battleship Cove

State Pier

Fall River

G "13"

Mount Hope Bay

G "11"

N "12"

REGION IV

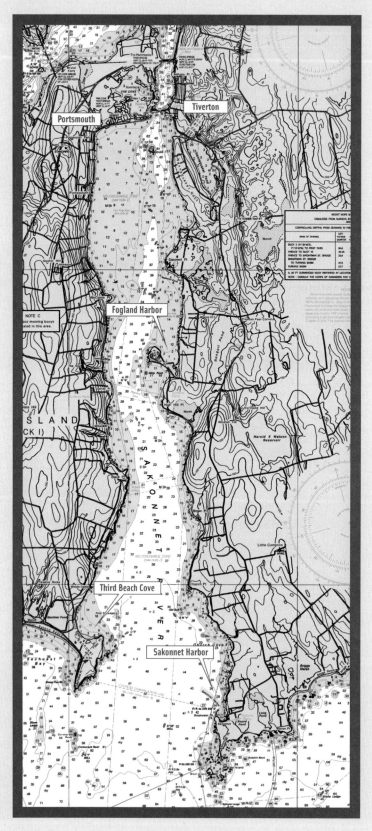

13221
57th ed., Feb. 08
NAD 83
Soundings in feet
1:40,000

THE SAKONNET RIVER

T he Sakonnet River is in fact not a river at all, but a 10-mile-long strait, or passage—the eastern-most and perhaps the most beautiful of the three passages into upper Narragansett Bay. It is also the least crowded of the bay's three passages—though it can still be busy—and it affords marvelous cruising for those inclined to wander from the beaten path that leads to Newport. A northerly or southerly blowing along the river's long axis can set up a chop in its comparatively shallow waters, but rolling hills on both shores offer protection from a breeze from any other direction. Sailors can enjoy fast sailing on smooth waters in the prevailing southwesterlies of summer, and the bucolic scenery of pastures, stone walls, orchards, vineyards, and old farmhouses creates a delightful backdrop to what often feels like a cruise on inland waters.

The outer approaches to Narragansett Bay from Rhode Island Sound are touched on in Region II. We have always found red-and-white whistle "SR" to be a safe and convenient starting point for an approach to the Sakonnet River. From the whistle, a northerly heading to red bell "2A" will leave 58-foot Sakonnet Light and the many shoals and ledges off Sakonnet Point well to starboard. Give a wide berth also to Cormorant Reef to the west (see chart page 94). The reef, which is exposed at all tides, is marked by green bell "1" and often by breaking surf.

Tiverton

The approach to Tiverton (see page 98).

SAKONNET HARBOR,
THIRD BEACH COVE, AND FOGLAND

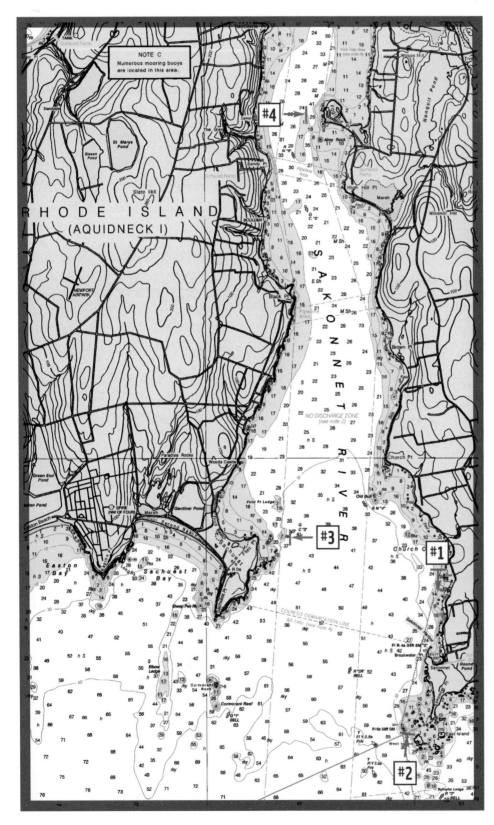

13221
57th ed., Feb. 08
NAD 83
Soundings in feet
1:40,000

LOCATED in the rural, undeveloped town of Little Compton, Rhode Island, just north of Sakonnet Point, Sakonnet Harbor provides good protection and reasonable access for those traveling to or from Newport. A northeasterly heading from red bell "2A" takes you toward the 34-foot light on the harbor breakwater and keeps you well off the numerous rocks and hazards surrounding Sakonnet Point. Little Compton is home to the Sakonnet Yacht Club, which does its best to be as hospitable as possible to visiting yachtsmen during the summer. Though anchorage is possible, there is very limited room, and you will be much better served to call ahead for a mooring. There are few facilities.

#1 Sakonnet Harbor   Sakonnet Light

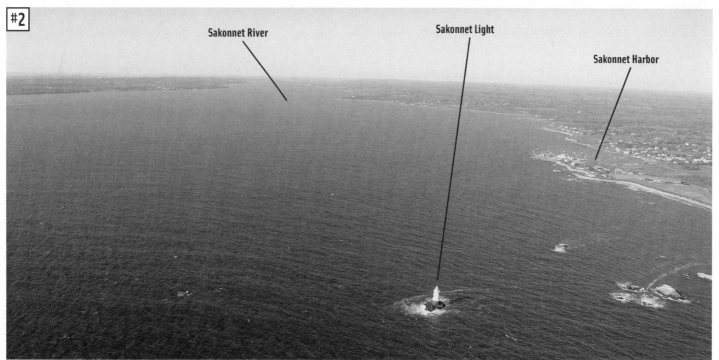

#2 Sakonnet River   Sakonnet Light   Sakonnet Harbor

THIRD BEACH COVE

ON the other side of the river, just north of the Sachuest peninsula and Flint Point, is a semicircular cove off Newport's busy Third Beach. This little cove, sometimes called Sachuest Cove, provides comfortable anchorage and good holding in the prevailing south-westerlies and wonderful access to the protected beach, though no services exist. The north end of the cove may provide some respite from the frenetic watersports you'll find in progress off the beach on most summer weekends. It's a great picnic stop.

#3 (See page 94.)

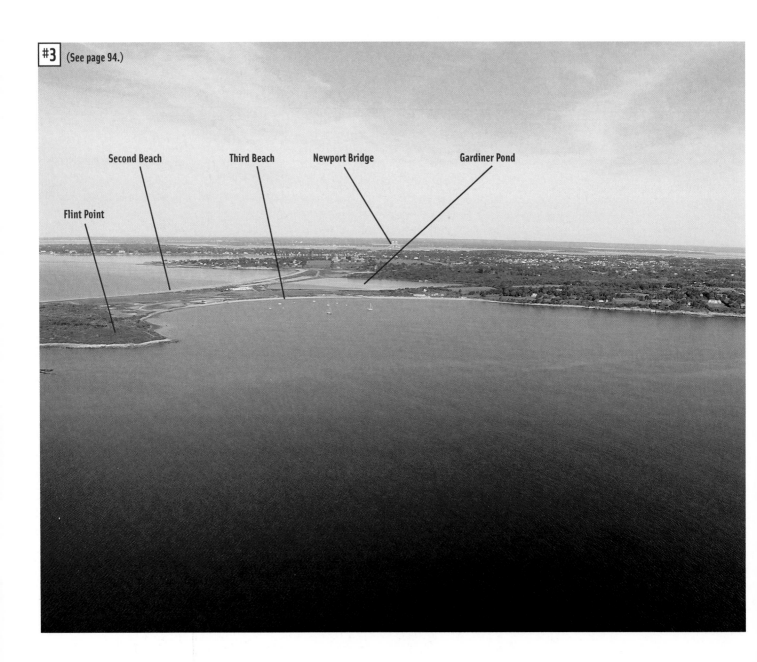

Flint Point

Second Beach

Third Beach

Newport Bridge

Gardiner Pond

FOGLAND HARBOR

SOME 4½ miles north of Third Beach Cove, on the eastern (Tiverton) shore of the Sakonnet River, is Fogland Harbor, with reasonable protection and anchorage. Though lacking accessible services, this pastoral harbor with its accessible swimming beaches (less crowded than Third Beach Cove) is nevertheless a good spot to lay over for a night. The approach into the harbor is best made from the center of the river, west of red nun "6." Note unmarked (but charted) Almy Rock to the east of the buoy. From nun "6," proceed east of north, staying near midchannel until well past Fogland Point. Once clear of the point, head east into the middle of the protected harbor and anchor along the eastern shore in 11 to 12 feet of water. Don't go too far in, as it shoals rapidly.

#4 (See page 94.)

Fogland Point

TIVERTON AND PORTSMOUTH

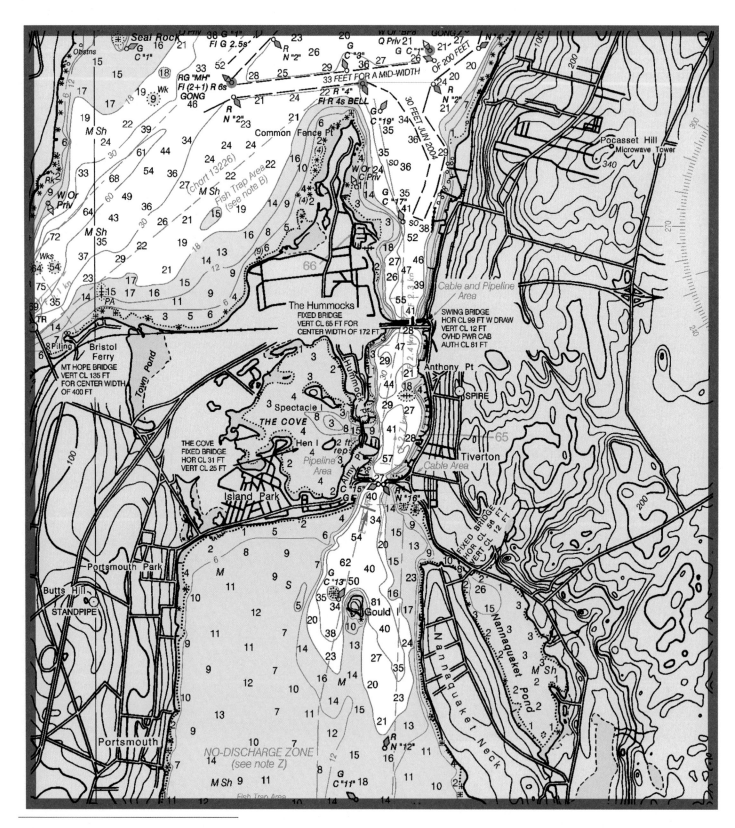

13221, 57th ed., Feb. 08, NAD 83, Soundings in feet, 1:40,000

AT its northern end, the Sakonnet River narrows abruptly to a constricted deepwater channel that opens to the north into Mount Hope Bay. From the bay, as we saw in Region III, you can head north to Fall River and the Taunton River, or west under the Mount Hope Bridge and into the East Passage of Narragansett Bay.

The channel between the Sakonnet River and Mount Hope Bay is constricted at its southern end by the breakwaters marked by green can "15" and red nun "16" (these breakwaters being the remaining stonework of a vanished bridge), and at its northern end by the abutments of a permanently open railroad bridge over which looms the highway bridge (with 65 feet of clearance under its center span) connecting Tiverton, on the east shore, with Portsmouth on the west shore. Through these constricted openings funnel currents of 2.5 knots or more—definitely a factor to include in your passage planning—with the current through the southern opening being especially notorious. (Also see photo page 93.)

Between these two constrictions is the unnamed harbor separating Portsmouth from Tiverton, and it provides a sheltered place to spend the night. There are marinas on both shores, and the Tiverton Yacht Club is on the eastern shore. These facilities can provide the transient yachtsman with moorings and dock space. Ashore are a couple of small eateries, a convenience store, a coffee shop, a gas station, and a few other shops, though major shopping requires a car or taxi. This harbor is a bit sleepier and quieter than some other anchorages in this area, providing a pleasant contrast. Anchoring is not recommended due to the swift currents and numerous moored boats. North of the high-rise highway bridge is another large marina facility on the western shore. From there it is just a 5-mile hop to Fall River (Region III), which makes yet another interesting stop.

Portsmouth

Tiverton

N "16"

C "15"

REGION V

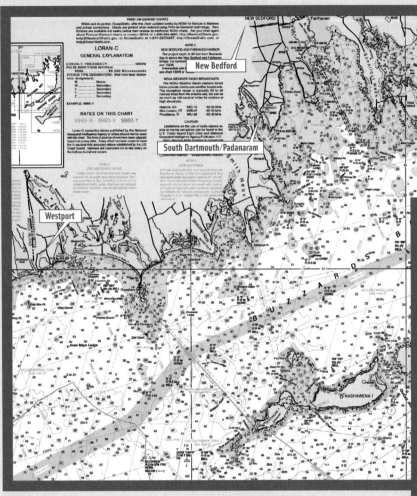

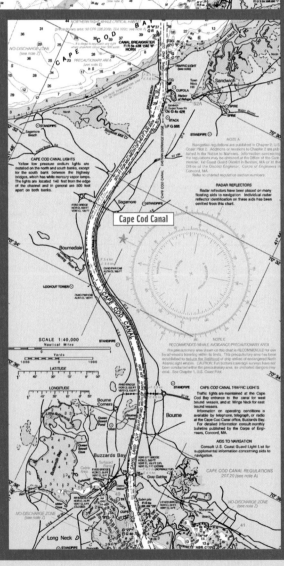

Westport: 102

South Dartmouth/Padanaram: 104

New Bedford: 106

Mattapoisett: 110

Marion/Sippican: 112

Wareham River: 114

Onset Harbor: 116

Cape Cod Canal: 118

Pocasset Harbor: 122

Red Brook Harbor: 124

Megansett Harbor/Fiddler's Cove: 126

West Falmouth Harbor: 128

13218
40th ed., Feb. 08
NAD 83
Soundings in feet
1:80,000

13229, 30th ed., Apr. 08, NAD 83, Soundings in feet, 1:40,000

BUZZARDS BAY AND THE CAPE COD CANAL

—WESTPORT, MA, TO WEST FALMOUTH HARBOR—

Coasting the shoreline east from Sakonnet Point, you soon pass the town and state boundary dividing Little Compton, Rhode Island, from Westport, Massachusetts. The shoreline doesn't change—dreamlike vistas of rolling hills and well-tended farmlands continue to unfold to port—but you are now sailing along the shore of Massachusetts' Southeast Corner. Does that mean you have entered Buzzards Bay? Well, maybe. Government publications seem to consider everything between Rhode Island Sound and Cape Cod Canal to be part of Buzzards Bay, a definition that includes the shoreline of Westport. That makes the bay some 25 miles long, about the same size as Narragansett Bay. On the other hand, NOAA's chart of Buzzards Bay does not extend as far as Westport, and many cruisers think of the bay as lying northeast of a line drawn from the southwest corner of Cuttyhunk Island to Gooseberry Neck, on the east side of Westport. Other cruisers shrink the bay even further, thinking of it as lying northeast of a line connecting Woods Hole with West Island. By the latter definition, the bay is only 10 miles long and 8 miles wide. Here we'll follow the government's lead and include Westport in the bay.

The harbors of Buzzards Bay have a special feel. Though varied in most ways, as a group they are not nearly as remote as the coasts of Maine or New Hampshire, and they convey a bucolic charm more reminiscent of English villages than northern New England. Yet there is a certain cosmopolitan feel in these waters. The Colonial remnants of early American settlements is everywhere you look—from Westport's villages to New Bedford's whaling and groundfishing origins and the traditional yachting centers of Padanaram and Marion. Storm-swept dunes give way to well-manicured upland pastures and vineyards, neat within their stone-wall boundaries. The blend of Colonial charm and worldly energy, old vision and new, is alluring.

Despite Buzzards Bay's deserved reputation as a wind factory, the bay's sandy shores and rolling uplands give it a gentler mien than the "stern and rockbound" shores north of Cape Ann. Still, you'll be challenged by shifting winds, tidal currents, and shoals. During the summer, there is almost always a stiff afternoon breeze, known locally as the "Buzzards Bay Trades," that makes this area particularly attractive to sailors—especially when eastbound. This afternoon southwesterly is usually stronger in the upper regions of the bay, and the chop there is steeper when the wind is opposed by an ebb tide from the Cape Cod Canal.

The bay is also well known for excellent bluefish and striper fishing, and records have been broken in the rocky waters surrounding Cuttyhunk Island. You are likely to see dolphins and whales as well, possibly even a great white shark. Great swimming beaches abound, and the waters are warm. Be sure to utilize your tide and current tables to make the trickier passages at the most favorable times. With plenty of harbors, marinas, and anchorages and all the services any cruiser could need, Buzzards Bay can be either a well-favored cruising ground you never wish to leave, or an intermezzo between the hubbub of Long Island Sound and the remote, rocky shores of Maine.

From Rhode Island Sound and points west, Westport Harbor is your first possible port of call on Buzzards Bay. If your approach is from the south and offshore, 87-foot Buzzards Tower, southwest of Cuttyhunk Island, makes an excellent landfall from which to plot your chosen course up the bay. From the east, you may enter the bay through one of the Elizabeth Island passages, taking due precautions with the tide. Your approach from the north may well be through the Cape Cod Canal.

■ WESTPORT ■

THOUGH often overlooked by cruisers, Westport Harbor, with its bordering village of Westport Point, is very well protected. Entering Westport presents some unique challenges and requires up-to-date charts, tidal current tables, and careful attention to avoid the many charted rocks and shoals, some of which are unmarked. From all points, the approach begins at red-and-white bell "WH," one-quarter nautical mile south of Two Mile Rock and about 1.75 miles southeast of the harbor entrance. Don't cut any of the buoys in this harbor approach without intimate local knowledge, as there are hazards lurking just outside the channel. From the bell, proceed on a northerly course, keeping green marker "3" at Two Mile Rock to your port. Continue on this course, picking up red nun "4" off Joe Burris Ledge, and

be sure to leave that to port as well. Looking northwest from there, you should be able to see 35-foot flashing green light "7" on The Knubble, the rocky highpoint capping the eastern extremity of the Acoaxet peninsula. Once you see the light, the narrow curving channel becomes more obvious. Still, you must be careful to maintain the delicate approach between Dogfish Ledge, marked by can "5,"and Halfmile Rock, marked by nun "6." (From the chart it would appear that an approach north of Halfmile Rock is possible for any boat drawing less than 7 feet, but this is not advisable without up-to-date local knowledge.) As of this writing, it is advised to favor the Halfmile Rock side of the channel as you begin the entrance around The Knubble, but be aware that there is a bar across the channel that may carry as little

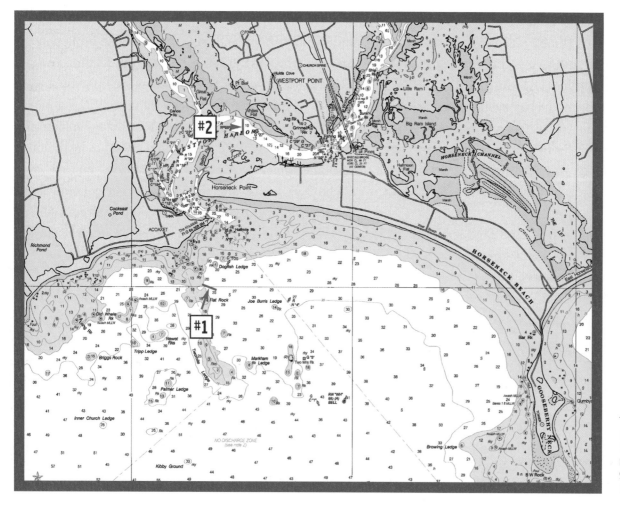

13228
11th ed., May 07
NAD 83
Soundings in feet
1:20,000

#1 Westport River | The Knubble | Horseneck Point | Horseneck Beach | Westport Harbor | Westport Point

N "6"

C "5"

as 6 feet of water, and the strong currents coming from or entering the Westport River (2.5 knots on standard tides and up to 3.5 knots on spring tides) will be felt. The bar breaks in heavy weather when the current is pouring out against the wind, and this is not an entrance to be taken lightly in a strong onshore blow.

After making the turn around The Knubble, you'll find the channel is well marked but still requires attention, and you will be either blasting along with a favorable current or fighting a stiff one. Periodically check over your stern to make sure you aren't being swept out of the channel by the current, and be aware that much of the harbor is a slow-speed, no-wake zone that is well enforced by the Westport Harbormaster.

Follow the curving channel around to the west, then northeast, and then east until you see the marina and boatyard to your right with rental moorings, fuel, a very good marine store, and all repair facilities. You will have a large fleet of moored boats to contend with, but the marina or its launch should be reachable by radio. Hospitable Westport Yacht Club, located on the northern side of Horseneck Point just beyond the marina, is worth a visit, but transient berths are limited. Anchoring in the river is not recommended due to the swift reversing currents. Many an unwary mariner has lept overboard for an evening swim only to find him- or her-

self heading out to sea with the tide. Your surroundings consist of beautiful marshland, drying sandbars, elegant New England homes ashore, and probably several osprey nests perched on poles. Contact the harbormaster if you are in need of any advice or assistance.

Westport provides an interesting stop that is extremely well protected. There are a couple of restaurants within walking distance of the marina, and the village of Westport Point, with further shops and restaurants, is a cab ride away. Three-and-a-half-mile-long Horseneck State Beach and Reservation is a great treat.

#2 Westport Point | Yacht Club | Horseneck Beach | Marina

■ APPROACH TO SOUTH DARTMOUTH ■

FROM the south, the approach to South Dartmouth, New Bedford, and the Fairhaven region generally begins from flashing red bell "8," midway between Dumpling Rocks (with its green flashing 52-foot light)

and Great Ledge. From there, a northerly approach through well-buoyed waters into South Dartmouth (locally known as "Padanaram" but labeled on the chart as Apponagansett Bay) or a northeasterly approach into New Bedford and Fairhaven can easily be made.

A passage east from Westport will have to take you out around Gooseberry Neck and its offlying ledges, the Hen and Chickens. If in any doubt you might as well circle outside The Wildcat and south of can "1" as well. Then you can run northeast to flashing green gong "5" off Slocums Neck, then continue northeastward toward the approach buoys off South Dartmouth and New Bedford.

SOUTH DARTMOUTH/ PADANARAM

PADANARAM, on the northwest shore of Buzzards Bay, is home to the New Bedford Yacht Club and the Concordia Company, builder of the famous Concordia yawls. As mentioned above, an approach from the south is most safely made via red flashing bell "8" just east of Dumpling Rocks. Head north from the vicinity of the bell, picking up red-and-green flashing gong "AB." From there, Ricketsons Point, on the north side of the Apponagansett Bay entrance, and the breakwater running south from the point should be visible, along with 25-foot red flashing light "8" on the breakwater's southern end. Leaving the light to starboard will take you through the mouth of Apponagansett Bay and into the center of Padanaram Harbor.

13230
49th ed., Aug. 08
NAD 83
Soundings in feet
1:40,000

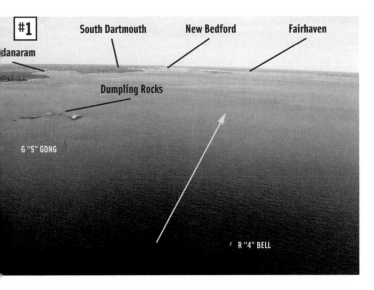

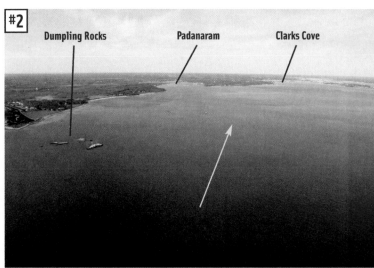

Once you're past the breakwater, channel markers will indicate the passage to the New Bedford Yacht Club. Many boats anchor and moor off the yacht club and its neighboring boatyards, and depending on the season, transient moorings may be available. The small, tidy village center of South Dartmouth (Padanaram) lines the streets behind the marine facilities.

In addition, the southwestern side of the harbor is a permitted anchorage spot. A number of services, shops, and restaurants are available ashore. Needless to say, this popular harbor is crowded during the summer, despite the fact that it can get quite uncomfortable during a rare southeasterly blow.

■ NEW BEDFORD ■

AS the largest commercial marine port in Massachusetts south of Boston, New Bedford can provide important emergency services, but in the past has not been considered a prime destination for visiting cruisers. This is a shame. The harbor is well protected and easily approached in all weather, and the marinas on Popes Island and the Fairhaven shore provide convenient access to the remarkable historic districts of both cities. Here you'll find the New Bedford Whaling Museum, New Bedford Whaling National Park, the Nantucket lightship, and the schooner *Ernestina*, a former Grand Banks fishing schooner and Arctic explorer. Ferries sail from here to Cuttyhunk and Martha's Vineyard. When hunger strikes, you'll find fresh seafood in the many restaurants near the waterfront, all with specials right off the numerous commercial fishing boats tied up nearby. We never miss a chance to enjoy fresh scallops.

The approach to New Bedford follows the well-marked entrance channel, which, for all practical purposes, begins with flashing green gong "7" off Brooklyn Rock and flashing red buoy "6" off Henrietta Rock. From there, a well-buoyed fairway leads you directly to the breakwater and the "hurricane gates" that close off the harbor to protect it from the destructive storm surge associ-

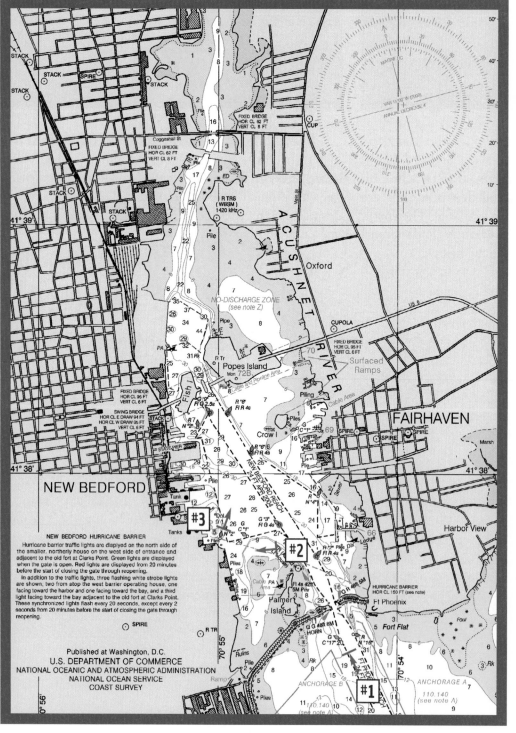

NEW BEDFORD HURRICANE BARRIER

Hurricane barrier traffic lights are displayed on the north side of the smaller, northerly house on the west side of entrance and adjacent to the old fort at Clarks Point. Green lights are displayed when the gate is open. Red lights are displayed from 20 minutes before the start of closing the gate through reopening.

In addition to the traffic lights, three flashing white strobe lights are shown, two from atop the west barrier operating house, one facing toward the harbor and one facing toward the bay, and a third light facing toward the bay adjacent to the old fort at Clarks Point. These synchronized lights flash every 20 seconds, except every 2 seconds from 20 minutes before the start of closing the gate through reopening.

Published at Washington, D.C.
U.S. DEPARTMENT OF COMMERCE
NATIONAL OCEANIC AND ATMOSPHERIC ADMINISTRATION
NATIONAL OCEAN SERVICE
COAST SURVEY

13229
30th ed., Apr. 08
NAD 83
Soundings in feet
1:40,000

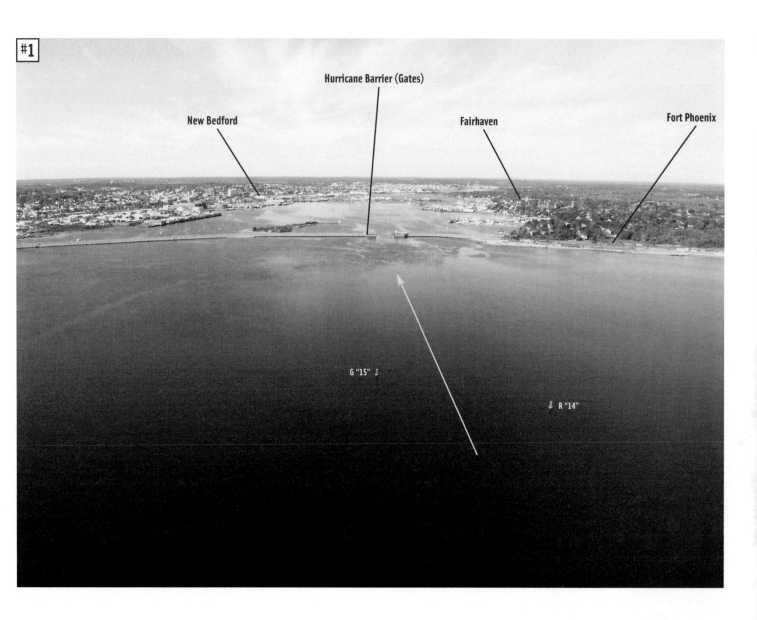

#1

New Bedford   Hurricane Barrier (Gates)   Fairhaven   Fort Phoenix

G "15"   R "14"

ated with a hurricane. The flood and ebb through the gates are both about 2.4 knots.

After passing through the open gates (a no-wake zone), the channel, here called the New Bedford Reach, continues up the Acushnet River to the more commercial sections of the harbor on the New Bedford shore to your port and the marinas to your starboard on Popes Island and the Fairhaven shore (see photos pages 108 and 109). There are rental moorings available (contact the harbormaster) and plenty of room to anchor, though you must stay clear of the numerous docks and channels, and the harbor is busy with commercial traffic.

New Bedford is the fifth-largest city in Massachusetts with much to see, do, and enjoy. Its Quaker and whaling roots are everywhere, including the Seaman's Bethel, the chapel described in Herman Melville's *Moby-Dick*. This was once the largest whaling port in the world. Many of the grand old houses in Fairhaven, across the river, were built by wealthy sea captains.

#2

Fairhaven

Fort Phoenix

Palmer Island Light

#3

Acushnet River

Popes Island

Fairhaven

G "9"

R "8"

R "6"

MATTAPOISETT HARBOR

EAST of New Bedford Harbor, Nasketucket Bay is shallow and rocky, and is more popular for sportfishing and daysailing than as a cruising destination. East of Nasketucket Bay is well-known Mattapoisett Harbor, a special anchorage spot along the northwestern shore of

Buzzards Bay. Uncomplicated and easily navigated, the Mattapoisett approach usually begins from flashing green bell "1" off Nye Ledge. From the bell, a north-westerly course takes you straight up the harbor. Keep green cans "3," "5," and "7" on your port side and nuns

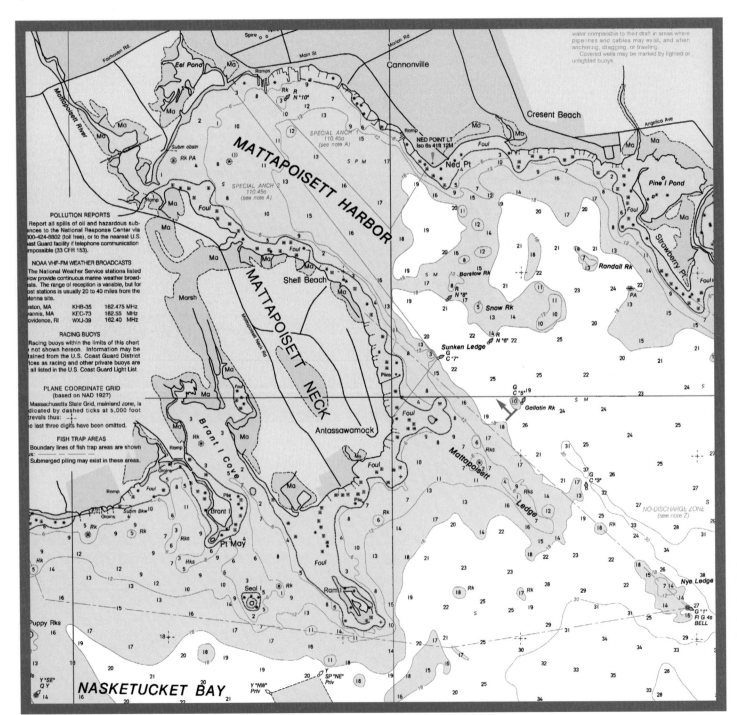

Mattapoisett Neck

C "7"   N "6"

"6" (off Sunken Ledge) and "8" (off Barstow Rock) on your starboard side as you make your way to the comfortably deep water.

Possible anchorages can be found along both the western and eastern shores, and there are transient rental moorings—contact the harbormaster. In addition to the hospitable Mattapoisett Yacht Club on Ned Point, a short tender run from the anchorages or moor-ings can take you to the town dock located near nun "10." The major marine facilities are all located along the northern side of the harbor. Ashore are shops and restaurants, with many more within a short cab ride.

Mattapoisett Harbor is exposed to the southeast, but in any other weather it's a quiet, comfortable anchorage. Go elsewhere for hubbub. Stop at Mattapoisett to relax.

13232
4th ed., June 01
NAD 83
Soundings in feet
1:20,000

■ MARION HARBOR ■

ANOTHER of our favorite spots is Marion Harbor, otherwise known as Sippican Harbor. Well protected and beautiful, Marion provides the visiting yachtsman a wonderful stopping-off point on any cruise. The approach into the harbor is best made from flashing red "2" off Centerboard Shoal, which sits midway between Bird Island and the Bow Bells indicated on the chart. Though it's tempting if you're approaching from the east, one should not try to cut the corner between Butler Point and Bird Island, as the 2- to 4-foot depths are real. A northerly course from red "2" will take you into Sippican Harbor, but be sure to leave green "3" and "5" to port. Don't worry if you can't make out the exact path into Marion Harbor from green "5." It becomes visible only as you near Ram Island and red nun "6." From red "6" the approach requires some attention and is a bit counterintuitive—i.e., the channel does not run where the shoreline trend would lead you to believe—so be sure to follow the navigation aids precisely, keeping the green on your port and the red on your right.

We have to say that Marion Harbor is one of our favorite stopovers—though the members of the harbor's Beverly Yacht Club may not be happy to read this, since the harbor is always extremely crowded. But the harbormaster and the yacht club do a wonderful job managing summer traffic, and we've never had a difficult time finding a mooring for the night. In the rare case when a mooring is not

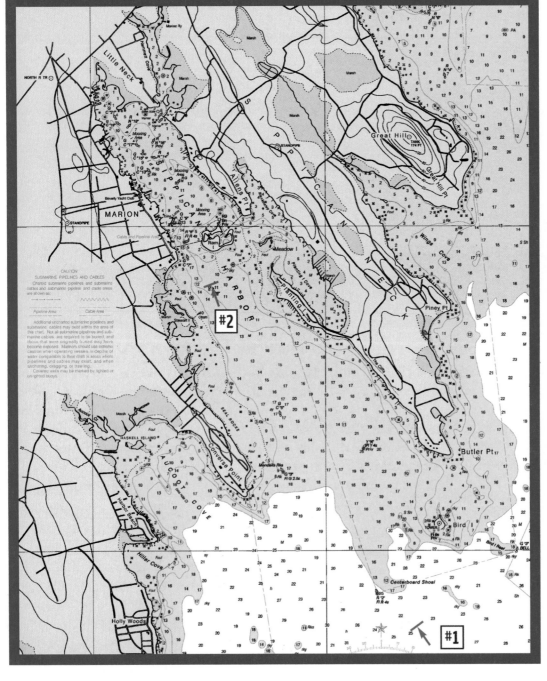

13236
30th ed., March 06
NAD 83
Soundings in feet
1:20,000

available, anchorage can be had outside Ram Island or off Allens Point, but a mooring is much preferred. The yacht club—which, along with the marine facilities, is on the harbor's west shore—provides frequent launch service, and once you're ashore, exploring the surrounding walks, upscale homes, and town is a must. The driveways to some of the homes are made of crushed shells—a vivid reminder that Cape Cod and the islands are close at hand.

You'll also find wonderful boatbuilders along the harbor's west shore, which is also home to the Tabor Academy and its training vessel, the 92-foot schooner *Tabor Boy*.

■ WAREHAM RIVER ■

HAVING recently visited the Cape Cod Shipbuilding Company in Wareham to look at one of their classic boats, we know that the Wareham River offers great protection for shoal-draft boats. Cruisers often bypass Wareham, and indeed, the 2-mile approach into and up the Wareham River isn't for the faint of heart. Careful attention to tide and current is a must, as the current can run at up to 4 knots. The river is prone to shoaling but can provide an incredibly safe haven near the Cape Cod Canal.

The best approach to Wareham begins from red nun "2" off Dry Ledge. From there, follow a northwesterly course to leave Great Hill Point to port and red nun "4" to starboard, then thread your way carefully past nun "6" and cans "7" and "9" off Cromeset Point. Leaving nuns "10" and "12" close aboard to starboard will get you safely past Long Beach Point and into the river. Watch the current and faithfully observe the well-buoyed channel as you proceed upriver to Wareham.

Marine services are available, including moorings and some dock space, but space is limited.

13236
30th ed., March 06
NAD 83
Soundings in feet
1:20,000

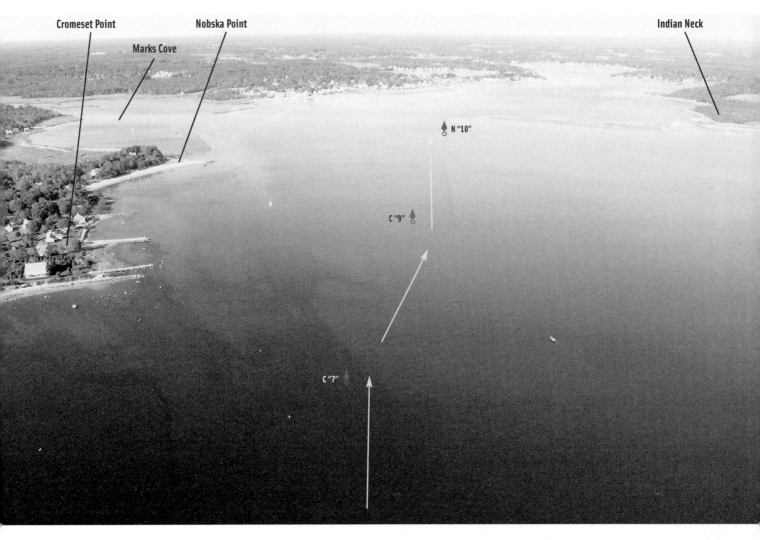

Cromeset Point

Marks Cove

Nobska Point

Indian Neck

N "10"

C "9"

C "7"

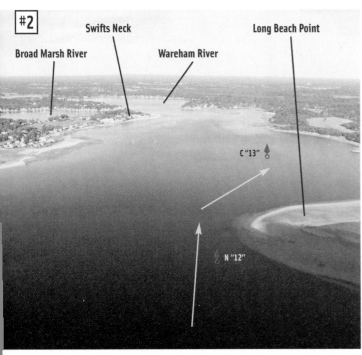

#2

Broad Marsh River

Swifts Neck

Wareham River

Long Beach Point

C "13"

N "12"

#3

Broad Marsh River

Quasuet Point

Wareham

Parkwood Beach

N "20"

C "19"

C "17"

■ ONSET HARBOR ■

WE have found Onset Harbor to be very protected, particularly in the special anchorage area indicated on the chart just off Point Independence. Onset also provides convenient access to stores and services as well as a marina. The downside is that the approach into the harbor is no piece of cake and requires careful attention even in daylight and clear weather. In addition, as anyone who has navigated the Cape Cod Canal knows, it is not uncommon upon exiting the southwest end of the canal to encounter significant waves and currents just off Hog Neck, conditions that present a not-insignificant challenge to entering Onset Bay.

To enter the bay from the canal, a shoal-draft boat might proceed westerly from green light "23"to nun "8" and green can "5" off Burgess Point, keeping south of the line between green "23" and nun "8," but this approach is risky for any boat drawing more than 4 feet. The safer approach—which is also the more convenient approach for any northbound boat—begins from green flashing "21" off Hog Neck. Leave green "21" to starboard (because it marks the Cape Cod Canal channel, not the Onset Bay channel), passing between it and can "1," taking care to compensate for any tendency of an ebb current from the canal to set you toward shore. From there the navigation aids will lead you past the north shore of Hog Neck and then north to Burgess Point. There the channel narrows, and you will turn to port to follow the buoys into the inner part of Onset Bay.

Once there, the special anchorage area off Point Independence can be accessed easily via a buoyed side channel. There is a marina with a fuel dock there, on the northeastern shore of the harbor. For the even more adventurous with shallow draft, limited access to Sunset Cove can be made by navigating around the "hook" on the northern side of Great Neck, but the many shoals and submerged pilings showing on the chart in this passage strongly suggest that it be navigated only by tender.

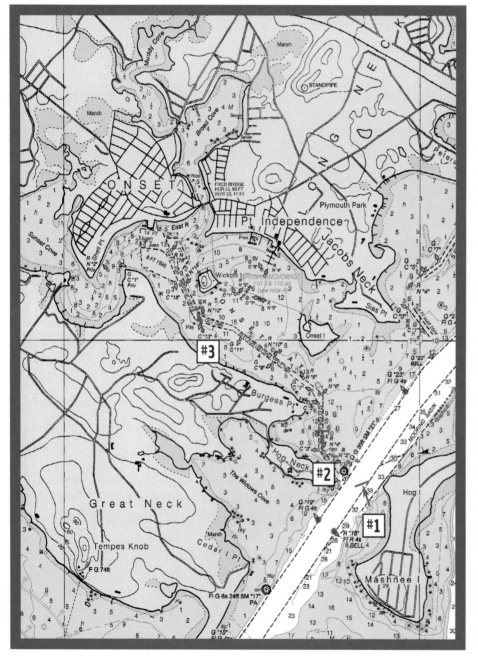

13236
30th ed., March 06
NAD 83
Soundings in feet
1:20,000

#1

Burgess Point

Onset

Onset Island

C "3"

N "4"

N "2"

G "21"

Hog Neck

C "1"

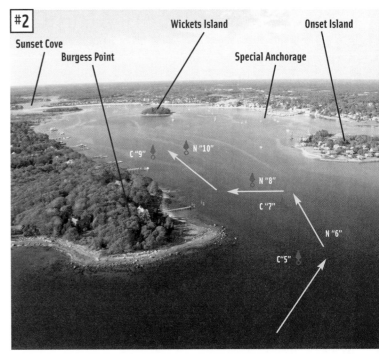

#2

Sunset Cove

Burgess Point

Wickets Island

Special Anchorage

Onset Island

C "9"

N "10"

N "8"

C "7"

N "6"

C "5"

#3

Sunset Cove

Shell Point

Onset

N "16"

C "15"

N "14"

Wickets Island

■ CAPE COD CANAL ■

PERHAPS the most famous waterway on the East Coast, the Cape Cod Canal opened in 1914 and was purchased by the federal government in 1928. According to the Army Corps of Engineers, the canal was dredged to nearly 500 feet wide and 32 feet deep, which required the removal of 30 million cubic yards of earth. This seven-mile link from Sandwich on the east side to Bourne and Buzzards Bay on the west provides one of the most appreciated shortcuts in the annals of boating. Easily navigated on a favorable tide, the canal provides quick passage and a unique historical glimpse of early 20th century ingenuity. The main challenge in transiting the canal is an accurate forecast of the currents, which greatly assist you in the right direction, but for sailboats in particular can stop all forward progress if you are fighting them. The flood sets eastward at an average of 4.0 knots, and the ebb sets westward at an average of 4.5 knots.

Note that you are not allowed to sail through the canal—you must use auxiliary power—and there is a maximum speed limit of 10 m.p.h. No excessive wakes are allowed. Keep to the starboard side of the canal. Vessels larger than 65 feet must obtain permission to transit the canal from the control office (monitoring VHF channels 12, 13, 14, and 16). Boats smaller than 65 feet must stay clear of bigger vessels, and vessels traveling against the current should give way

(continues on page 120)

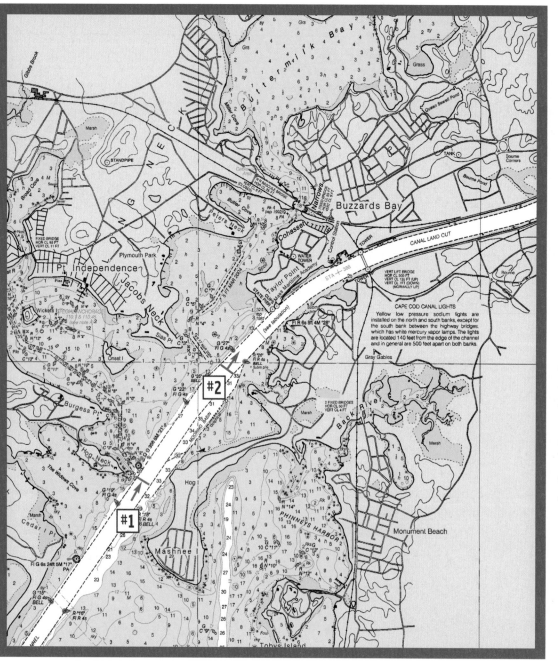

13236
30th ed., March 06
NAD 83
Soundings in feet
1:20,000

#1 — Sias Point · State Pier · Canal · G "21"

#2 — Butler Cove · Massachusetts Maritime Academy · Railroad Bridge · Cape Cod Bay · G "27" · R "26"

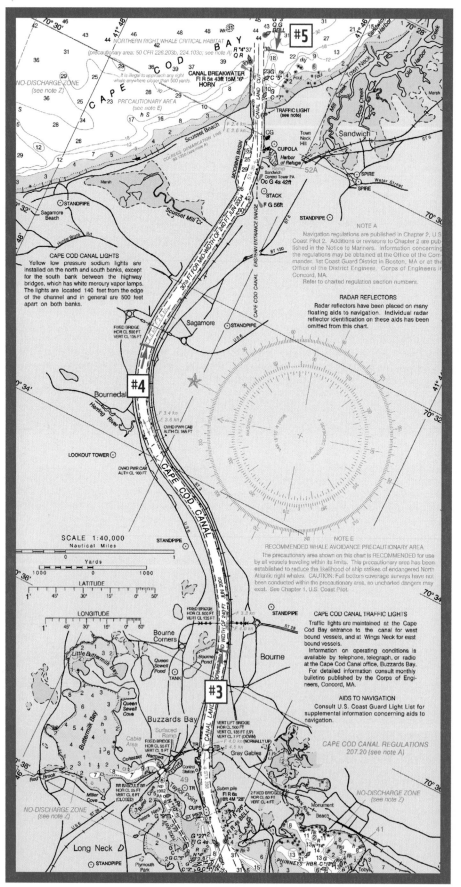

to vessels traveling with the current, just as on inland waterways.

There are two other challenges to note. The first is the railroad bridge, which is normally in the raised position (vertical clearance 135 feet) but is lowered on rare occasions (vertical clearance 7 feet). Pay attention to any horn blasts or radio commands you hear, and to the designated stop signs on each side of the bridge. Due to the swift currents, it can be difficult to wait while the bridge is down. The second challenge is the likelihood that, as you exit to the west on an ebb current, Buzzards Bay will welcome you with a pounding—often seemingly endless choppy waves set up by the typical strong afternoon southwesterly meeting the currents pouring out of the canal. You can duck into Onset Bay and wait for conditions to improve, or you can endure the pounding, secure in the knowledge that the chop will diminish as you get farther away from the canal.

Near the canal's eastern end is a small dredged basin known as the Harbor of Refuge which provides a marina with a fuel dock; this can be a good layover when the wind is blowing up at either end of the canal. Just be sure to listen and watch carefully for any large commercial traffic when entering or leaving the nearly blind channel into the basin. Once inside, you are out of the current, but be prepared for swift currents hitting you on the beam near the harbor entrance.

13229, 30th ed., Apr. 08, NAD 83, Soundings in feet, 1:40,000

#4

Cape Cod Bay

Harbor of Refuge

Sagamore Bridge

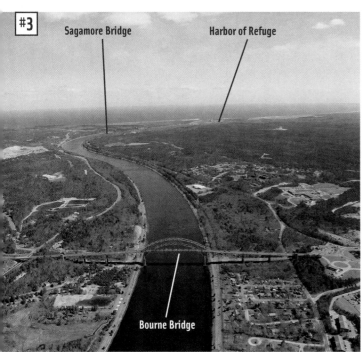

#3

Sagamore Bridge

Harbor of Refuge

Bourne Bridge

#5

Sandwich

Harbor of Refuge

■ POCASSET HARBOR ■

TURNING our attention from the Cape Cod Canal to the east side of Buzzards Bay, we know from experience that Pocasset Harbor, with its private homes on the shoreline, provides a peaceful refuge for those seeking an alternative to its busier neighbors. The approach into

Pocasset is best made from green flashing "1" (marking the southern end of the Hog Island Channel leading to the Cape Cod Canal), south of Abiels Ledge. From this point, an easterly heading will take you directly to the traffic light control tower and the abandoned lighthouse

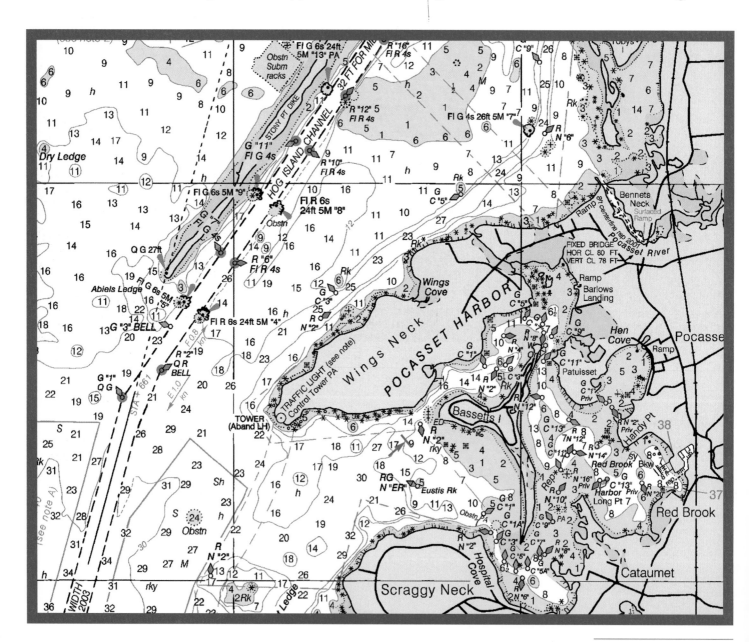

13229
30th ed., Apr. 08
NAD 83
Soundings in feet
1:40,000

tower on the western edge of Wings Neck. Once you pick up this visual marker, continue around the southern shore of Wings Neck, giving a wide berth to the shore and its off-lying rocks, until you reach nun "2" west of Bassetts Island. Swing to a northeasterly course there, into the harbor entrance, leaving nun "2" to starboard and holding to the middle of the entrance channel to avoid the hazards on both sides. The current can run hard through the entrance, so pay attention.

The anchorage area is just inside the harbor. You can dinghy ashore at a town landing toward the head of the harbor, near the charted "Barlows Landing." There are no services in the harbor.

■ RED BROOK HARBOR (CATAUMET) ■

CLOSELY associated with Pocasset Harbor is its neighbor to the southeast, Red Brook Harbor. This harbor is in the village of Cataumet, which, like the village of Pocasset, is part of the town of Bourne. Though accessible through a northern entrance from Pocasset Harbor, the principal entrance to Red Brook Harbor is the southern one, skirting the northern shore of Scraggy Neck. Not only is this entrance more direct, it is also easier to navigate, with more moderate currents.

Red-and-green nun "ER" off Eustis Rock provides a point of approach to the outer end of the southern entrance. Leave can "1" close to port, then swing south to leave nun "2" close to starboard and can "1A" close to port as you begin the hook around Bassetts Island's southern stem. Though the channel is somewhat prone to shoaling, the navigational aids are updated locally and provide clear guidance into the harbor. On our last visit, we had no difficulty picking up a mooring. We saw boats anchoring on the east side of Bassetts Island. With launch service and easy access, this harbor is a favorite for those looking for a refuge for the night close to the canal. Several marine facilities are farther in to the east, including one of the larger marinas in the region. There is a restaurant in the marina.

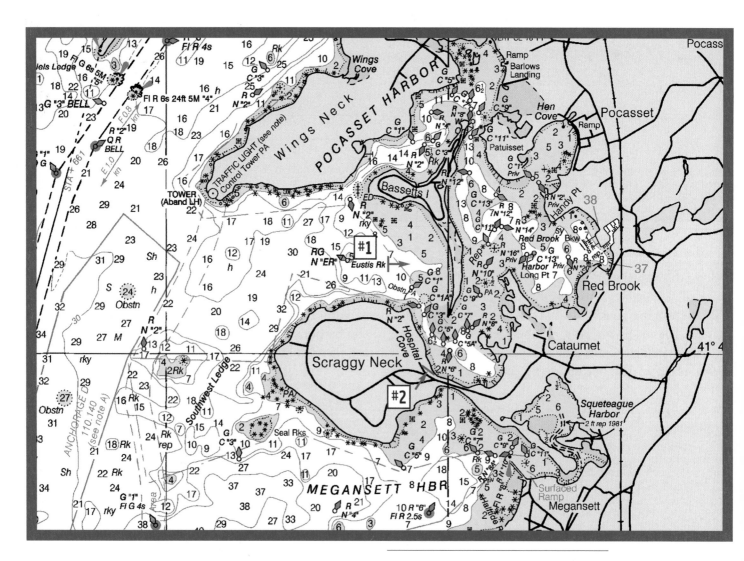

13229, 30th ed., Apr. 08, NAD 83, Soundings in feet, 1:40,000

#1

Bassetts Island   Red Brook Harbor   Scraggy Neck

C "1"

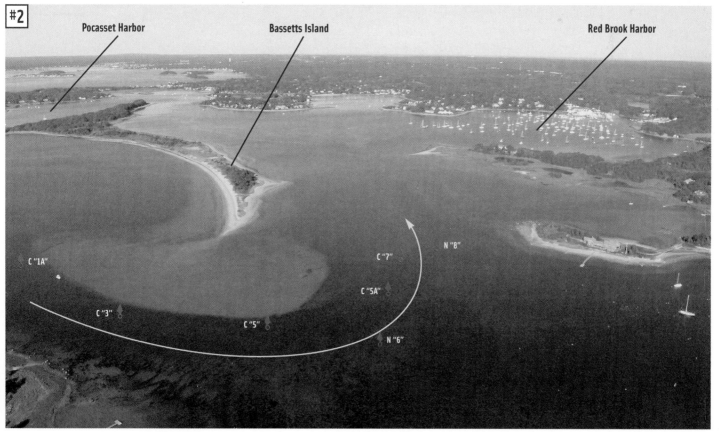

#2

Pocasset Harbor   Bassetts Island   Red Brook Harbor

N "8"

C "7"

C "1A"

C "5A"

C "3"

C "5"

N "6"

■ MEGANSETT HARBOR ■ AND FIDDLER'S COVE

BOTH Megansett Harbor (the northernmost of Falmouth's fourteen harbors) and Fiddler's Cove are easily accessible from the northern shore of Nyes Neck. The entrance is wide. Just keep red nun "4" off Cataumet Rock safely on your starboard side.

If you are looking to enter Fiddler's Cove (photo #2) with its large marina, the unmistakable arrowhead-shaped channel on Megansett Harbor's southern shore leads directly in. If you choose instead to head into Megansett's inner harbor, follow an easterly course midway between

can "5" to port and flashing red "6" to starboard, and you will find yourself in center channel with flashing red light "8" on the northern end of the breakwater directly ahead. Observe the remaining buoys. Though prone to shoaling, Megansett Harbor has ample anchorage on either side of the breakwater. The water close in on the west side of the breakwater is shoaler, however, and the western side of the breakwater is better protected. Adventurous and shallow-draft boats can choose a favorable tide and head farther in to totally protected Squeteague Harbor.

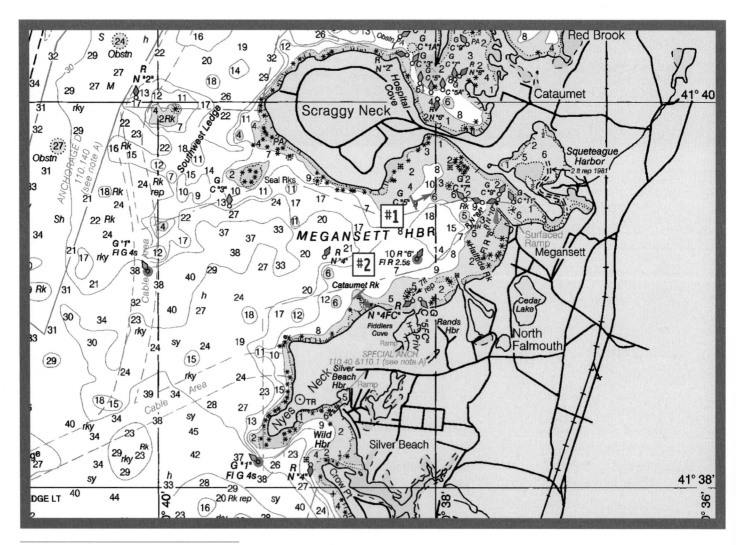

13229, 30th ed., Apr. 08, NAD 83, Soundings in feet, 1:40,000

#1

Squeteague Harbor

Breakwater

R "8"

C "7"

#2

C "5FC"

N "4FC"

■ WEST FALMOUTH HARBOR ■

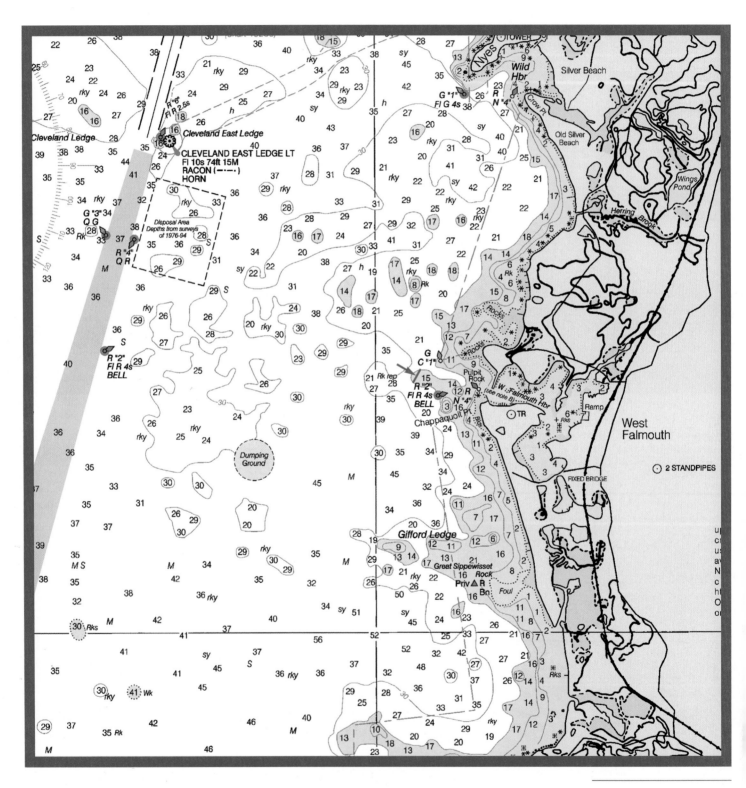

13230
49th ed., Aug. 08
NAD 83
Soundings in feet
1:40,000

WILD Harbor, just south of Megansett Harbor, is exposed to the prevailing southwesterlies and provides poor holding for anchoring. For boats with shoal draft, however, West Falmouth Harbor—just over 2 miles southeast of 74-foot Cleveland East Ledge Light marking the Cleveland Ledge Channel approach to the canal—may provide a comfortable spot to spend the night. The entrance is clearly marked by flashing red bell "2" and green can "1." From a point midway between these buoys, an easterly course will take you to nun "4"

off Pulpit Rock and the breakwater protruding from the northern shore. As of this writing there was sufficient depth to anchor comfortably inside the breakwater, if you can negotiate a spot between the local moored boats and the various rocks and shallows.

Quisset Harbor, the southernmost harbor on the east shore of Buzzards Bay, is delightful but small and crowded, and lacks transient anchorage. You might be able to get a guest mooring there.

West Falmouth Harbor

Chappaquoit Point

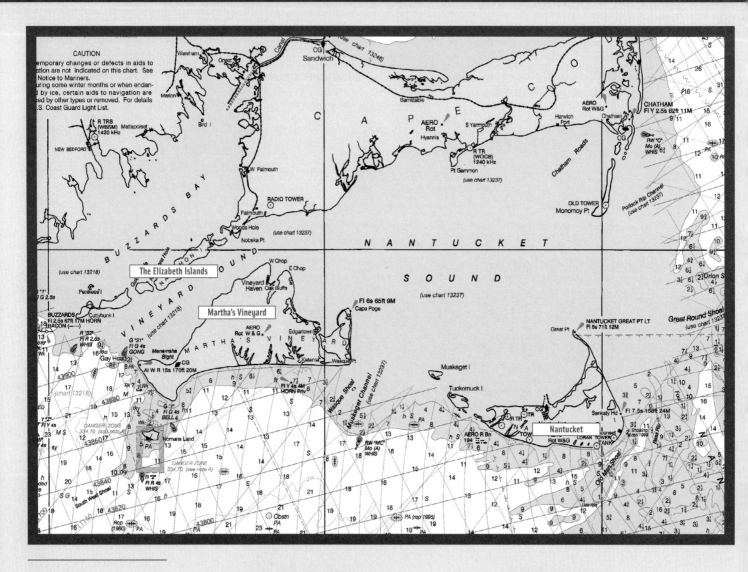

13200
37th Ed., April 09
NAD 83
Soundings in feet
1:400,000

THE ELIZABETH ISLANDS, MARTHA'S VINEYARD, AND NANTUCKET

The Elizabeth Islands, Martha's Vineyard, and Nantucket—known collectively as "the Islands"—were left behind some 12,000 years ago by the same retreating glacier that deposited Block Island and Montauk Point to the west. Now they emerge from the sea as if by magic, fragile amalgams of sand, salt marsh, and salt pond that somehow manage to persevere against the winter storms from the open Atlantic. The south coasts of Martha's Vineyard and Nantucket have been beaten flat and smooth by the sea as if by a smith's hammer—there are no harbors there. To find safe harbor you must seek the islands' northern coasts.

Close enough to be attainable, remote enough to be irresistibly alluring, the Islands are a cruiser's dream. Island-hopping cruisers—those happy to cut the mainland umbilical cord, at least temporarily—can make the 31-mile passage across Rhode Island Sound from Block Island to the harbor on Cuttyhunk Island, the southwesternmost of the Elizabeth Islands, in a day's run, particularly with the summer's prevailing southwesterlies behind them. Menemsha, on Martha's Vineyard, is only 6 miles more distant, and Vineyard Haven Harbor is just 11 miles beyond that.

Cuttyhunk and Menemsha are 12 and 20 miles, respectively, from Sakonnet Point, while Vineyard Haven is only 4½ miles across Vineyard Sound from Falmouth Harbor. Edgartown is just 11 miles from Falmouth. An 8-mile passage across Buzzards Bay from South Dartmouth takes you to Cuttyhunk, or you could take the Quicks Hole passage through the Elizabeth Islands and be in Vineyard Haven Harbor after 22 miles.

Nantucket is the most remote of the Islands, and so also the most compelling to many cruisers. It is the most "of the sea," seeming to exist in a tenuous balance with the swift currents that surround it and the winter gales that roar over it. Nantucket Harbor lies 25 miles east southeast of Vineyard Haven and 22 miles southeast across Nantucket Sound from Hyannis. For a real taste of offshore sailing, there is the 70-mile passage east to Nantucket Harbor from Block Island—a passage that would carry you south of No Mans Land and Martha's Vineyard, north through the Muskeget Channel, then east among the shoals north of Nantucket. In the right weather and the right boat, it could be done in a long day, but the Muskeget Channel can be hazardous and nerve-wracking even in broad daylight, and you wouldn't want to be there with darkness coming on, or in the fog that frequently shrouds the island. The prudent navigator coming from Block Island or Narragansett Bay would opt instead for the Vineyard Sound route to Nantucket, with the more clearly marked waters and the many intermediate anchorages that route provides.

Each of these islands and special harbors invites cruisers from far and near to experience the pure pleasure of cool breezes and warm water, not to mention some incredible beaches. Islanders are understandably proud of their homes, and though welcoming, expect visitors to treat the Islands with the respect they deserve. No matter how many times we visit them, we always find some new spot that is more beautiful than the last one.

■ THE ELIZABETH ISLANDS ■

THE Elizabeth Islands (Cuttyhunk, Nashawena, Pasque, Naushon, and nine to twelve minor islands, depending on which you choose to count) stretch 14 miles from Woods Hole in the northeast into the open Atlantic in the southwest. They separate Buzzards Bay to the north from Vineyard Sound to the south, but the

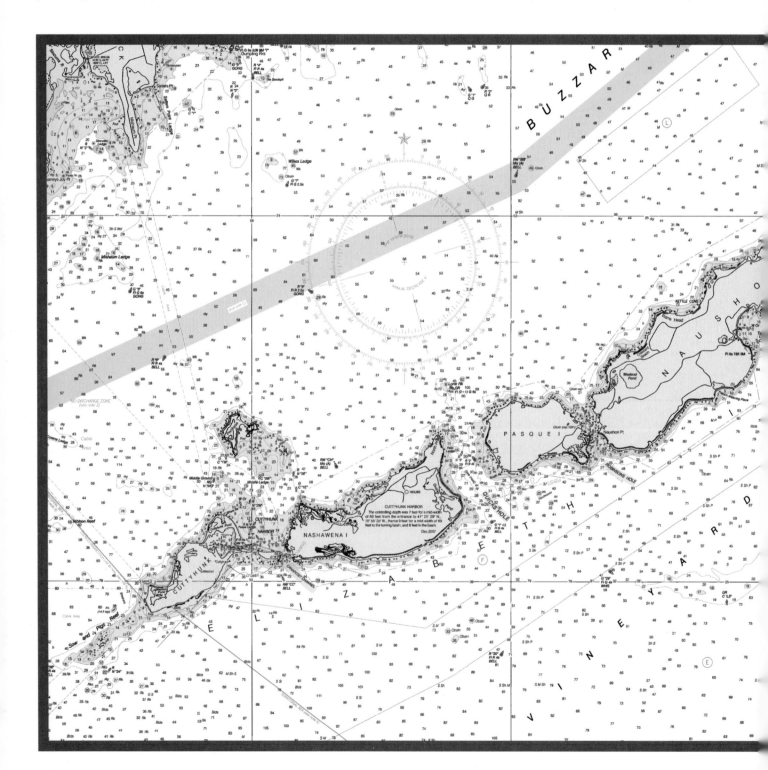

separation is, at best, incomplete, with four buoyed channels—Canapitsit, Quicks Hole, Robinsons Hole, and Woods Hole—that provide access between the bay and the sound. Woods Hole will be shown in the next chapter, but the others are touched on below.

Though the currents through the passages are tricky, the waters north and south of the islands permit idyllic coasting along the islands' bay or sound shores. The tide floods east and ebbs west in Vineyard Sound as well as Buzzards Bay.

Owned mostly by family trusts, the islands are largely wild and undeveloped yet open to respectful visitors. We'll cover them in order, from southwest to northeast.

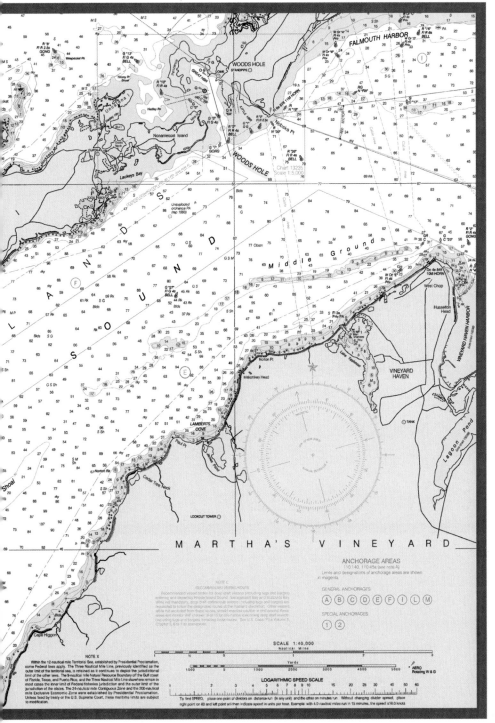

13230
49th ed., Aug. 08
NAD 83
Soundings in feet
1:40,000

CUTTYHUNK HARBOR

LIKE its sister Elizabeth Islands to the northeast, Cuttyhunk Island is a must for the visiting mariner traveling through Buzzards Bay. Though only five nautical miles from the Massachusetts mainland, it is remote and starkly beautiful. It teases visitors with an elusive sense of simplicity, like an answer just beyond the mind's grasp. Though often described as fragile, the essence of Cuttyhunk is today solidly preserved.

Our preferred approach is from the east, via a leisurely sail down the north coasts of Naushon, Pasque, and Nashawena islands. When approaching this way, give a wide berth either side to the flashing green gong off Lone Rock, and from there head southwesterly to red-and-white channel bell "CH" marking the center of the entrance into Cuttyhunk Harbor. As you approach the harbor, keep green "1E" off Nashawena's Knox Point to your port and red nun "2E" to starboard. From there, head approximately southwesterly to red bell "6" off the narrow, breakwatered entrance of Cuttyhunk Pond. Note small green marker "9" to port marking the end of a submerged rock breakwater. Stay in the center of the

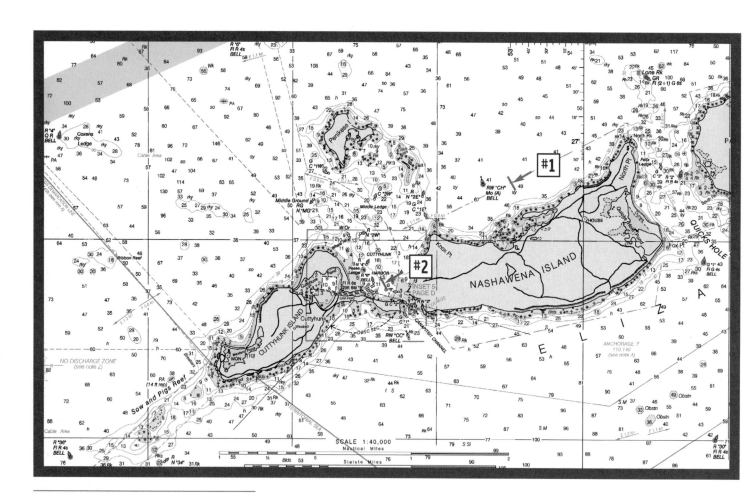

13229, 30th ed., April 08, NAD 83, Soundings in feet, 1:40,000

#1

Nashawena Island

Canapitsit Channel

Cuttyhunk Island

Cuttyhunk Pond

RW "CH"

channel for best water, and don't be surprised if you have to dodge dinghies and swimmers in the channel.

Cuttyhunk can also be approached from the west or southwest, though this requires a bit more caution. Sow and Pigs Reef extends 1½ miles west-southwest of Cuttyhunk, looking for all the world like what it no doubt is—the submerged seaward end of the island chain (which may at one time have been a Cape Cod peninsula). To give the reef the wide berth it deserves, use Penikese Island as your visual indicator for an approach from the southwest or west. As you approach Penikese in clear weather, you'll be able to see red-and-green nun "MG" marking the Middle Ground shoals. Leave that well to starboard, then leave nun "2W" off Edwards Rock and nun "4" off Pease Ledge to starboard as well, finally swinging around bell "6" and into the entrance (see page 136).

The Canapitsit Channel between Cuttyhunk and Nashawena islands, linking Vineyard Sound to Cutty-hunk Harbor, is narrow, poorly marked, beset by strong currents, and surrounded by rocks and shoals. Local boats barrel through at all hours, but it is not for the faint of heart or the newcomer. If you are interested in trying it, we suggest checking it out first in a dinghy on a calm day. There is generally plenty of water, if you can stay in it.

Once inside Cuttyhunk Pond, you will pass the ferry and fuel dock to port, at which point the mooring fields will become apparent to starboard. Moorings are first-come first-served and fill up quickly on summer weekends. Though the fee has fluctuated over the past few seasons, the visit is well worth the fee. Other options include calling the dockmaster for slip availability or to pick up additional moorings, or anchoring outside the main harbor. There is some anchoring room in the

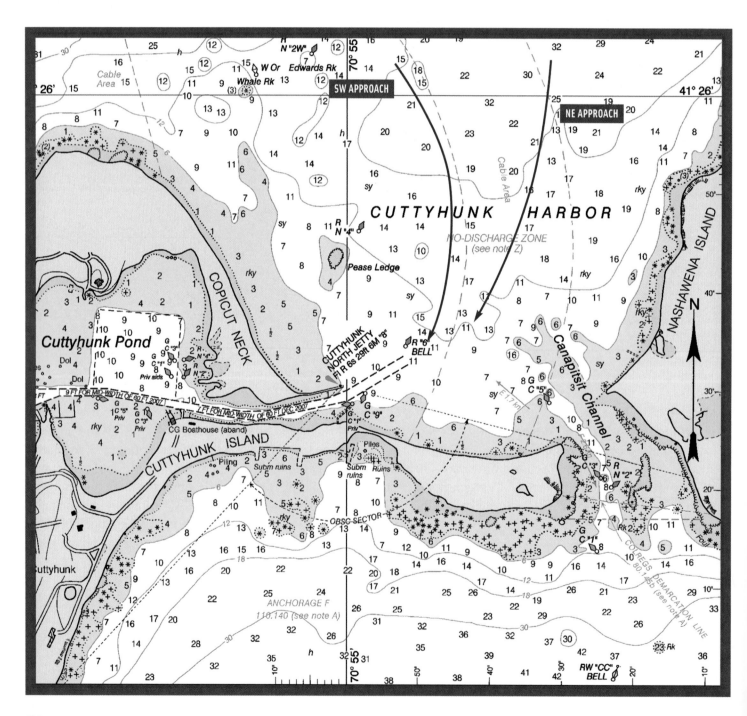

#2 (See page 134.)

Cuttyhunk North Jetty

Cuttyhunk Pond

Copicut Neck

R "6" BELL

northeastern part of the dredged square shown on the chart, outside the mooring field and clear of the buoyed channels.

Once your boat is safely put away for the night, a visit ashore is a must. You'll find easy hikes, stunning vistas, and endless places to explore. Over the past several years, restaurants and a bakery have come and gone, so when ashore, check to see what is available. There is also a post office, a library, a museum, a small general store, several nice gift shops, a fish market on the dock, public restrooms, and ice cream vendors. Every Friday night in the summer you can catch a movie in the town hall, and there is usually some fishing tournament, celebration, or parade on the schedule. Ask around.

Cuttyhunk recently celebrated the 400th anniversary of its discovery in 1602 by Bartholomew Gosnold, who attempted to establish a small settlement. The settlement was quickly abandoned, but tales of this expedition inspired other explorations, and some believe it was one of Shakespeare's inspirations for *The Tempest* as well. Today, you are in the Town of Gosnold when you visit Cuttyhunk, and the Elizabeth Islands are named after Gosnold's sister. Gosnold went on in 1607 to become part of the ill-fated settlement at Jamestown, where he died.

13229
30th ed., April 08
NAD 83
Soundings in feet
1:40,000

QUICKS HOLE

THE Quicks Hole passage between Nashawena and Pasque islands is a well-marked, easily navigated route between Buzzards Bay and Vineyard Sound. It is marked at its southern terminus by flashing green bell "1" and at its northern end by the flashing green light on the green-and-red buoy off Lone Rock. Strong currents flow through the passage—ebbing northward at 2.6 knots and flooding southward at 2.5 knots—and a transit against the tide can be a fight in a low-powered boat. If you're proceeding with the tide, be careful not to get swept onto one of the buoys. In the right weather, the anchorage area midway through Quicks Hole, off the beach on Nashawena, can make a wonderful stop, particularly if you arrive after the beach crowds have left. Nashawena's topography is conducive to beautiful sunsets in the anchorage. When approaching the beach from the north, be mindful of the rocks off North Point.

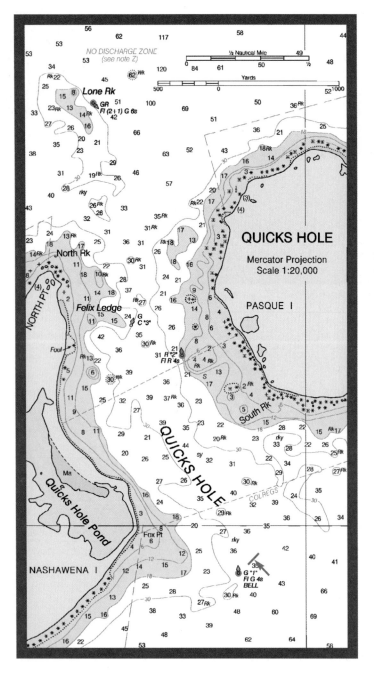

13230
49th ed., Aug. 08
NAD 83
Soundings in feet
1:20,000

ROBINSONS HOLE

ROBINSONS Hole between Pasque and Naushon islands is much narrower than Quicks Hole but nevertheless constitutes a viable passage through the islands. Navigating this route requires close attention, as the current-swept passage is not to be taken lightly. Newcomers should try to hit it at slack water in order to pass through slowly and under control. Quicks Hole is much preferred in low visibility. No recommended anchorages exist along this passage.

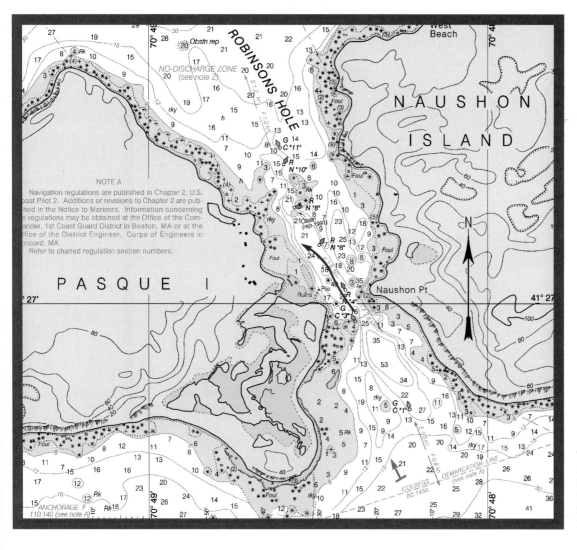

13229
30th ed., April 08
NAD 83
Soundings in feet
1:40,000

TARPAULIN COVE

THOUGH often forgotten, Tarpaulin Cove, on 8-mile-long Naushon Island, is one of our favorite spots. With no material obstacles, the approach into the cove is simple and straightforward. The cove is easily identified thanks to the highly visible 78-foot classic white lighthouse that guards the southerly hill. Just be sure to leave green can "1" to port on entry, and be aware that the holding is weedy in spots. The prevailing southwest breeze may die or change at night, leading to boats drifting strangely on the currents—leave plenty of room between boats at anchor. Feel free to dinghy ashore and explore along the beach and up to the lighthouse, but bear in mind that Naushon is private property, and

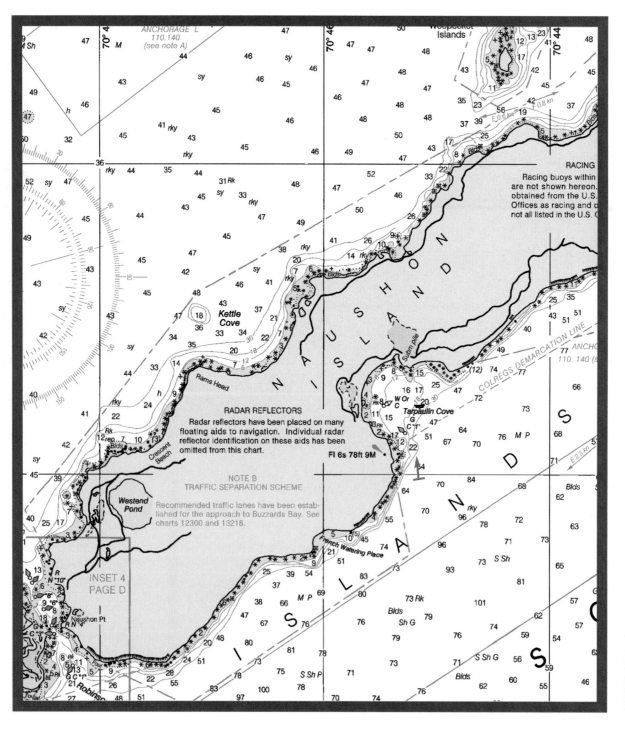

13229
30th ed., April 08
NAD 83
Soundings in feet
1:40,000

travel inland is forbidden. You may see one of the horse-mounted caretakers guarding the island and the homes ashore. The island is also home to many sheep and deer, and ticks are likely to be thick in the long grass. Lyme disease is prevalent, so wear long pants, spray the cuffs with bug repellent, and make frequent tick checks.

The cove is open to the east and southeast, and winds from those directions can raise an uncomfortable chop, but Martha's Vineyard blocks the groundswell from the Atlantic. This is a good fair-weather anchorage.

HADLEY HARBOR

BEAUTIFUL Hadley Harbor, Naushon Island's chief anchorage, must not be missed. Hadley is well-protected, truly beautiful, easily accessible, and literally just across the way from Woods Hole.

The best approach to Hadley is from the north and can be made from flashing green bell "13" marking the northern entrance to the Woods Hole Passage. Rather than continuing to flashing red "10" and the passage, head south from "13" toward the northwestern portion

13235, 6th ed., April 04, NAD 83, Soundings in feet, 1:5,000

Uncatena Island

Bull Island

Outer Harbor

Penzance

Inner Harbor

Woods Hole

Nonamesset Island

Goats Neck

Naushon Island

of Nonamesset Island. As you approach, you'll discover two choices to enter Hadley Harbor—either the center-line approach following the 11- and 12-foot depth contours (with shoals to starboard and a rock to port), or a more southerly approach using the channel marked by nun "2" and can "3." Either route takes you to the center of Hadley's outer harbor, where you'll find deepwater space to anchor.

For the more adventurous—and on less crowded nights—the inner harbor offers even more protection and quiet. You can make your way there by heading south through the middle of the channel between Bull and Nonamesset islands. Once past Bull Island's eastern shore, turn west toward the Northwest Gutter, giving the shoal water off the southern side of Bull a respectful berth, then turn southwest down the center of the inner harbor. There are numerous moorings there, and often the only place to anchor is south of Bull Island. Naushon Island is privately owned, and as of this writing the only place where visitors are welcome to go ashore is Bull Island, which is a nice place for a picnic. There are no facilities.

■ MARTHA'S VINEYARD ■

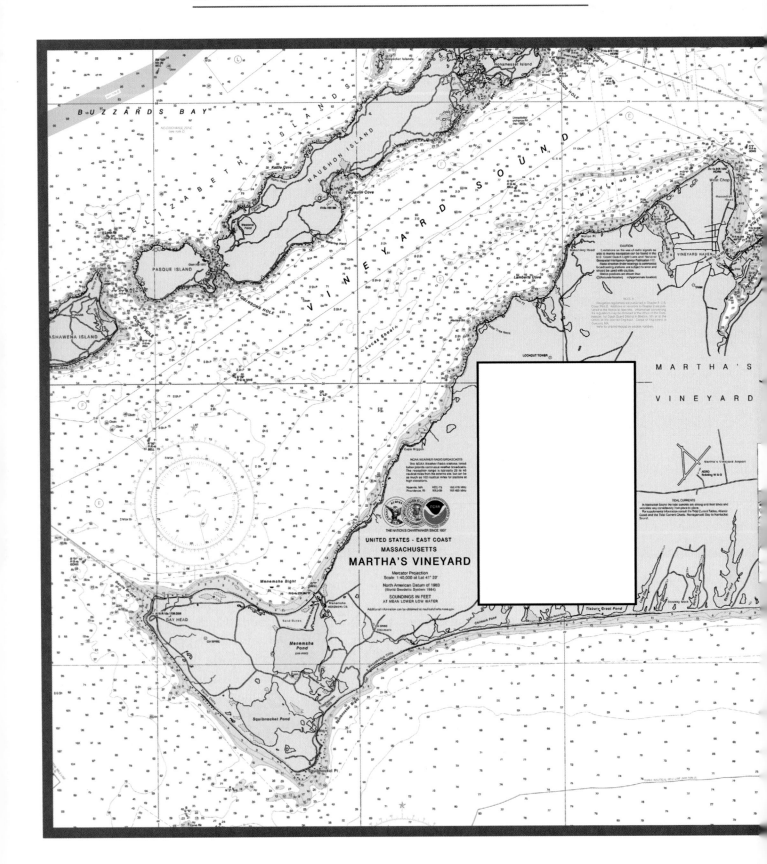

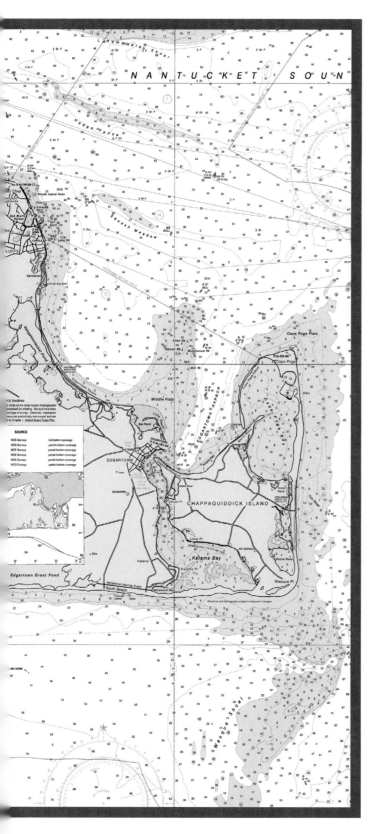

MARTHA'S Vineyard needs little introduction to cruisers—or to non-cruising vacationers, for that matter. The trip from Woods Hole to Vineyard Haven, on your own boat or on the Woods Hole ferry, is only 5 miles, and the delights that await on the island include superb beaches, bike trails, nature preserves, bluffs, unending seascapes, and varied restaurants, shops, and art galleries. A vacation destination that offers something for everyone (including presidents), the Vineyard's six towns can be crowded but are never boring.

Shaped like a rounded right triangle with its hypotenuse to the south, Martha's Vineyard is 17 miles long from Wasque Point (on Chappaquiddick Island) in the east to Gay Head in the west, and 9 miles wide at its widest. The northwest side of the triangle is bordered by Vineyard Sound, and the northeast side by Nantucket Sound, with the ill-defined transition between the sounds lying roughly between West Chop—the triangle's northern vertex—and Falmouth Harbor on Cape Cod. The island's three major harbors are all on the northeast side, and you can think of them as three mini-cities—each with a distinctive personality and its own offerings.

Strong currents complicate pilotage in the approaches to Martha's Vineyard. We'll begin our coverage with the two small, remote anchorages on the island's northwest coast, that being the coast you'll reach first when entering Vineyard Sound from the west or south.

13233
18th ed., Oct. 08
NAD 83
Soundings in feet
1:40,000

MENEMSHA BASIN AND POND

MENEMSHA Basin and its mostly inaccessible pond provide the first opportunity for the cruising yachtsman approaching from the south or southwest to experience the Vineyard. The basin has no anchorage and rarely a mooring for rent, but can be useful in an emergency or when fuel or supplies are urgently needed. We used it in one such emergency to pick up a replacement for a critical part that had failed as we made our way out to deeper waters. In calm weather, boats anchor outside the basin in Menemsha Bight.

Two miles east of Gay Head's dramatic clay bluffs and 170-foot-high lighthouse, Menemsha is easy to find but hard to see. Indeed, the entrance to the basin is nearly invisible until you reach green bell "1." From there the narrow entrance is apparent, as is the approach. Those with shoal draft, clear weather, and a strong heart can attempt the narrow channel from the basin into Menemsha Pond—but keep in mind that the constant shoaling and variations in current velocity and water depth through the channel will complicate your pilotage. The deepest water lies southeast of the privately maintained red and green day markers that are just past navigation buoys red "6" and green "5." Marine heads must be sealed in the pond.

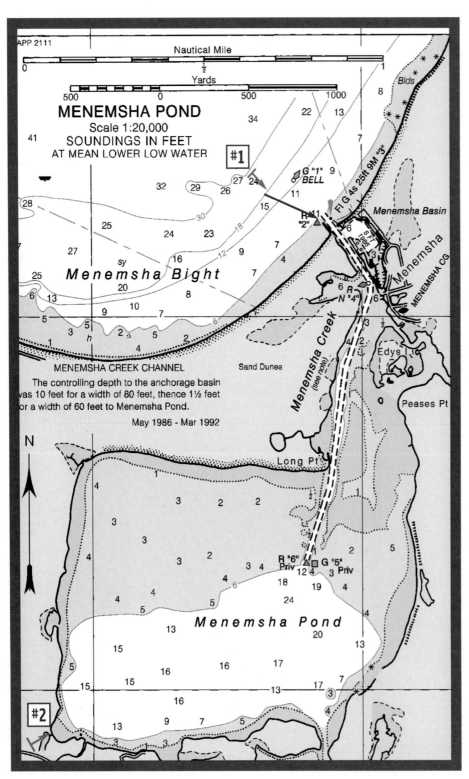

13233
18th ed., Oct. 08
NAD 83
Soundings in feet
1:20,000

#1

Menemsha Basin

Menemsha Pond

G "1" BELL

#2

Menemsha Creek

LAKE TASHMOO

NORTHEAST of Menemsha, almost due east of Tarpaulin Cove on Naushon Island, and just west of Vineyard Haven Harbor is the narrow entrance to Lake Tashmoo, a completely protected but very small anchorage with limited water depths in the entrance. Avoid the tide rips over the Middle Ground shoals just offshore. Making your approach at high-water slack will simplify your pilotage.

East Jetty Light   Vineyard Haven Harbor   Lake Tashmoo

Almost undetectable until you are right in front of it, the entrance is marked by its East Jetty lighthouse. Though dredged to 5 feet in 2000, the channel is prone to significant shifts in depth, but privately maintained buoys inside the entrance will lead you to deeper water and the anchorage area in the southern part of the lake. The mean tidal range here is 2.1 feet, and making your entrance near high water will give you more depth to work with. Once safely inside, consider yourself lucky. There is a public dock and ramp on the east side of the lake, complete with a trash can and water. From there it is a moderate and pleasant walk across the island to Vineyard Haven. Like Menemsha Pond, Lake Tashmoo is a no-discharge zone.

VINEYARD HAVEN HARBOR

VINEYARD Haven Harbor is the most commercial of the Vineyard's three main harbors. It is the terminus for large car ferries from Woods Hole, the point of embarka-

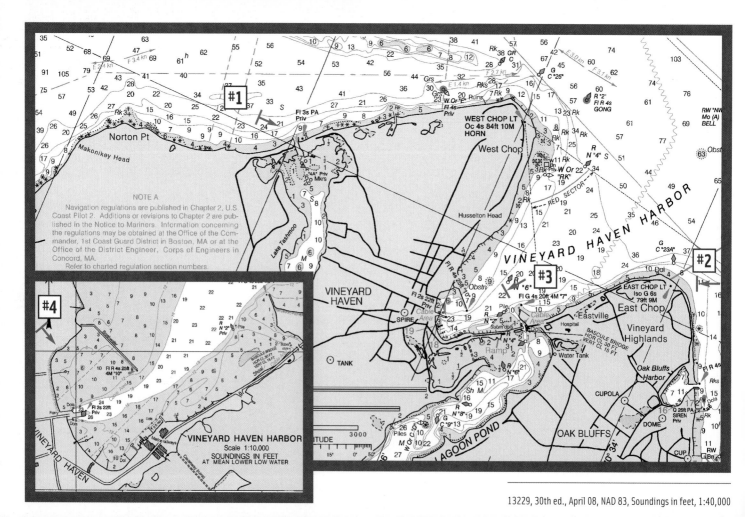

tion for nearly a half-million passengers per year. On the plus side, the harbor is easily accessible despite the strong currents outside, which can run over 5 knots off West Chop—the strongest currents you will encounter in Vineyard Sound. Though the inner harbor is typically extremely busy, a mooring or a slip may be available, and if not, anchorage is possible outside the breakwater in the outer harbor—which is, however, exposed to the north.

Once you're moored or anchored, you'll enjoy easy access to the town wharf (north of the ferry dock in the inner harbor) and plenty of services, including grocery stores, restaurants, bakeries, and shopping for every taste. This is the best place on the Vineyard to re-provision, and you can take comfortable buses from Vineyard Haven to anywhere else on the island. Scooter and bicycle rentals are also available.

The approach to the harbor is made easily via a southwesterly heading midway between East and West Chop. Follow this course between nun "6" and flashing green light "7" off the entrance to Lagoon Pond, by which point the Vineyard Haven Inner Harbor will be apparent, as will flashing red "4" on the end of the main breakwater and the many boats moored behind it. There may be dockage at the marina to port on entry, and there is an alternative anchorage in Lagoon Pond (sealed heads only), though it requires negotiating a restricted opening bridge.

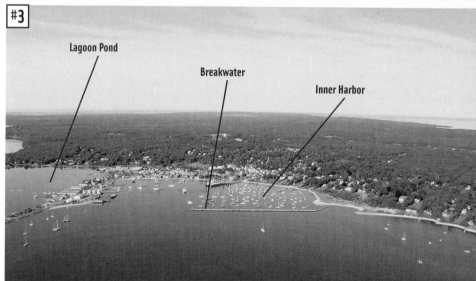

OAK BLUFFS HARBOR

HISTORIC Oak Bluffs lies around the corner from Vineyard Haven and just southeast of East Chop. The harbor is approached through the narrow gap between the breakwaters, with 30-foot flashing red light "2" marking the starboard breakwater. Though tempting, the harbor is incredibly small, and no anchoring is allowed. On a busy summer night the moorings are likely to be taken, and many boaters form moored rafts two or three boats wide. There are also some slips around the circumference of the small basin.

For those lucky enough to find a slip or mooring, this beautiful little village with its historic architecture, numerous shops and restaurants, and variety of services is just a short stroll away. The centerpiece of the town is the tiny 19th century "gingerbread" houses (still occupied today) built on tiny streets surrounding a beautiful Methodist camp meeting ground complete with large roofed auditorium, where numerous events are staged in the summer.

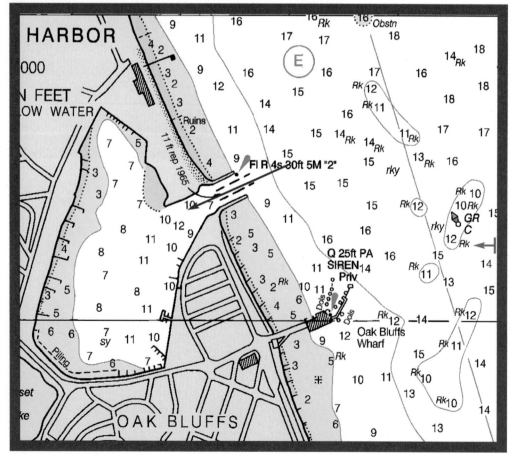

13238
16th ed., Aug. 07
NAD 83
Soundings in feet
1:10,000

EDGARTOWN

THE approach to Edgartown Harbor is straightforward, but don't cut straight across from Oak Bluffs. When coming from the northwest, it is safest to head out to red bell "2" and then turn south to red nun "4." (It is possible to cut inside bell "2," but you must take care not to stray too *far* inside. One glance at the chart will show you why.) From "4," head farther south to red flashing "6," then follow a south-southwesterly course to pick up red nun "8" just east of Edgartown Light.

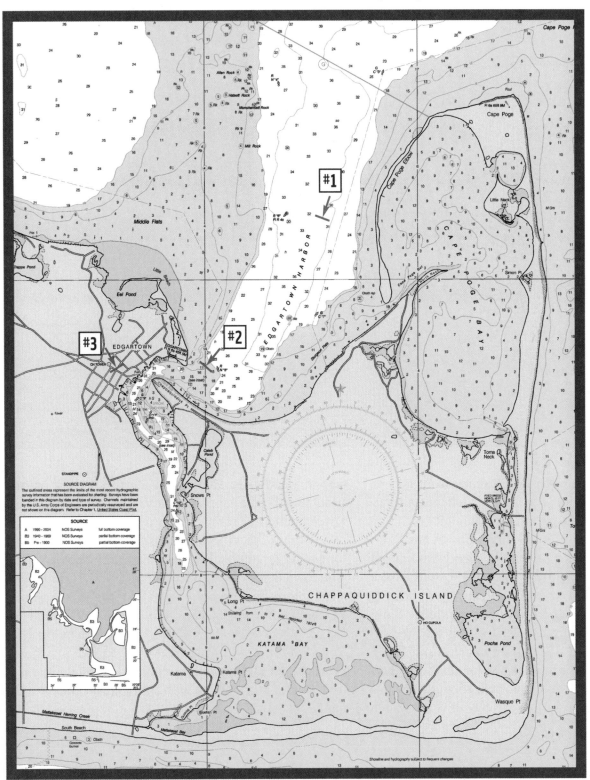

13238
16th ed., Aug. 07
NAD 83
Soundings in feet
1:20,000

#1 (See page 151.)

Chappaquiddick Island   Katama Bay   Edgartown Harbor   Eel Pond

Turn west into the harbor entrance from nun "8," and pay careful attention as you round Chappaquiddick Point. The harbor is busy almost all the time, with ferry and boat traffic moving in all directions. A small, fast ferry (sometimes two in opposite directions) zooms across the main channel from the town to starboard to the point to port—give it the right of way. Follow the well-marked channel around Chappaquiddick Point, giving special attention to the sharp turn required just past the lighthouse, and you'll see numerous moorings stretching down the channel toward Katama Bay. Check with the harbormaster for a mooring, though they may be hard to get in season. Alternatively, it is possible in settled weather to anchor outside the harbor, off the beach north of Chappaquiddick Point. This is our preferred anchorage for more privacy

Perhaps the Vineyard's most famous harbor, with a long sailing tradition, Edgartown is a very popular place. The town is replete with wonderful places to shop, eat, and explore, and it provides great hospitality to visitors. Recognize, however, that the hustle and bustle of Edgartown at its busiest can be a bit overwhelming. Like Vineyard Haven, this is a great place to take in a movie on a summer night, stroll streets lined with restored historic homes, or just to sit with an ice cream cone watching people stroll by.

#2 (See page 151.)

Chappaquiddick Point   Edgartown

#3 (See page 151.)

Katama Bay   Chappaquiddick Point

■ NANTUCKET ■

SOUTHEAST of Martha's Vineyard, like an advance scout probing the Atlantic, is its famous sister, Nantucket Island. "Take out your map and look at it," wrote Herman Melville in *Moby-Dick*. "See what a real corner of the world it occupies; how it stands there away off shore, more lonely than the Eddystone Lighthouse. Look at it—a mere hillock, an elbow of sand; all beach without a background."

Though less than 6 nautical miles separate Muskeget Island (Nantucket's western outlier) from Chappaquiddick Island (the Vineyard's eastern outlier), it's a 30-mile passage or ferry ride from Woods Hole to Nantucket Harbor, and 22 miles from Hyannis—and most of those miles are to seaward. Certainly there is no question in Nantucket residents' minds that *their* island is the most remote as well as the most beautiful, and that a difficult journey is the proper price of admission.

Nantucket itself (minus Muskeget and Tuckernuck islands off its western end) is 13 miles long from west to east but low-lying and treeless, just as in Melville's time, and your first impression upon landfall may be of a sandbar on the horizon. If you're unlucky enough to approach in the fog that frequently shrouds Nantucket Sound, you won't see even that. The island is best approached from the north or northwest, through Nantucket Sound. The approach from the south, through Muskeget Channel with its shifting, poorly marked shoals and swift currents, should only be attempted in clear, settled weather with a capable boat and a competent and well-equipped navigator.

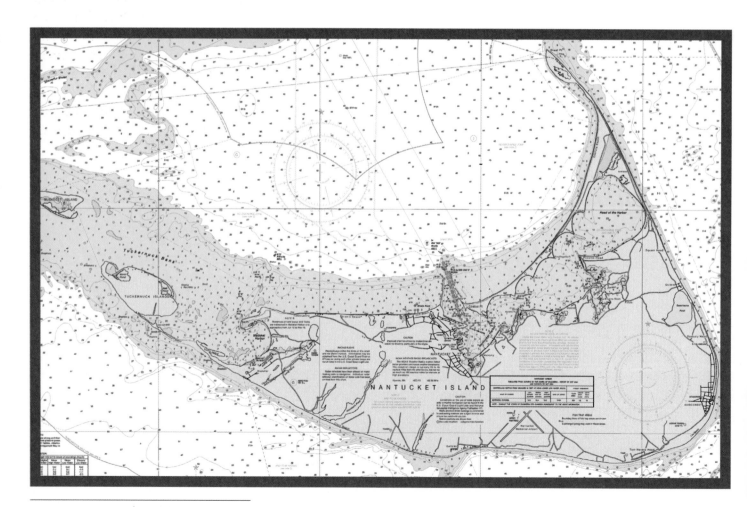

13241, 16th ed., Nov. 05, NAD 83, Soundings in feet, 1:40,000

MADAKET HARBOR

FOR adventurous cruisers coming from the northwest and looking to avoid the summer craziness of Nantucket Harbor, Madaket Harbor provides a true taste of wild, remote beauty. The approach to Madaket is best made from flashing red bell "2," approximately 2 miles north of Eel Point. From there, follow a southwesterly course to red "4" and red "6," keeping can "3" and the grassy shoals to your port and the nuns to starboard. Once past "6," proceed down the channel centerline, avoiding the 5-foot and 3-foot soundings and favoring the Eel Point side as you make an easterly turn around the point. You can then proceed southeasterly across the harbor through the charted finger of deeper water, and on the harbor's southeast shore you'll find, as of this writing, a limited number of guest moorings available. It is also possible to anchor in the charted deeper water south of Eel Point. There are limited facilities and gasoline for small boats at a marina all the way in. For those with patience, the visit is well worthwhile.

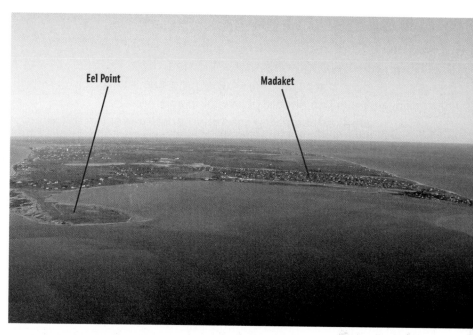

Eel Point   Madaket

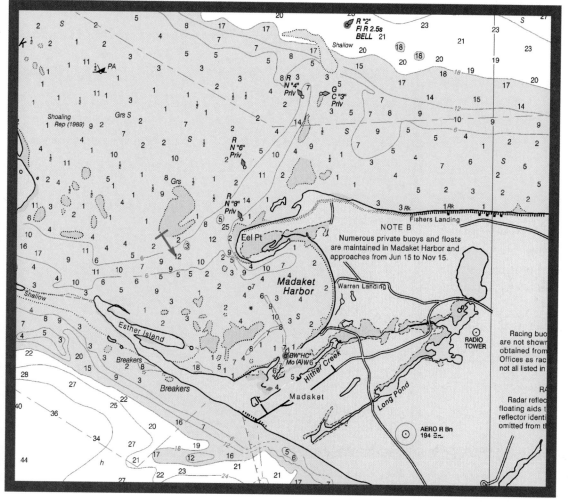

13238
16th ed., Aug. 07
NAD 83
Soundings in feet
1:20,000

NANTUCKET HARBOR

NANTUCKET is often the end point of a cruise for cruising sailors and powerboaters. Getting there can mean a tricky voyage across and around the many charted and marked shoals between it and Martha's Vineyard. Study the charts carefully, preplot your courses, have the waypoints loaded into the GPS, and don't be surprised if the fog closes in. A sail to Nantucket can have the feel of a short offshore voyage.

Nantucket Harbor offers something for everyone. With its large number of moorings, slips, and anchorages, spending a few nights is generally an easy proposition, though the huge harbor can be exposed when winds are up.

Approached from red-and-white bell "NB," the harbor entrance couldn't be better marked; navigational aids form a straight 1.5-mile corridor from there to famous Brant Point Light. Beware the submerged but well-marked entrance jetties on both sides of the channel, and be aware that currents up to 5 knots have been reported between Brant Point and Coatue Point. From Brant Point, buoys guide you into the inner harbor. There are numerous moorings off the town waterfront but little room to anchor unless one is willing to dinghy some distance from points farther to the northeast.

From the town, the island and its highlights are easily accessed via taxi or public transportation, and bicycles of all kinds are readily available, not to mention some of the best restaurants and shops in New England. You'll stumble over the cobblestone streets while trying to recall your favorite passages from *Moby-Dick*. Nantucket was a famous whaling port—in the early 19th century some 88 whalers sailed from here, making it the busiest whaling port in the world. A visit to the Nantucket Whaling Museum is a must.

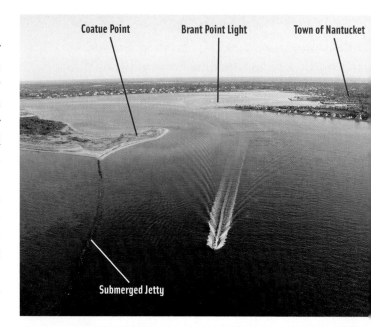

Coatue Point   Brant Point Light   Town of Nantucket

Submerged Jetty

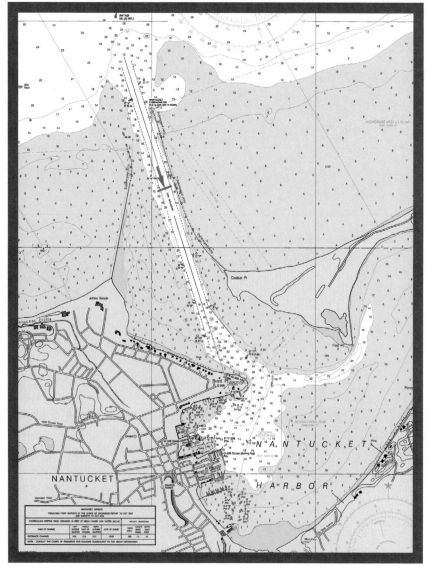

13238
16th ed., Aug. 07
NAD 83
Soundings in feet
1:20,000

HEAD OF THE HARBOR

JUST to the east of the main harbor there are anchorage opportunities to the south of Coatue Point, or you can go farther east and anchor at the Head of the Harbor, Nantucket's northeasternmost point. From our experience, the charted depths remain reasonably reliable, and the downside of distance from town is outweighed by the relative quiet and access to one of the island's most beautiful spots—Great Point and the dunes maintained by the Trustees of the Reservation. There may be some small, privately maintained buoys marking narrow spots as you travel toward the Head of the Harbor.

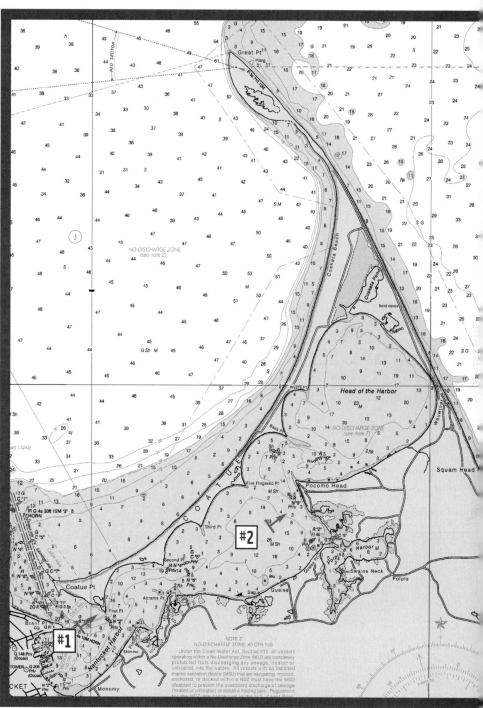

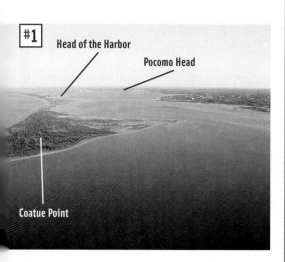

#1

Head of the Harbor

Pocomo Head

Coatue Point

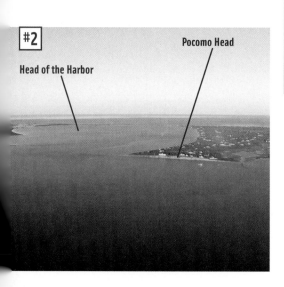

#2

Pocomo Head

Head of the Harbor

13241, 16th ed., Nov. 05, NAD 83, Soundings in feet, 1:40,000

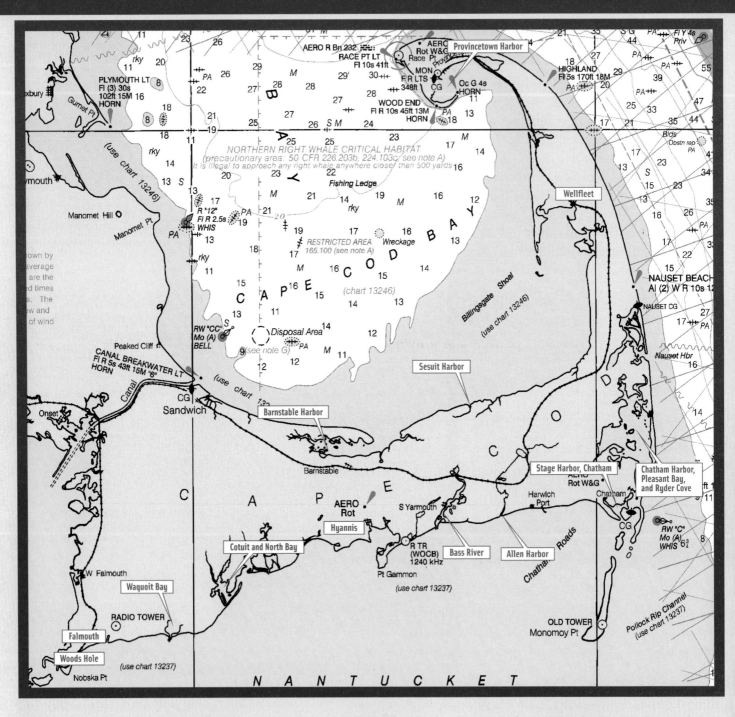

13200
37th ed., April 09
NAD 83
Soundings in feet
1:400,000

CAPE COD

When most cruisers think of Cape Cod anchorages, they think of the harbors on the South Cape, facing Nantucket Sound. You know you're getting closer to these classic harbors from Buzzards Bay or the Cape Cod Canal as you approach the three main passages through the Elizabeth Islands, namely, Woods Hole Passage, Robinsons Hole, or Quicks Hole. From Block Island or Narragansett Bay, your approach is likely to be via Vineyard Sound, the first sign of which may well be the lighthouse atop Gay Head on the Vineyard's western extremity.

Cape Cod's northern coast also offers harbors, and we cover Barnstable, Sesuit, Wellfleet, and Province-town in this region as well. But these anchorages are a world apart from the South Cape harbors. More than seventy hard miles separate any of the South Cape anchorages from Provincetown, the first viable North Cape anchorage you'd encounter in a counterclockwise circumnavigation of the cape. But, first you'd have to get around Monomoy Island and Handkerchief Shoals, requiring a passage of about 12 miles southeast from Hyannis Harbor or about 14 miles south-southwest from Stage Harbor. Then another 14 miles northeast would get you through Butler Hole and Pollock Rip. These are all anxious miles through shifting shoals, tide rips, and frequent fogs—waters almost as notoriously hazardous as Cape Hatteras—and then you'd still face the daring 45-mile passage along the cape's outer shore—a potential lee shore all the way, beaten flat and devoid of safe anchorages just as the south shores of Martha's Vineyard and Nantucket have been—and still you have to go around Race Point and Provincetown's hook to finally find safety in the approaches to Provincetown Harbor.

This helps explain why few cruisers choose to navigate the two charted and buoyed channels between Nantucket Sound and "the outside." The Nantucket Shoals extend roughly 23 miles east of Nantucket, and a big parcel of the Atlantic Ocean pours west to east through the Pollock Rip and Great Round Shoal channels on every flood tide (which itself is counterintuitive) and east to west on every ebb (again, the opposite of what you might expect). Current velocities of 2.5 knots are common in the channels, and the greater mean tidal range on the Atlantic side (about 3 feet greater than the Nantucket Sound side) causes overfalls in the channels. Needless to say, getting and keeping your bearings out there isn't easy.

These channels are certainly navigable—the racing crews in the Sails Around Cape Cod sailboat race, run each summer by the town of Harwich, do it with gusto—but cruisers can find more relaxed and more rewarding destinations within Nantucket Sound. Thus, the usual approach to Provincetown is from the Cape Cod Canal (see Region V on page 100) or from Boston or points farther downeast.

■ WOODS HOLE ■

LONG considered by many to be the front door to Martha's Vineyard and Nantucket, Woods Hole Passage is one of the classic passages of cruising annals, and shooting "The Hole" is a sort of ritual for sailing in this fantastic area. With segments named the "Branch," "The Strait," and "Broadway," the passage looks like no walk in the park when you study it on the chart, an impression that is likely to be confirmed on your first trip through.

Two critical points are worth emphasizing: (1) The buoys are numbered from southeast to northwest, and therefore the red navigation aids should be left to starboard when you transit from the Vineyard Sound side and to port when you enter from Buzzards Bay; and (2)

the tidal current—which reaches velocities of up to 6 knots—is a major consideration when choosing a time to make your passage. You want the current to be slack or favorable (i.e., setting you in the direction you are traveling). Note that the direction of the flood is from Buzzards Bay to Vineyard Sound, and the ebb is from the sound to the bay. This is the opposite of what you might imagine. Once you begin a passage from either direction, you're committed to continuing. Things happen remarkably fast in the passage.

With those cautions under your belt, and after careful study of the charts and tidal current tables, you will find that The Hole is easily navigable. Shooting through Robinsons Hole instead can take you 15 miles

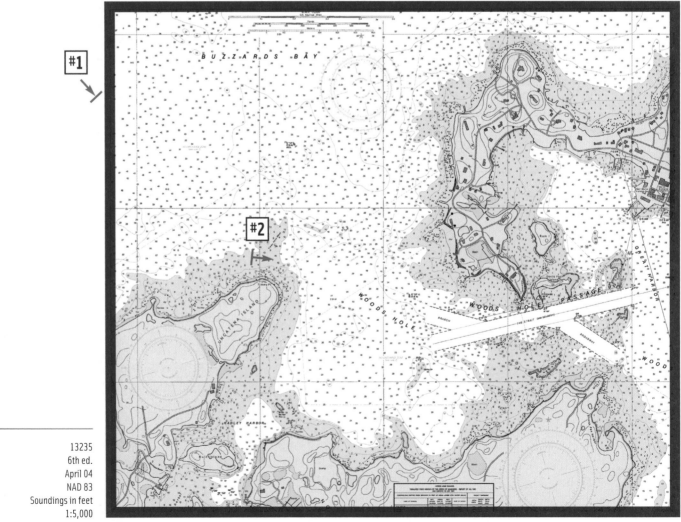

13235
6th ed.
April 04
NAD 83
Soundings in feet
1:5,000

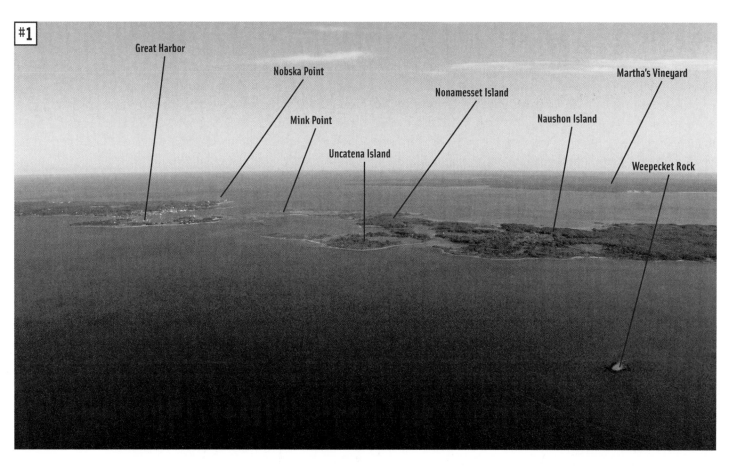

#1

Great Harbor

Nobska Point

Mink Point

Uncatena Island

Nonamesset Island

Naushon Island

Martha's Vineyard

Weepecket Rock

#2

Penzance

Great Harbor

Nonamesset Island

Uncatena Island

R "10"

out of your way, and Robinsons Hole might be more hazardous than Woods Hole. Quicks Hole is a more relaxed passage but even farther out of the way for Buzzards Bay traffic. Going all the way around the Elizabeth Islands would tack on 30 miles and put you in way of the Sow and Pigs Reef southwest of Cuttyhunk. Over the decades we have enjoyed the beauty and convenience of the Woods Hole Passage, and with a little planning you will too.

If you're approaching from Buzzards Bay, the entry point is flashing green bell "13," midway between the northeastern tip of Uncatena Island and the southwestern tip of Penzance. At this point you still have time to change your mind—to wait for clearer weather or a more favorable tide, perhaps heading south into beautiful Hadley Harbor (Region VI) until conditions improve.

From green bell "13," a south-southeasterly course takes you to the entry point of the Branch and flashing red "10." A course of roughly 120 degrees magnetic from this point takes you directly into The Strait, as indicated on the chart. At this point you're fully committed. Leave red nun "6" to port and can "7" and 34-foot flashing light "W" to starboard—and from there it's a short easterly trip (roughly 90 degrees magnetic) to the "Y" intersection with Broadway. This is the crux of The Hole, the area of swiftest currents and diverging channels. If you're there during maximum current, you'll see navigation buoys leaning at 45 degrees, sometimes nearly dragged under or describing crazy back-and-forth arcs while they spin on their mooring chains. When you check your back bearings, you may be amazed how much you are being set to one side or an-

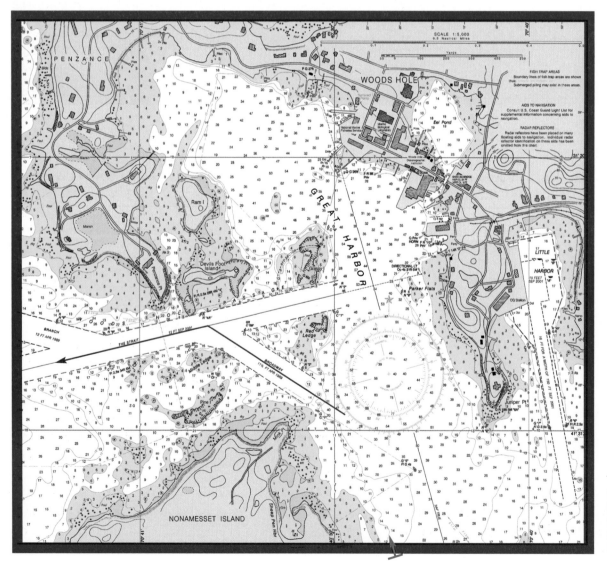

13229
30th ed., April 08
NAD 83
Soundings in feet
1:40,000

Penzance · Great Harbor · Little Harbor · Eel Pond · The Strait · C "1" · Mink Point · Nonamesset Island · G "5"

other of your course. You must take care not to be set onto Middle Ledge, which lies just south of the "Y."

At the intersection of The Strait and Broadway, you can turn to starboard onto Broadway and exit into Vineyard Sound, or you can follow The Strait directly into Great Harbor and the town of Woods Hole.

If you take the right turn into Broadway, follow a southeasterly heading to its exit point, from where you'll see flashing green "5" in the middle of Woods Hole. A southerly heading from "5" takes you between Great Ledge on your port and Nonamesset Shoal on your starboard. Set your course to pass between flashing red bell "2" and green gong "1." Alternatively, if your destination is Falmouth Harbor or Nantucket Sound, you can pass north of Great Ledge, toward Nobska Point, for a more direct route.

If, instead of turning into Broadway, you follow The Strait into Great Harbor, leave the light off Grassy Island and red nun "2" to port, then turn north into the harbor.

Though the Woods Hole Yacht Club (on the road to Penzance) will allow a short tie-up, and you can land a dinghy there, the services are limited and the harbor

can be very busy. The moorings are mostly local, but anchoring is possible along the northwest sector of the harbor. Avoid the finger of shallow water extending north from Ram Island nearly halfway across the harbor. You'll be amazed that an anchorage just off current-riven Woods Hole Passage can be so nearly free of current.

A marina and other rental moorings are located in Eel Pond, which is accessed via a narrow channel that is spanned by an opening bridge. Eel Pond is always crowded at the height of the season, and you'll have to work around the bridge opening schedule to get in there.

Once ashore, you'll find interesting exhibits at the Woods Hole Oceanographic Institution, at the Woods Hole Science Aquarium, and at the Marine Biological Laboratory. In addition, there are numerous restaurants, galleries, bookstores, and specialty shops. From Woods Hole you can catch a car ferry to Martha's Vineyard or Nantucket.

Little Harbor, just east of Great Harbor, is home to a large Coast Guard station and to many moored yachts, but you'll find no room to anchor there and no transient marine facilities.

■ FALMOUTH INNER HARBOR ■

WELL-PROTECTED Falmouth Harbor is rarely used by sailors as a quiet spot to spend the night, given its crowds and boat traffic. Having said that, as of this writing, Falmouth Marine and MacDougall's provide great emergency services for those who need more than a peripheral fix. The entrance to the inner harbor is as straightforward as it looks on the chart, with jetties that extend seaward protecting the entrance channel.

When approaching from the west—around Nobska Point with its famous 87-foot lighthouse—you can go either north or south of red-and-green nun "FW." Remember that the tide floods eastward and ebbs westward through Vineyard and Nantucket Sounds, and current velocities off Falmouth Harbor reach 2.5 to 3 knots on both flood and ebb. If you are making the approach in fog or at night, it's best to pick up flashing red bell "16," and from there follow a northerly heading to the flashing green light on the western jetty. Leave privately maintained nuns "2" and "4" to starboard, make the short trip past the jetties, then a starboard turn will

take you into the inner harbor and the marine services. Whenever we've needed a spot, we've always been able to find dock or slip space. Depending on how long you intend to stay, a walk into Falmouth will take you to any additional services needed.

GREEN POND

LIKE so many other Cape Cod harbors, Green Pond tempts cruisers with its protruding jettied entrance and glimpses of well-sheltered boats within. Indeed, it is a protected, peaceful spot. During the summer, however, there is little likelihood of finding space to anchor, and you will find few transient slips and no services within. The entrance is subject to shoaling, requiring frequent dredging, and it can also be subject to strong currents. We suggest visiting Green Pond after Labor Day, when space will likely be available and entrance dredging will have been completed, and then only if you require no services at all.

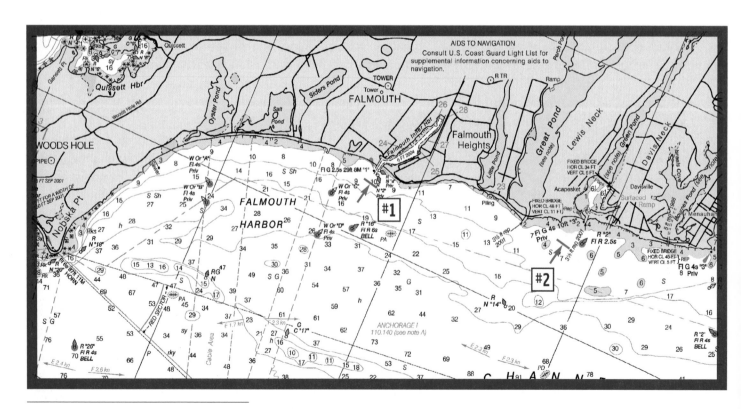

13229, 30th ed., April 08, NAD 83, Soundings in feet, 1:40,000

#1

Falmouth Inner Harbor

#2

Fixed Bridge

Green Pond

R "2"

■ WAQUOIT BAY ■

WAQUOIT Bay is like a Disneyland for shoal-draft vessels, completely protected from the tidal currents that pile through Nantucket Sound's North Channel outside. Make your approach just east of flashing red bell "2," and from there the light that protrudes at the end of the jetty will be clear. From the jetties, a slight dogleg to port takes you to red nun "2" on the southern edge of the bay, and a series of cans and nuns along the centerline of the bay permits passage to the Quashnet River. We've included photographs of both the jetty entrance and the western entrance through Eel Pond, but we recommend the jetty entrance. Once you anchor inside the bay, you owe it to yourself to take your tender along the western side of Washburn Island and into Eel Pond if the tide permits.

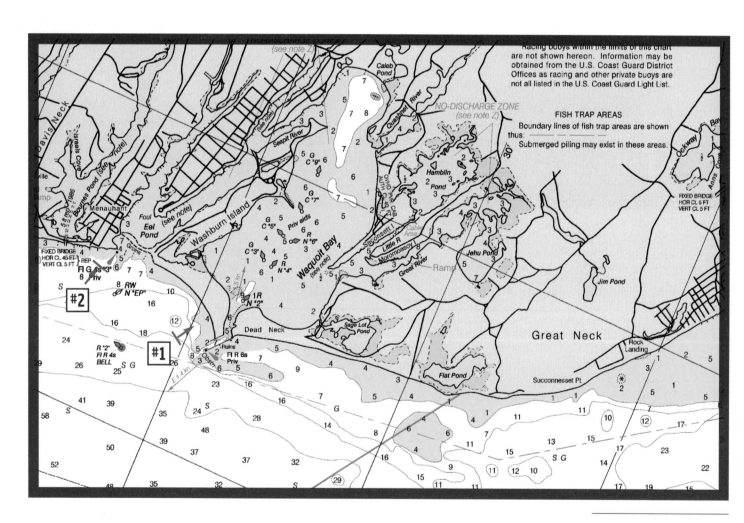

13229
30th ed., April 08
NAD 83
Soundings in feet
1:40,000

#1

Washburn Island

Waquoit Bay

R "2"

#2

Eel Pond

Washburn Island

Waquoit Bay

■ COTUIT BAY AND NORTH BAY ■

COTUIT Bay is worth the trip, but its entry is challenging. Enter on a high tide just west of the Cotuit roadstead anchorage marked on the chart, which lies north of red-and-white bell "C." Your approach to the entrance will be northwesterly from the bell. You'll be surrounded by shoal water, so keep one eye on the fathometer.

Once in the entrance, with Cotuit Highlands to port, you've completed the easiest part of the approach. From there, a turn to the northeast around Sampsons Island (a Massachusetts Audubon sanctuary for shorebirds) and then another turn to port around Bluff Point (with its town beach) will take you into the deep water of Cotuit Bay and eventually into the small and narrow entrance into North Bay. The town dock for Cotuit (which is actually a village in the town of Barnstable) lies on the northwestern side of Cotuit Bay, and an oc-

casional rental mooring can be found, as well as anchorage space when the bay is less crowded.

WEST BAY AND OSTERVILLE

THE safest approach to West Bay is from red-and-white bell "C" marking the approach to Cotuit Bay. A northeasterly course from the bell, leaving Lone Rock well to port, will lead you to flashing green bell "1" east of Lone Rock. From there, swing northwest, leave green can "3" close aboard to port, and continue north so as to keep the flashing red light at the entrance to starboard. The entrance jetties mark the centerline into West Bay. As the chart indicates, depths are limited, so mind your fathometer accordingly.

Osterville, another of Barnstable's villages, is home to a number of marinas, and depending on the season,

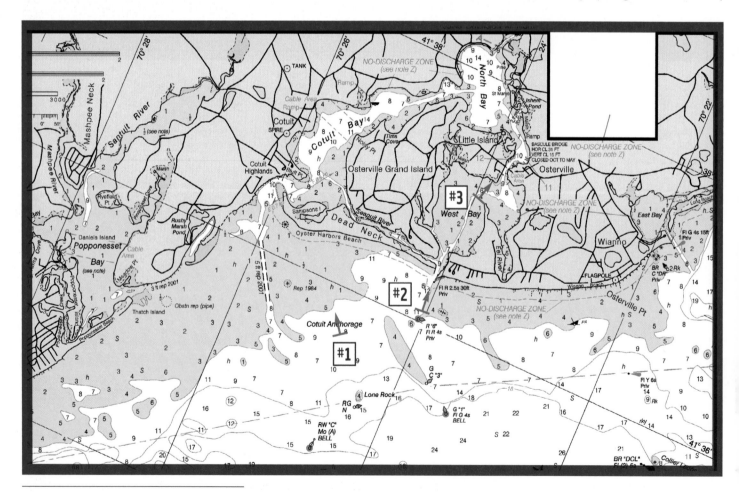

13229, 30th ed., April 08, NAD 83, Soundings in feet, 1:40,000

#1

Cotuit   Cotuit Bay

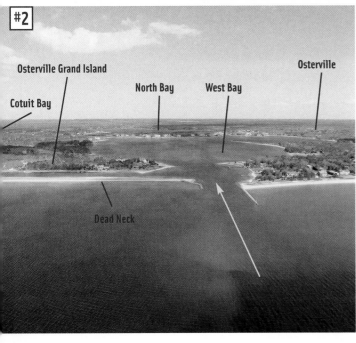

#2

Osterville Grand Island   North Bay   West Bay   Osterville
Cotuit Bay   Dead Neck

#3

North Bay   Little Island   Osterville

space can be found. The main anchorage area, over-looked by the Wianno Yacht Club, is south and east of the opening bascule bridge between West Bay and North Bay. Most of the facilities, however, are just north of the bridge. Though other cruisers generally bypass Osterville, we've found it to be very hospitable.

■ HYANNIS ■

HYANNIS is full of activities and lots of traffic, but it's worth the trip. The primary approach is from red-and-white bell "HH" southwest of Point Gammon on Great Island. A northerly heading from the bell takes you to flashing red "4" off Great Rock, and from there, a turn to starboard takes you into the dredged channel that extends all the way into Lewis Bay.

North of the dredged channel's seaward end is the Hyannis Port breakwater, marked by flashing red 31-foot light "H" at its outer edge. If you need a quick place to duck in, you can find anchorage room just to the northwest of the channel, inside the breakwater, where you'll be lying just offshore from the Kennedy family summer compound.

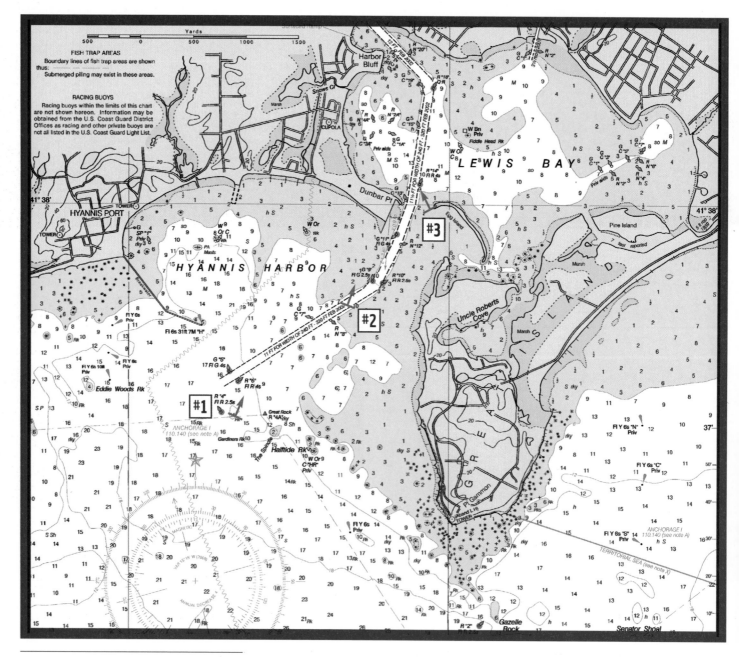

13229, 30th ed., April 08, NAD 83, Soundings in feet, 1:40,000

Our preference, however, is to follow the channel past Dunbar Point and into Lewis Bay, where you can anchor wherever there is room. Extremely well protected and generally less crowded than Hyannis's busy inner harbor, it's a perfect spot. You may be able to secure a transient mooring from the Hyannis Yacht Club, which lies just south of Harbor Bluff.

The west shore of the inner harbor is lined with charter and commercial fishing boats and ferry terminals, along with restaurants and bars. The town docks are at the head of the harbor. There's plenty of shopping and nightlife ashore, and you may even run into one of the Kennedy clan.

171

■ BASS RIVER ■

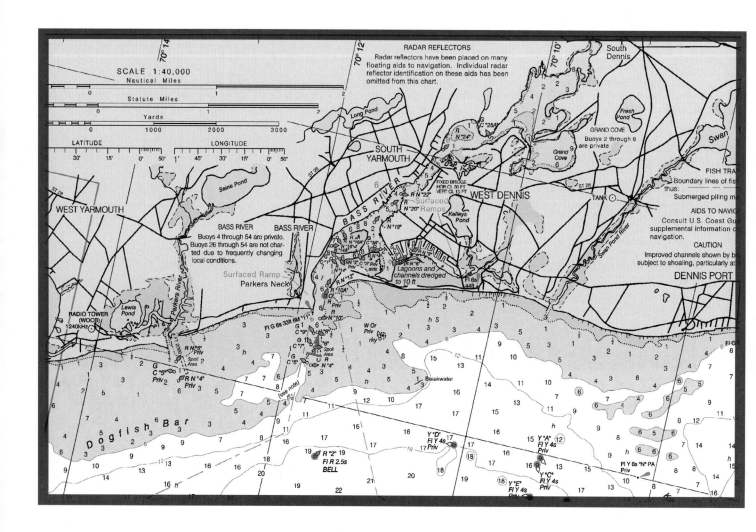

GIVEN its limited and constantly changing depths, the Bass River and its access into the villages of South Yarmouth and West Dennis should only be used by boats with shoal draft and favorable tides. Approach from flashing red bell "2" east of Dogfish Bar, following a northerly course into the buoyed channel that will lead you to the 33-foot light at the end of Parkers Neck. From there, the Bass River continues along the eastern shore of South Yarmouth.

The fixed bridge connecting South Yarmouth with West Dennis, with 15 feet of vertical clearance, marks the limit of navigation for many boats.

13229
30th ed., April 08
NAD 83
Soundings in feet
1:40,000

■ ALLEN HARBOR ■

WE'VE included Allen Harbor, in the town of Harwich, because it is attractive, well protected, and offers several powerboat facilities as well as town docks, but we have never entered it. Anchoring is not allowed—the harbor is too small—and it is a crowded harbor with uncertain availability of transient dockage. This and the challenging entrance have discouraged us from calling there.

WYCHMERE AND SAQUATUCKET HARBORS

A MILE east of Allen Harbor, Wychmere and Saquatucket Harbors share an approach from the northwestern edge of Chatham Roads. Begin the approach from green can "1" at the southern end of the dredged channel. Follow a northerly midchannel course to red-and-green can "5," east of the breakwater and its visible light. At this point you have a choice of turning to the port for the "L"-like approach into tiny Wychmere Harbor (or possibly to anchor behind the breakwater), or continuing along the dredged channel to red nun "8" and then making a starboard turn into Saquatucket Harbor. For an overnight berth, Saquatucket is the only viable option, with an occasional transient slip available. Nevertheless, these are beautiful and very well-protected spots, and Saquatucket does provide easy access to limited services.

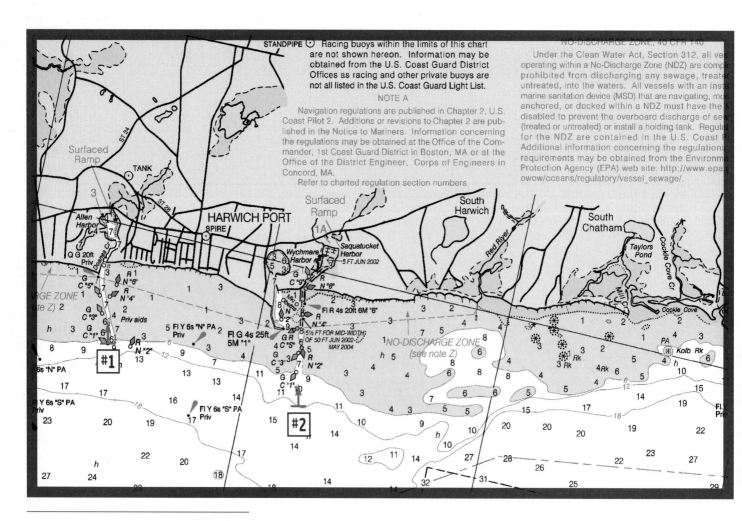

13229, 30th ed., April 08, NAD 83, Soundings in feet, 1:40,000

#1 Allen Harbor Harwich Port

#2 Harwich Port Wychmere Harbor Saquatucket Harbor

■ STAGE HARBOR, CHATHAM ■

THE entrance to Stage Harbor is approached from Chatham Roads and from red-and-white bell "SH" sitting to the west of the dredged harbor channel's seaward end. From there, enter the well-buoyed channel. Once inside, it will become apparent that this is a busy commercial fishing harbor with limited services for the cruising yachtsman. Occasionally transient moorings may be available either from the yacht club or through the harbormaster. If not, there is limited anchorage south of the dredged channel, inside Harding Beach Point.

What isn't apparent from the charts is just how difficult the entrance to Stage Harbor can be, given the confused and shifting sand and the likelihood that in a southwest blow strong waves will break around the entrance, making it look particularly fearsome. Further, the difficult passage from Nantucket Sound to the Atlantic Ocean via Butler Hole and Pollock Rip Channel makes Stage Harbor something of a dead end for any cruiser coasting eastward along the South Cape. For these reasons, many travelers bypass Stage Harbor.

If you can get situated in the harbor, however, you will enjoy wild and lovely surroundings. It is worth a dinghy trip up into Little Mill Pond to see the sights and to tie up for a walk into the town of Chatham, which offers many very nice shops and restaurants.

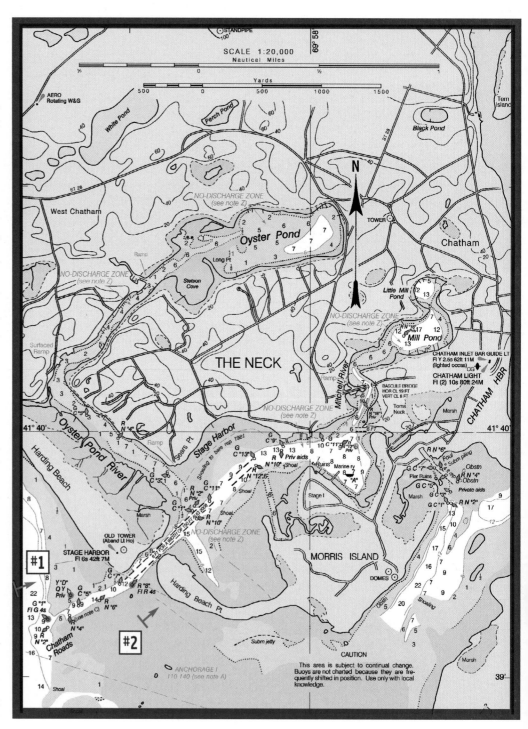

13229
30th ed., April 08
NAD 83
Soundings in feet
1:20,000

#1

Oyster Pond River

Chatham Harbor

Mill Pond

Stage Harbor

G "1"

RW "SH"

#2

Stage Harbor

Town of Chatham

Stage Island

Chatham Harbor

Harding Beach Point

Oyster Pond River

#1A

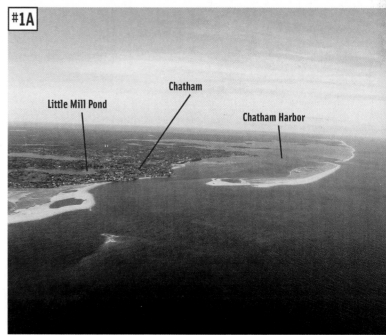

Little Mill Pond

Chatham

Chatham Harbor

(See chart on page 178.)

CHATHAM HARBOR, PLEASANT BAY, AND RYDER COVE

A MERE half-mile walk through the town of Chatham separates Chatham Harbor from the headwaters of Stage Harbor in Mill Pond, yet the journey by sea from Stage Harbor to the Chatham Harbor entrance is about 40 miles—a journey that would take you south-southwest around Monomoy Island and Handkerchief Shoal, northeast through Butler Hole and Pollock Rip Channel and into the open Atlantic, then northwest to the cape's outer shore. The hazards of this journey are touched upon in this region's introduction. It's a journey few boaters ever make.

The only reasonable approach to Chatham Harbor and Pleasant Bay begins from red-and-white whistle "C" southeast of Chatham's Coast Guard station with its two navigation lights. Anyone attempting this entrance must have absolutely up-to-date local knowledge of water depths and the favored sides of the town-maintained navigation channel that winds its way through the harbor, around Allen Point, and past the entrance to Ryder Cove, Crows Pond, and Pleasant and Little Pleasant Bay. Though spectacular in almost every way, the challenging passage and the water depths (assume no greater than 4 feet) limit access. For skippers with shoal boats and access to local knowledge, the opportunity to explore this region is tempting. Those who have done so have never been disappointed.

Given the vagaries and the constant changes wrought by the sea upon these sandy shores, we can't provide detailed pilotage instructions. You must weigh the beautiful environment against the challenges of entry.

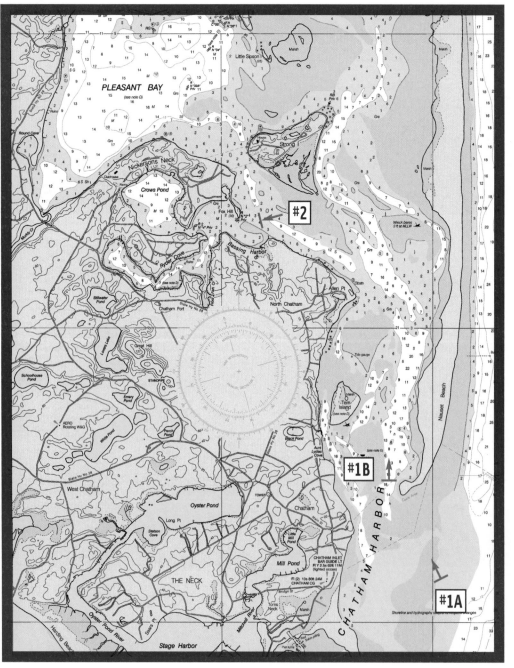

13248
10th ed., March 01
NAD 83
Soundings in feet
1:20,000

#1B

Bassing Harbor

Strong Island

Tern Island

#2

Ryder Cove

Crows Pond

Pleasant Bay

Bassing Harbor

Fox Hill

■ PROVINCETOWN HARBOR ■

PROTECTED Provincetown Harbor perches at the northern terminus of Cape Cod. Provincetown's sandy hook is unmistakable from any direction, and the approach is easy under almost any conditions, but don't underestimate the distance and time required to get all the way into the inner harbor. The final approach is likely to feel endless.

The standard approach from the direction of the Cape Cod Canal, which is 21 miles southwest—or from Plymouth Harbor, which is about the same distance due west—begins from flashing green bell "1." If you approach from Boston Harbor or points downeast, your landfall is likely to be on Race Point with its 41-foot-high light and horn, but from this direction, too, it's advisable to begin your final approach into the harbor from bell "1." The town's Pilgrim Monument—a granite tower commemorating the Pilgrims' landfall there and the Mayflower Compact—rises 348 feet above sea level and is visible from all directions.

From bell "1" you'll see the 45-foot light (and hear the horn) on Wood End, three-quarters of a mile to the north. A northeasterly heading will take you to green bell "3" off the northeastern tip of Long Point, the spit of land that protects the harbor. You'll see 36-foot-high Long

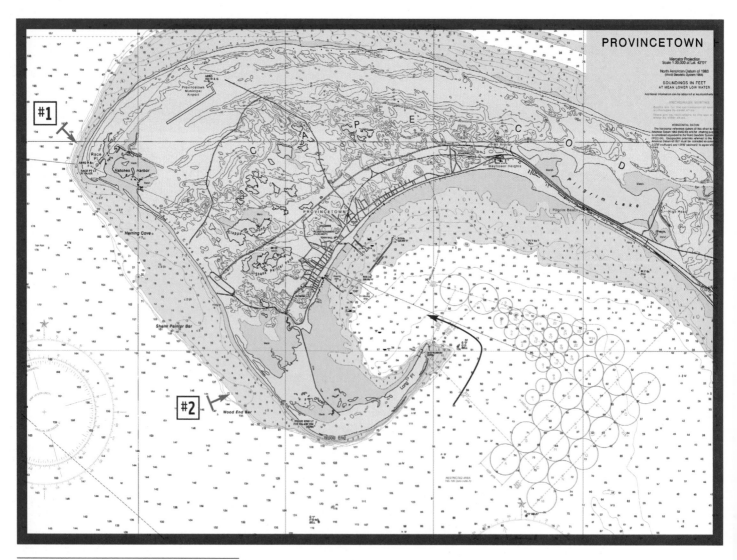

13249, 13th ed., April 07, NAD 83, Soundings in feet, 1:20,000

Point Light (and hear its horn) at the end of the spit. A northwesterly course from bell "3" takes you into the center of the harbor, where you'll find any number of moorings and services, all located behind the breakwater. We've never had a problem finding a spot for the night. There are numerous slips, moorings, and places to anchor. One peaceful spot is tucked in behind the hook along Long Point spit.

Provincetown is well known for its busy gay summer community, which supports many interesting galleries, shops, and restaurants. In juxtaposition with the commercial fishing fleet, transient boaters, and visitors from all over, the resulting scene is a colorful and entertaining pageant. Cape Cod National Seashore is nearby, and there are many bike paths worth exploring.

■ WELLFLEET ■

WELLFLEET Harbor, north of Cape Cod's inner elbow, is clearly out of the way. Six-mile-long Billingsgate Shoal, projecting southwest into Cape Cod Bay from the harbor's western shore, prevents a direct approach from the west and forces a long, circuitous approach from the south instead. As a result, the harbor is more distant than Provincetown from the Cape Cod Canal, and the journey from Provincetown to Wellfleet is a lot longer by sea than by road. Still, Wellfleet offers the traveling yachtsman deep water, a navigable entrance (though shifting sands and strong currents require diligent navigation), and reasonable protection.

From green flashing bell "1" southwest of Billingsgate Shoal, an east-northeasterly course will take you along the southern edge of the shoal to flashing green "3" off Stony Bar, to the north of black-and-red "DJ." From

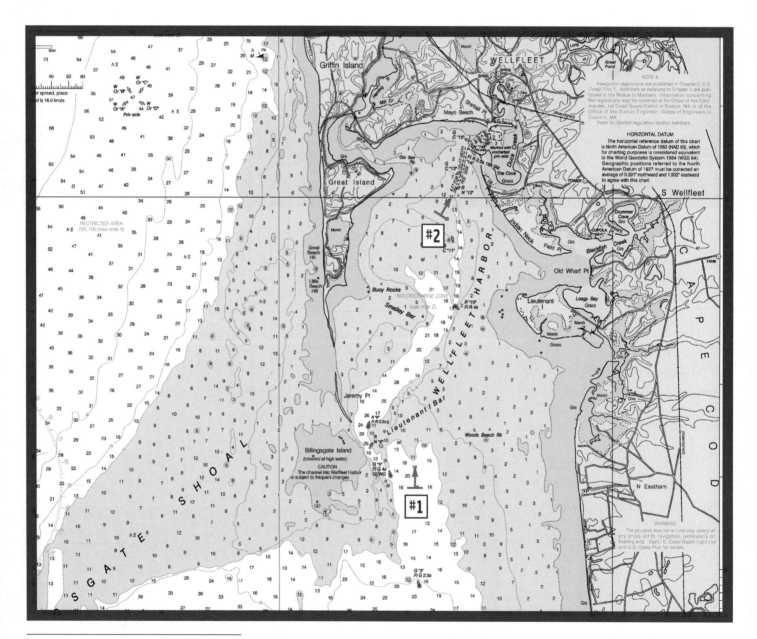

13250, 8th ed., Oct. 01, NAD 83, Soundings in feet, 1:20,000

"3," continue north to flashing green gong "5" east of Billingsgate Island, but note that this "island" is underwater at high tide. From there, leave red nuns "6" and "8" to starboard as you navigate around Lieutenant Island Bar, then turn to a northeasterly heading to flashing red "10." A northerly course from "10" will take you to the dredged channel into the inner harbor. Observe the buoys in the channel, then turn to the starboard flashing red "14" marking the end of the harbor jetty.

Once inside, you can usually obtain a mooring by contacting the harbormaster, but there is no room to anchor in the inner harbor. For a remote and somewhat sheltered nearby anchorage, head west from green can "11" to anchor east of Great Beach Hill and north of Smalley Bar.

Wellfleet is a charming town with a whaling, fishing, and oystering heritage. Commercial fishing continues, but tourism is now the town's primary source of employment and income. There are numerous shops and restaurants ashore.

■ SESUIT HARBOR ■

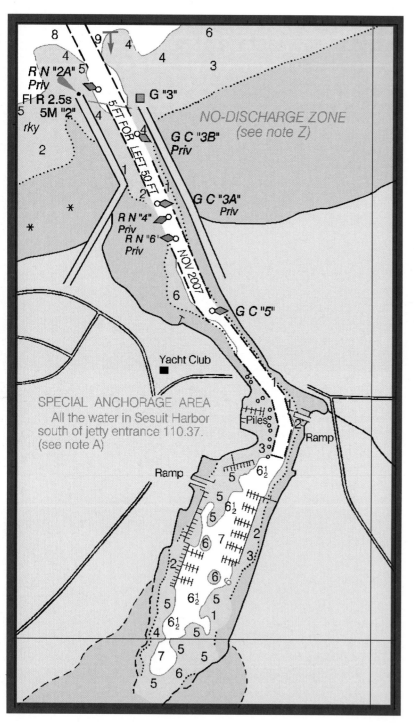

SESUIT Harbor, just west of the cape's inner elbow, is 15 miles east of the Cape Cod Canal, 12 miles south-southwest from Wellfleet Harbor, and less than 3 miles south and a little east of green bell "1" off the southwest end of Billingsgate Shoal. The final approach to this East Dennis harbor can be made from flashing green bell "1S" north of the entrance.

The harbor entrance, like many others on Cape Cod, is sheltered by protruding jetties. It has a charted dredged depth of 5 feet, but this is a hazardous entry when the wind and seas are coming in off Cape Cod Bay to the north, and should not be attempted in such conditions. The narrow harbor inside is overwhelmed by slips and a marina, and there is no room for anchoring.

13250
8th ed., Oct. 01
NAD 83
Soundings in feet
1:10,000

■ BARNSTABLE HARBOR ■

JUST 10 miles east of the Cape Cod Canal and fronted by a lovely town, Barnstable Harbor is certainly tempting. Nevertheless, we have generally avoided it due to the challenges and circuitousness of the approach. The channel through the entrance bar is narrow, and seas break over the bar in a northerly blow. The chart warns that the bar and harbor channels are subject to continual changes and shoaling, and the navigation buoys have to be moved frequently to follow the shifting channel. Without local knowledge, you shouldn't attempt this entrance in anything other than ideal conditions.

For those tempted to make the trip, the approach begins from flashing red-and-white bell "BH," 1.4 miles north of Beach Point. From this bell, a southerly course will take you to green can "3" and then red nun "4." Con-

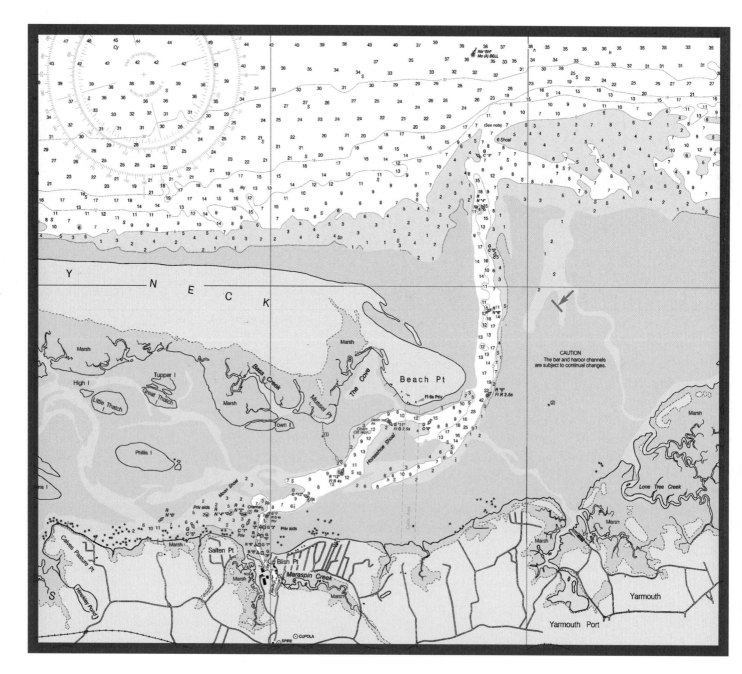

tinue south through the narrow passageway to flashing red "8" off Beach Point, then turn to starboard, leaving green cans "9" and "11" to port as you make the turn around Horseshoe Shoal. After leaving flashing red "12" to starboard and green can "13" to port, you'll eventually reach the dredged channel, marked by flashing green "1" at its northern end.

Narrow, and without room to anchor, this is mainly a small-boat harbor, popular for sea kayaking, sportfishing, and whale-watching excursions. Barnstable is the county seat of Barnstable County, which encompasses all of Cape Cod, and the village features stately colonial homes, attractive gardens, and a selection of nice restaurants.

13251
15th ed., Sept. 04
NAD 83
Soundings in feet
1:20,000

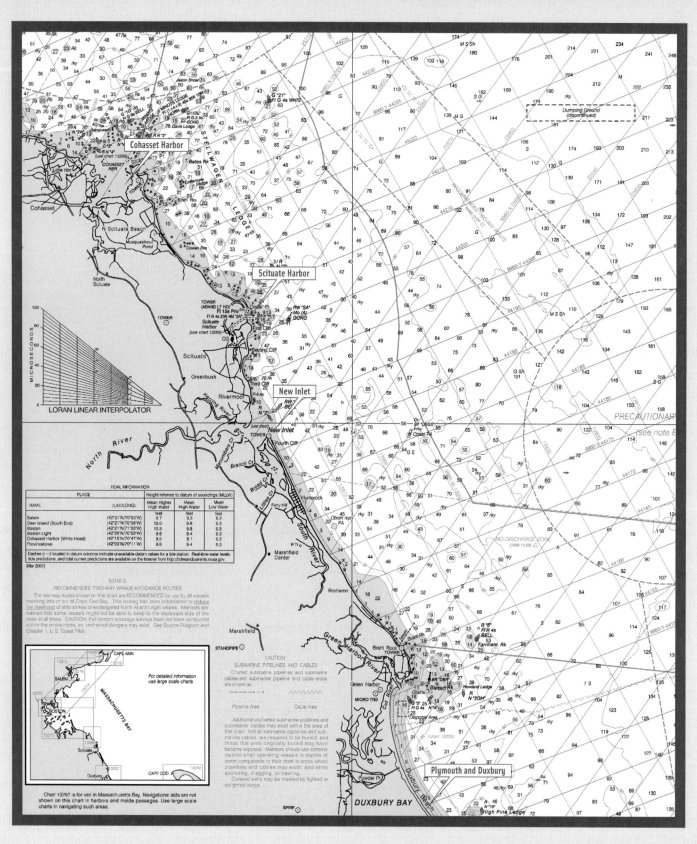

SOUTH OF BOSTON
—PLYMOUTH TO COHASSET—

The South Shore of Massachusetts—the roughly forty miles of coast between Boston Harbor and the Cape Cod Canal—becomes a dangerous lee shore in a northeast gale but is otherwise a varied, interesting, and pleasant place for cruising. This coast offers several good harbors with short runs between them—only 22 miles separate Cohasset Harbor in the north from Plymouth Harbor in the south. Shelter is never far away. Plymouth and Scituate, in particular, are worthwhile diversions for cruisers traveling between the Cape Cod Canal and Boston or points downeast.

13267
34th ed., May 07
NAD 83
Soundings in feet
1:80,000

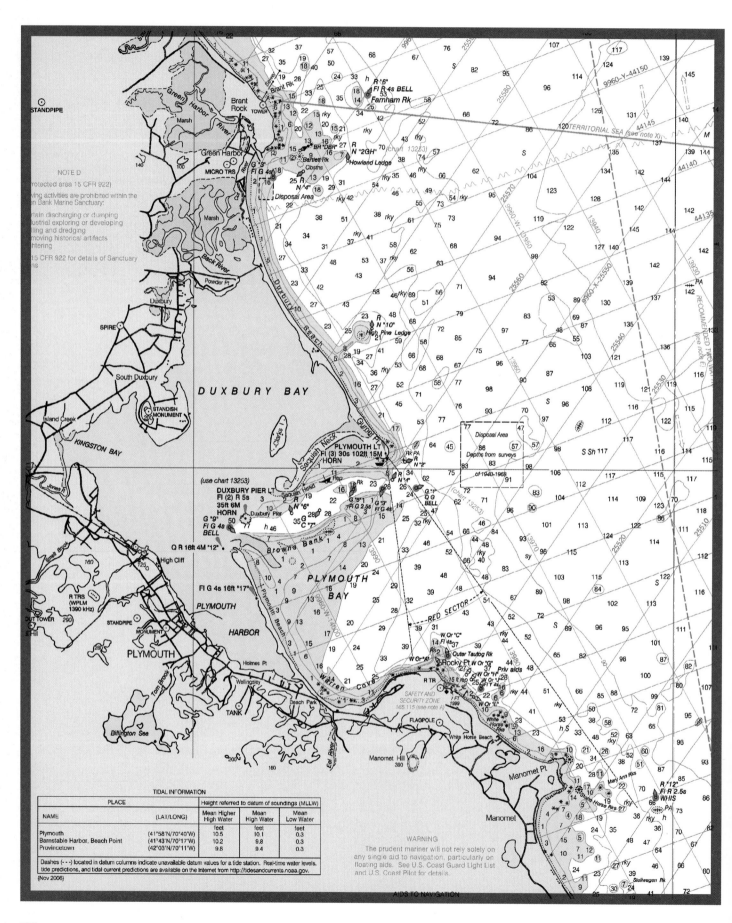

TIDAL INFORMATION				
PLACE		Height referred to datum of soundings (MLLW)		
NAME	(LAT/LONG)	Mean Higher High Water	Mean High Water	Mean Low Water
		feet	feet	feet
Plymouth	(41°58'N/70°40'W)	10.5	10.1	0.3
Barnstable Harbor, Beach Point	(41°43'N/70°17'W)	10.2	9.8	0.3
Provincetown	(42°03'N/70°11'W)	9.8	9.4	0.3

Dashes (- - -) located in datum columns indicate unavailable datum values for a tide station. Real-time water levels, tide predictions, and tidal current predictions are available on the Internet from http://tidesandcurrents.noaa.gov.

(Nov 2006)

WARNING
The prudent mariner will not rely solely on any single aid to navigation, particularly on floating aids. See U.S. Coast Guard Light List and U.S. Coast Pilot for details.

AIDS TO NAVIGATION

APPROACHES TO PLYMOUTH AND DUXBURY ■

FROM almost any vantage point more than a mile or two offshore, the entrance into Plymouth or Duxbury can be confusing, as the long, south-projecting Saquish Neck and north-projecting Plymouth Beach hide the interior approaches to Duxbury and Plymouth, respectively. The cut between these two long spits must be approached north of Browns Bank even if you're arriving from the south, so Gurnet Point, topped by 102-foot Plymouth Light (with horn) provides the first precise landmark for cruisers entering Plymouth Bay from Cape Cod Bay.

Southeast of Gurnet Point you'll find flashing green bell "1" surrounded by good water, and from there a short run west takes you to flashing green "3" and "5" just north of Browns Bank. Head west and a little south from "5," staying in midchannel for your approach to the prominent Duxbury Pier light and horn, which is unmistakable in virtually any weather. This so-called pier marks the channel intersection at which you turn north for Duxbury or south for Plymouth Harbor.

13246
38th ed., Dec. 06
NAD 83
Soundings in feet
1:80,000

PLYMOUTH HARBOR

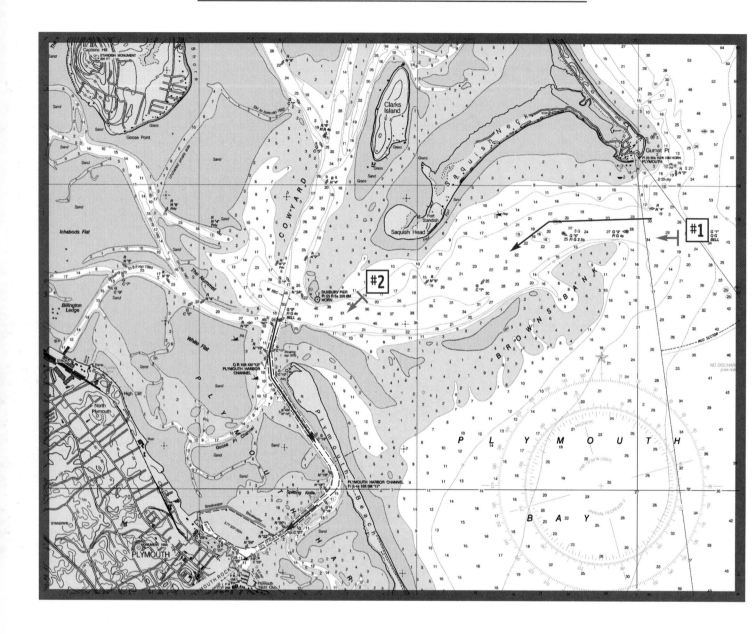

#1

Plymouth

Plymouth Beach

Saquish Head

Clarks Island

Gurnet Point

G "5"

G "3"

R "4"

FORTY-FOUR miles southeast of Boston and about the same distance east and a little north of Providence, Plymouth is a popular stopover for cruisers and home to a large fleet of recreational boats. The many shoreside attractions in this thriving town, settled by the Pilgrims in 1620, include the *Mayflower* replica (docked at the state pier), Plimouth Plantation (the living history mu-

seum south of the harbor), Plymouth Rock (on the harbor waterfront), and the many shops, restaurants, and other attractions of the busy Plymouth Center downtown district adjacent to the harbor. A seasonal ferry runs to Provincetown, and whale-watching and deep-sea fishing excursions also leave the harbor. Plymouth Beach, the three-mile-long barrier beach that shelters

13253
19th ed., May 07
NAD 83
Soundings in feet
1:20,000

Plymouth

C "11"

N "10"

N "8"

G "9"

To Duxbury

N "2A"

Duxbury Pier

the harbor from Plymouth Bay, is the largest of the town's nine public beaches. With bus, rail, plane, and convenient highway connections, Plymouth is a good place to drop off or pick up crew.

If the Plymouth approach channel seems tricky today, imagine what it was like for Colonial-era sailing vessels navigating with fewer navigation aids and no engines. In *George Washington's Secret Navy: How the American Revolution Went to Sea*, James L. Nelson tells the story of the schooners commissioned and manned by General Washington to harass British merchant shipping in the Boston Harbor approaches while he had the British garrison in Boston under siege in 1775. One of the schooners, newly refitted, attempted to leave Plymouth Harbor in a fresh northwesterly breeze in late October but ran aground within a half-mile despite the presence of a local pilot on board—and indeed, looking at a chart today, one wonders how a ship of that day or this could possibly work clear of the harbor's narrow channel under sail against a headwind from the northwest. A few days later the *Harrison's* commander, Captain William Coit, tried again but promptly ran aground again, and did not float free until the following afternoon. On his third attempt in early November he ran aground yet again, but floated free soon after and finally cleared the harbor that evening.

Today, thankfully, it is easier. When you reach the Duxbury Pier in the approach to Duxbury and Plymouth, flashing green bell "9" will be just to your south. Pass between it and red nun "8" to enter the dredged channel leading to Plymouth Harbor. Head toward 16-foot red quick-flashing Plymouth Harbor Channel Light "12" until you pass between can "11" and nun "10," then turn gently to port to stay in the dredged channel with Plymouth Beach close aboard to port. You may at some point begin to think that the approach is endless, but stick with it—you're getting there. Sixteen-foot flashing green Plymouth Harbor Channel Light "17" marks a hard turn to starboard around Splitting Knife shoal, and now the inner harbor breakwater should be in sight ahead. At red nun "22" you'll pass the breakwater's eastern end, and from there, Plymouth Rock lies straight ahead. The Plymouth Yacht Club is just to the left of the rock.

Marinas can provide transient moorings, and even in summer we've had no difficulty finding space. Haulout and other marine services are available. There is no room to anchor in the inner harbor, but you may find room between marks "17" and "19" or elsewhere in Plymouth or Duxbury bay. This is a busy harbor and town but a very interesting place to visit.

■ DUXBURY ■

HAVING traversed the Plymouth/Duxbury approach on numerous occasions, we've learned to give great respect to the trip into Duxbury. From the Duxbury Pier's 35-foot flashing red light and horn, a wide turn to starboard between green can "1" and red nun "2A" marks the beginning of the Duxbury channel. Given the vagaries of currents and the constant shoaling, it is important to pay particular attention and ensure that you account for and observe each and every charted navigation aid. At flashing red "6" you reach another fork in the channel; the right-hand branch leads to a potential anchorage with reasonable protection north of Clarks Island, and the left-hand branch is the main channel into Duxbury Bay and Duxbury Harbor.

To reach Duxbury Harbor, follow the buoyed main channel from flashing red "6" until you pick up red nun "12," where a 90-degree turn to port leads into the narrower channel to Duxbury Harbor and its yacht club. The harbor is small, but the yacht club is hospitable, and on several occasions we've found space to spend the night. The village is charming and welcoming and worth the trip. But remember, it's a long way back out in the morning to Gurnet Point.

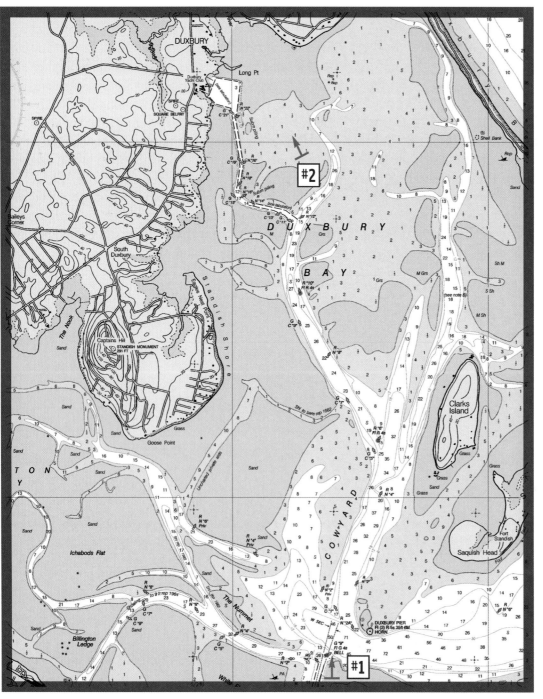

13253
19th ed., May 07
NAD 83
Soundings in feet
1:20,000

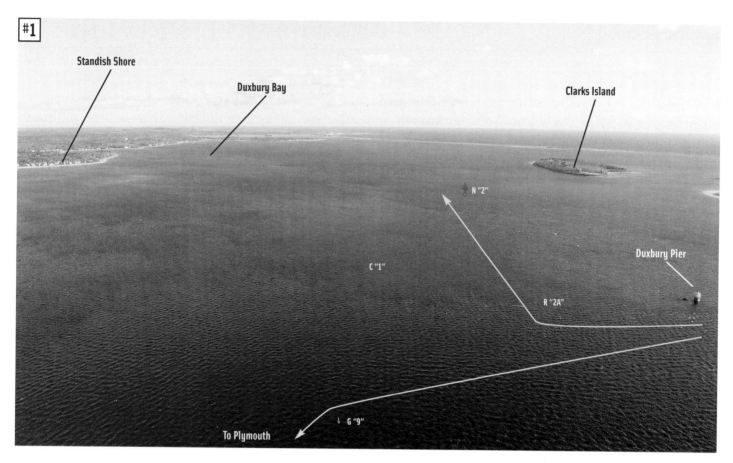

#1

Standish Shore

Duxbury Bay

Clarks Island

N "2"

Duxbury Pier

C "1"

R "2A"

To Plymouth

G "9"

#2

Duxbury Yacht Club

Bluefish River

Powder Point

NEW INLET (NORTH AND SOUTH RIVERS)

TEMPTING only for those with shoal-draft boats and good local knowledge, New Inlet—11 miles north of Gurnet Point—provides access to the North River and the South River, with the former having far more navigable soundings than the latter. New Inlet is subject to shoaling, forcing frequent relocation of the entrance

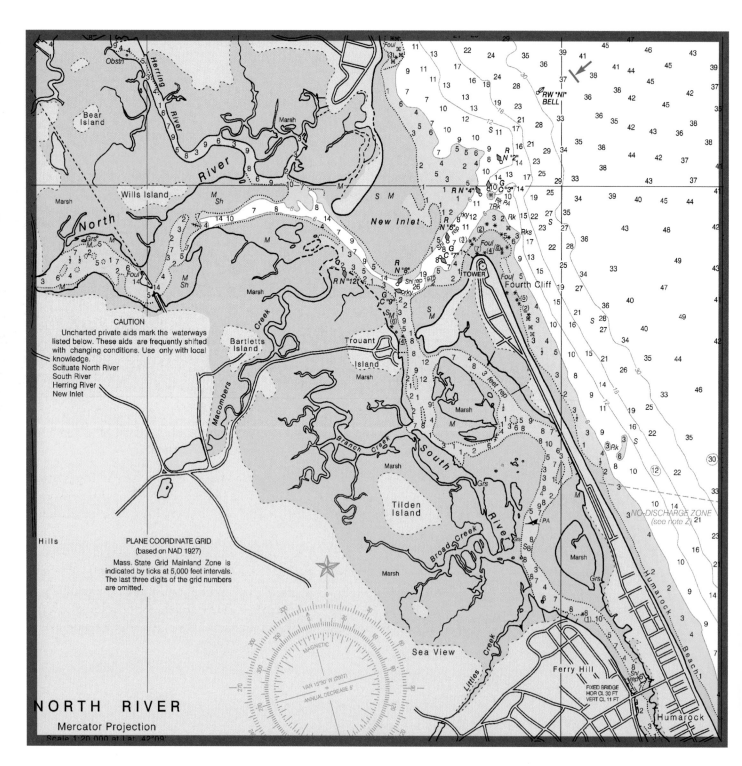

NORTH RIVER

Mercator Projection

Scale 1:20,000 at Lat. 42°09'

buoys, and seas may break over the inlet bar on an ebb tide in heavy weather.

The approach to New Inlet is made from red-and-white bell "NI," a southwesterly course from which leads first to red nun "2" and then to green can "3" off the northern end of Fourth Cliff. Follow the buoyed entrance channel from can "3," leaving nuns to starboard and cans to port. The entrance to the South River branches south from can "9" and nun "8;" and privately

maintained buoys mark the shallow, challenging passage down the river. The North River passage through peaceful salt marsh is less winding and somewhat deeper.

There is dockage for small powerboats at marinas in either river, but little else. Given the navigational challenges, the lack of services within, and the availability of Scituate Harbor just to the north, New Inlet is seldom used by transient yachtsmen on their way east or south.

13267
34th ed., May 07
NAD 83
Soundings in feet
1:20,000

■ SCITUATE HARBOR ■

POPULAR Scituate Harbor, 20 miles southeast of Boston and 2 miles north of New Inlet, is a favorite stopover for boaters of all stripes. With its protected deep water, ease of access, wide range of services, and the hospitable Scituate Harbor Yacht Club, this harbor can provide an overnight berth to a cruiser even in the busiest of times.

The approach into Scituate is made from red-and-white gong "SA" due east of the harbor entrance. A westerly course from the gong leads you between green can "1" and red nun "2." You'll leave 21-foot flashing red light "2A" on the southeastern end of the breakwater to starboard, and First Cliff to port. The dredged channel leads into the main harbor at nun "6," then bends southward into the back harbor between First and Second Cliffs.

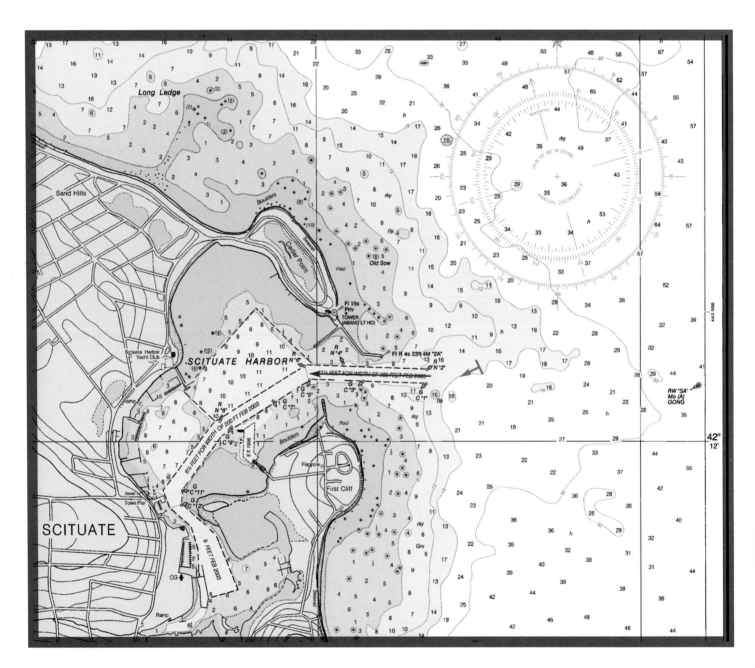

Back Harbor

Main Harbor

Scituate Harbor Yacht Club

First Cliff

N "4"

C "3"

C "1"

N "2"

13269
10th ed., Feb. 06
NAD 83
Soundings in feet
1:10,000

■ COHASSET HARBOR ■

THOUGH providing the first real shelter south of Boston, Cohasset Harbor, 5 miles north of Scituate, requires careful navigation through its shoal- and ledge-strewn approaches. The harbor can be approached via the Western Channel, the Gangway, or the Eastern Channel, but our strong preference has always been the Western Channel, which keeps cruisers well clear of The Grampuses—notorious ledges in the Gangway—and infamous Minots Ledge in the Eastern Channel.

(Outer Minot Ledge is marked by 85-foot Minots Light, successor to the original lighthouse that was built by the federal government after more than forty ships went aground on the ledge in the early 1800s.)

The Western Channel approach begins from green can "3" off Chittenden Rock. Take a southerly heading from this marker, leaving the green day marker off Barrel Rock to port. Avoid the 6-foot soundings just south of the rock, then turn east to leave red nun "6W" off Sut-

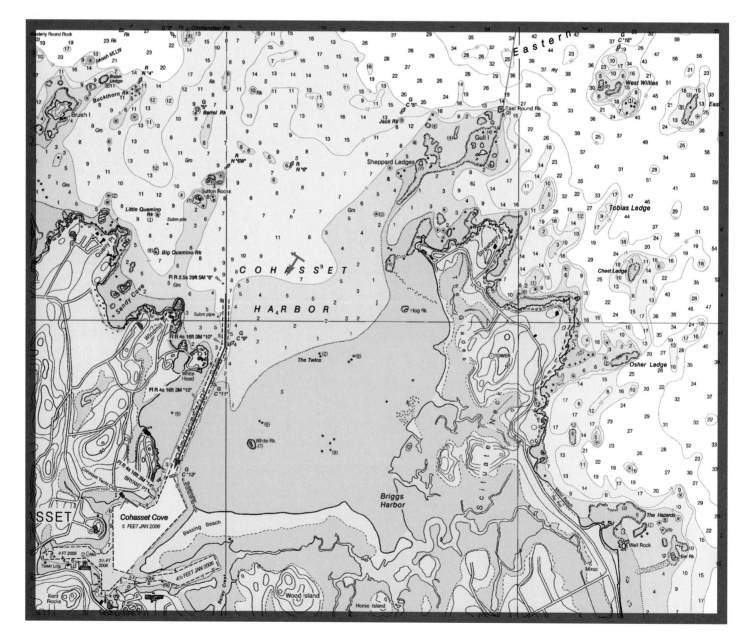

Outer Harbor

Cohasset Cove

White Head

FL R "12"

C "11"

FL R "10"

C "9"

FL R "8"

ton Rocks to starboard. A southerly course from the nun will lead you across Cohasset's outer harbor (too shoal and exposed for overnight anchoring) to 29-foot flashing red light "8" at the mouth of the dredged channel into the inner harbor.

Once you're in the channel, Windmill Point and White Head will be on your starboard side. Follow the channel between Bryant Point and the entrance breakwater extending northwestward from Bassing Beach, and you'll arrive in Cohasset Cove and the inner harbor. Given its small size, lack of transient facilities, and large local fleet, Cohasset is not often used as an overnight stay, but a call to the harbormaster may yield a mooring or slip for the night.

13269
10th ed., Feb. 06
NAD 83
Soundings in feet
1:10,000

REGION IX

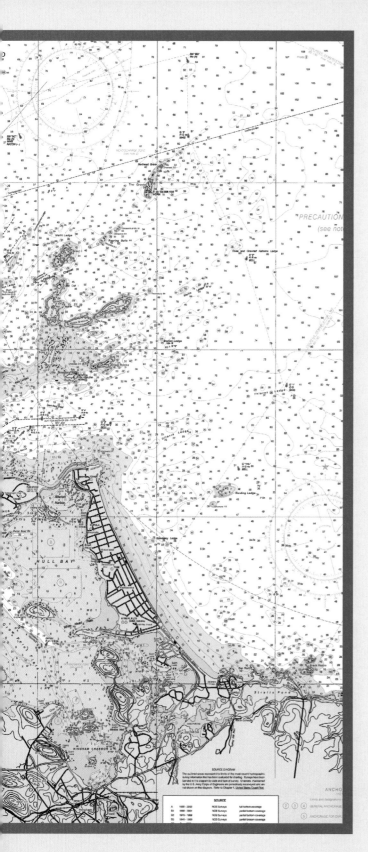

Despite surrounding the largest city in New England, Boston Harbor is often considered a place for the visiting mariner to avoid. We couldn't disagree more. Boston Harbor contains countless passages, numerous anchorages and hidden lunch spots, and endlessly varied and interesting activity. It is a major commercial and financial hub, a leading port, a center of commercial fishing, host to numerous colleges and universities, and one of our country's most historic cities and leading tourist destinations. It features a vibrant waterfront, a walkable downtown, a rich menu of ethnic restaurants and cultural attractions, sports events, and a good public transportation system that will take you anywhere you want to go in the metro region. In short, it's well worth adding a day or two— or more—to a cruise downeast to sample Boston Harbor's inexhaustible offerings.

There are two primary approaches to Boston Harbor. One is to the north, through one of two clear channels from Massachusetts Bay to the President Roads passage and from there into downtown Boston and Charlestown. The other is to the south through Nantasket Roads, past the Hull peninsula and the harbors of Hull, Quincy, Hingham, and Weymouth. The north and south approaches are interconnected by three channels, the most popular and easily navigable of which is The Narrows.

13270
63rd ed., Aug. 08
NAD 83
Soundings in feet
1:25,000

■ ENTERING BOSTON HARBOR FROM ■ THE SOUTH VIA NANTASKET ROADS

THE Nantasket Roads approach begins between green bell "3" off Point Allerton and 102-foot Boston Light (known as the "ideal" American lighthouse) on Little Brewster Island. From that point, the wide-open and

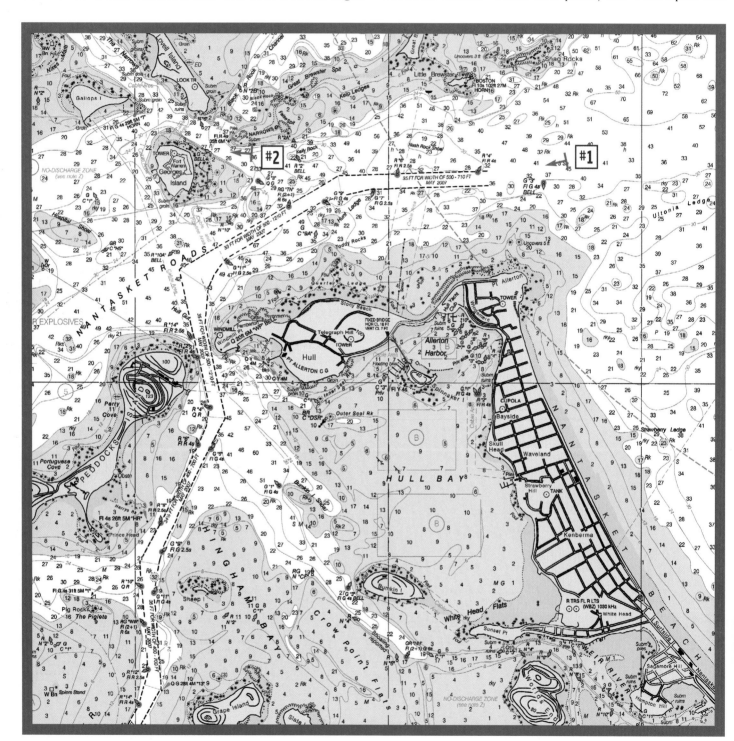

13270, 63rd ed., Aug. 08, NAD 83, Soundings in feet, 1:25,000

#1

Allerton Harbor
Hull
Peddocks Island
Georges Island
The Narrows
Boston
Deer Island
Hull Gut
Boston Light
R "4"
G "3"

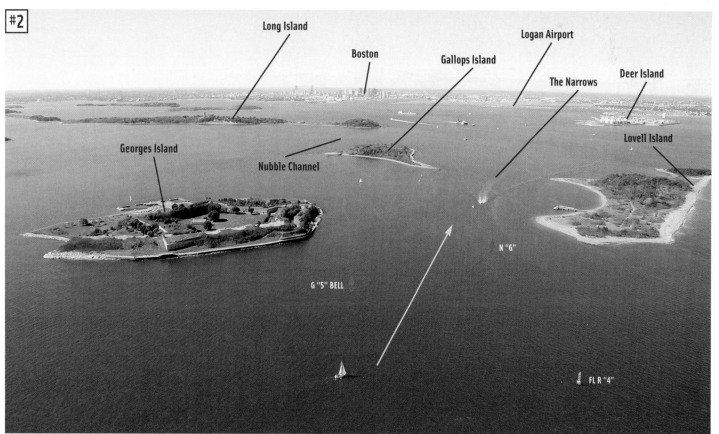

#2

Long Island
Boston
Gallops Island
Logan Airport
The Narrows
Deer Island
Georges Island
Nubble Channel
Lovell Island
N "6"
G "5" BELL
FL R "4"

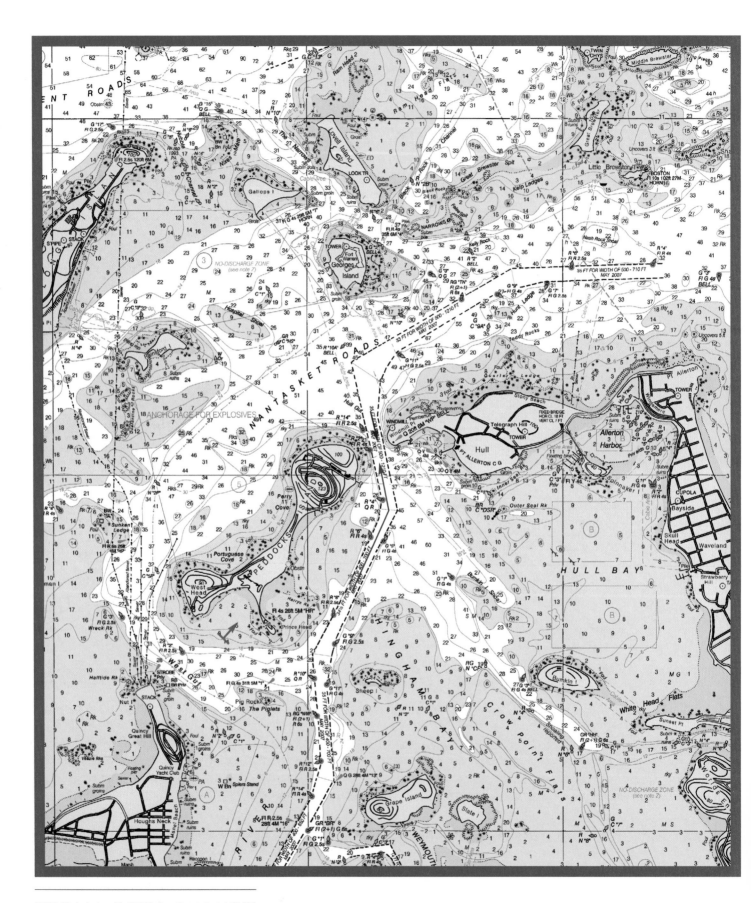

13270, 63rd ed., Aug. 08, NAD 83, Soundings in feet, 1:25,000

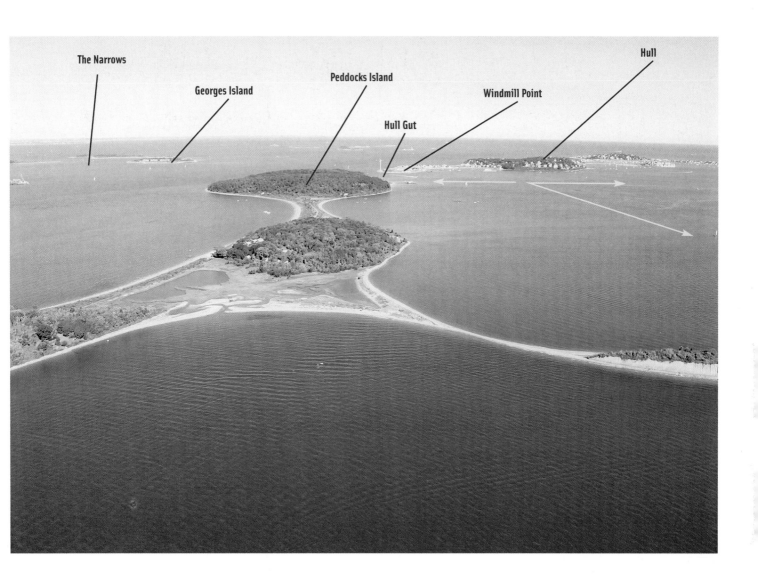

well-buoyed dredged channel ahead is obvious. If you have time for a slight diversion, Calf, Middle Brewster, and Outer Brewster islands enclose a nice little bight that makes a great spot in settled weather for a midday picnic or a late-afternoon pre-dinner anchorage. It's far enough out to feel remote, yet the Boston skyline is ever present (as are the planes approaching Logan International Airport). There are dangers around this bight, so approach it with chart in hand.

Back in Nantasket Roads, after leaving flashing red "4" and "6" to starboard (see photo #2, page 207), you'll need to decide whether to pass east or south of Georges Island, on which historic Fort Warren can be seen. East of the island is the little passage called The Narrows, which will take you northwest between Lovell and Gallops islands and into President Roads. This waterway makes an easy shortcut for the cruising mariner who has approached Boston from the south and wants to connect with the President Roads passage into downtown Boston. Deep and easy to follow, with a clearer channel and far less ship traffic than in the outer approaches, The Narrows is preferable in this circumstance to approaching the President Roads passage from outside the harbor. Watch the tidal current in The Narrows, however; it can be strong, and you can be set by cross currents.

Ferries from the Boston waterfront carry tourists to Lovell and Georges islands. There are a few moorings off Georges and historic sites on the island, including the gun emplacements of Fort Warren and a Civil War prison where Confederate prisoners of war were confined.

If, on the other hand, you intend to follow Nantasket Roads into Hull, Hingham, or Weymouth, you'll turn

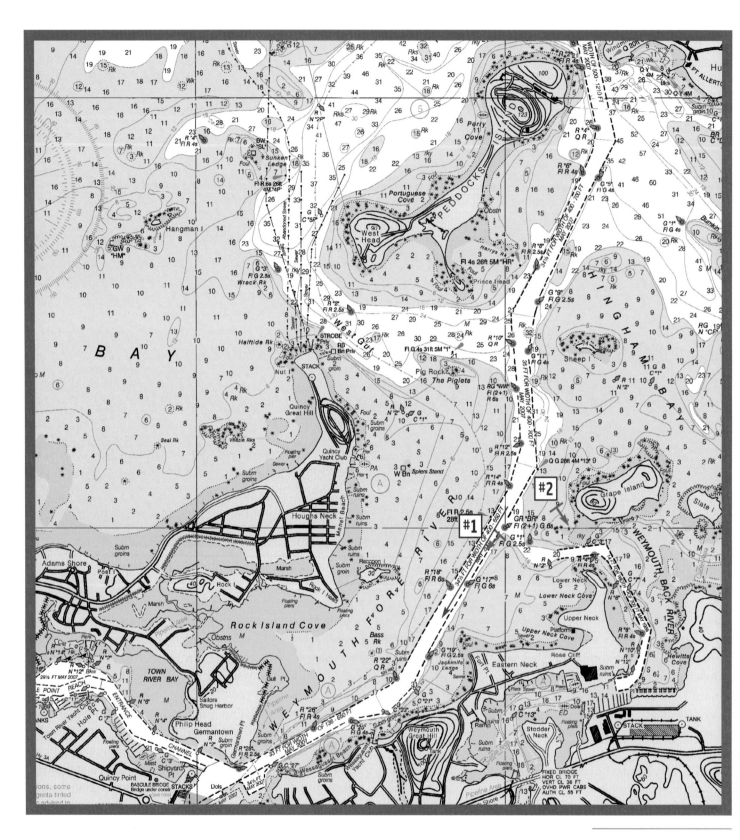

13270
63rd ed., Aug. 08
NAD 83
Soundings in feet
1:25,000

to a southwesterly heading shortly after leaving flashing red "6" to starboard, following the buoyed channel south of Georges Island. This approach is quite straightforward. From flashing green bell "11" midway between Georges Island and Windmill Point, a southerly heading will quickly take you through Hull Gut, the narrow passage between the northeastern end of Peddocks Island and Windmill Point (the western end of the Hull peninsula). There the channel splits, with clearly marked branches leading into Hull Bay and Allerton Harbor; the Weir River and World's End (a wonderful public property maintained by the Trustees of the Reservations); Hingham Bay and Hingham Harbor; Weymouth; and Quincy (see photo page 209).

Yet another alternative is to turn northwest at flashing green bell "11" and pass west of Georges and Gal-

lops islands before transiting Nubble Channel (shallower and narrower than The Narrows) into President Roads. Finally, you can reach President Roads west of Long Island by passing beneath the fixed bridge connecting Moon Head with Long Island (51 feet of vertical clearance under the channel span) and using either Sculpin Ledge Channel along Long Island's western shore or the Western Way on the west side of Spectacle Island. The Western Way gives you access to Dorchester Bay, which is bordered by the Southeast Expressway, with its constant traffic, and is beneath the flight paths of low-flying commercial jets approaching and leaving Logan. This is not a quiet anchorage, nor does it give convenient access to downtown Boston. Visually it's dominated by the Kennedy Library (on the point west of Thompson Island) and by the Boston Gas Tank,

the rainbow painting on which is the world's largest copyrighted work of art.

If, from Hull Gut, you elect to enter Allerton Harbor, you will see the Hull Yacht Club, an active club that sponsors a lot of racing in the summer. The harbor is well protected by Point Allerton and the breakwater connecting Hull to Spinnaker Island, and the narrow entrance channel is well buoyed. Anchorage is available but tight in the summer. The harbor is frequented more by recreational fishing boats and Hull's active local fleet than by cruising mariners.

The islands of Hingham Bay offer several possible picnic anchorages. In particular, Peddocks Island is inviting. The shallow bight on its south side is one possibility, and Portuguese and Perry coves on the west side of the island are also promising. There are good picnic spots ashore. Southeast of Peddocks, farther into the bay, Bumkin and Grape islands are easily accessible and make good lunch stops. Both have gravel beaches and limited dinghy docking, and both permit overnight camping if your crew wants to get off the boat for a night and pitch a tent ashore.

From Hingham Bay you can follow the dredged and buoyed channel south into the Weymouth Fore River as far as Quincy Point (photo page 211), or you can go farther, following Hole Point Reach through Town River Bay into downtown Quincy—an interesting trip, though neither bucolic nor well-groomed. Or you can branch off the Weymouth Fore River channel to travel southeasterly into the smaller dredged channel of the Weymouth Back River (photo above), curling around to the south, then west, then south again past Stodder Neck. Two marinas

(Text continues on page 215.)

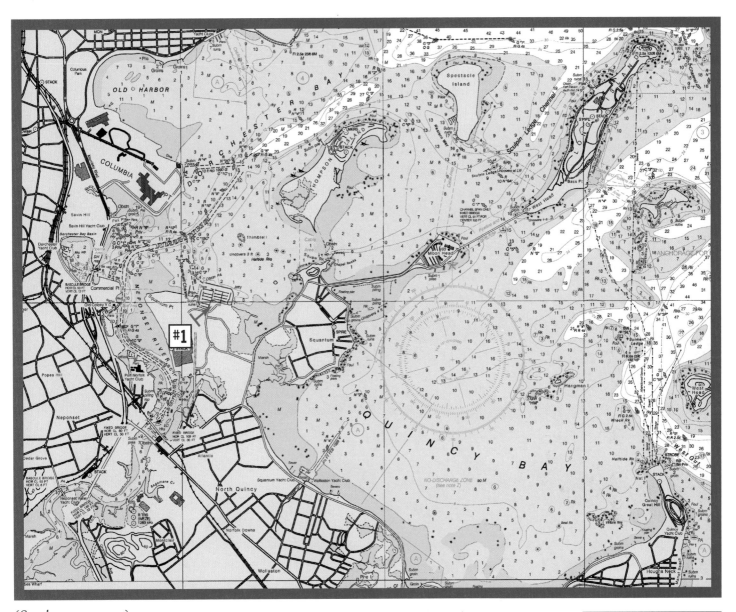

(See photo page 214.)

13270
63rd ed., Aug. 08
NAD 83
Soundings in feet
1:25,000

(See chart page 213.)

provide slips, moorings, and services. The South Shore Yacht Club is just before the fixed bridge with 36-foot clearance connecting North Weymouth with Hingham.

Hingham Yacht Club is a popular stop. From Hingham Bay, head southeasterly from the Weymouth Fore River approach channel, leaving flashing green bell "1" off Bumkin Island Shoal to port. Continue southeasterly through the buoyed channel, leaving Bumkin Island to port. You'll reach a "Y" in the channel at flashing green, green-and-red buoy "HH" and can "1," with the easterly leg leading to Worlds End and the Weir River and the southerly leg leading to Hingham Harbor and the Hingham Yacht Club on Crow Point. A line between Crow Point and the north end of Worlds End can be thought of as dividing navigable Hingham Bay from shoal and tricky Hingham Harbor. Local knowledge is a great asset when negotiating the harbor. Making your approach at low tide will show you where the exposed mudflats are. The inner harbor features a town dock and a friendly harbormaster, but getting there through the twisty channel is a challenge. There are moorings available off the yacht club, and the club provides a launch service. You can walk or take a cab into town from the club to enjoy Hingham's fine restaurants.

Scenic Worlds End dominates the visual horizon from Hingham Harbor and from the Weir River. If you follow the easterly channel out of Hingham Bay into the Weir River, you're likely to have plenty of company. East of Worlds End the Weir River channel divides around a midriver mudflat, with the eastern branch being the main, buoyed channel. The western branch, known locally as the Old Channel, carries reported depths of 7 to 8 feet at low water and is used as an anchorage. Local yacht clubs maintain moorings there, and it is not uncommon to see cruising boats rafted on these balls. With spectacular Worlds End close at hand, there is not a better place to spend a summer evening. The Trustees of the Reservations welcome all visitors ashore on Worlds End, and it is truly a memorable place to visit. The anchorage is less crowded during the week. If you anchor, anchor well, as the current runs briskly through the Old Channel.

■ BOSTON HARBOR CHANNEL APPROACH FROM THE NORTH VIA PRESIDENT ROADS ■

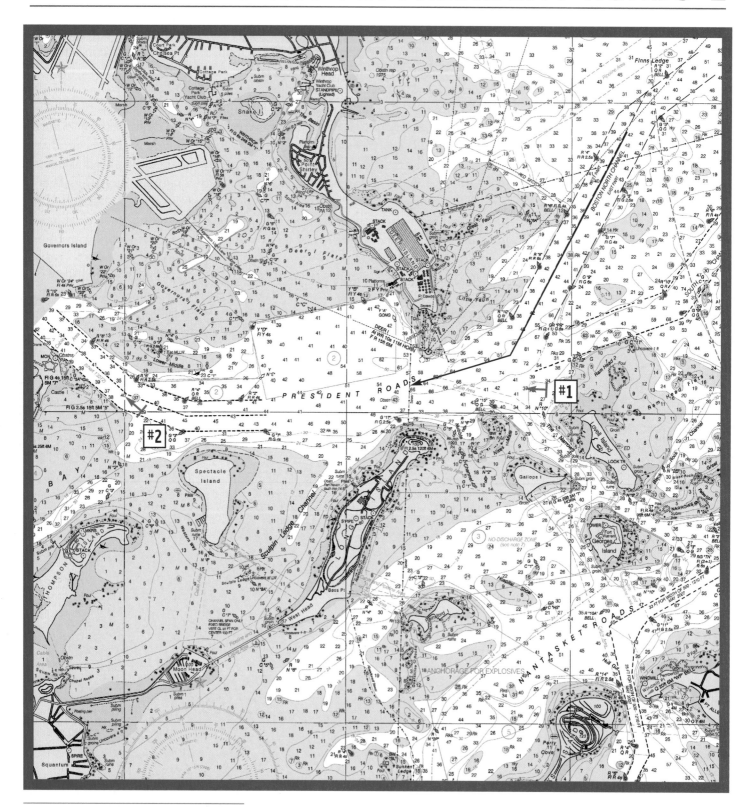

13270, 63rd ed., Aug. 08, NAD 83, Soundings in feet, 1:25,000

WHETHER you take the North Channel or the South Channel from Massachusetts Bay into President Roads, the approach is clear and well defined. Red-and-white whistle "NC" marks the seaward beginning of the North Channel and is useful for the approach to the South Channel as well. The channels converge east of the southern end of unmistakable Deer Island, with its many tanks and stacks, and President Roads runs west from there between 15-foot Deer Island Light off the southern tip of Deer Island on one side and the northern tip of Long Island with its 120-foot lighthouse on the other. From there, the visiting cruiser continues west and then northwest through President Roads, leaving Governors Island and Logan Airport to starboard and Castle Island, Fort Independence, and South Boston to port.

#2

South Boston

Back Bay

Fort Independence

Boston

C "5A"

Charlestown

East Boston

Logan Airport

R "8"

R "6"

■ BOSTON'S INNER HARBOR ■

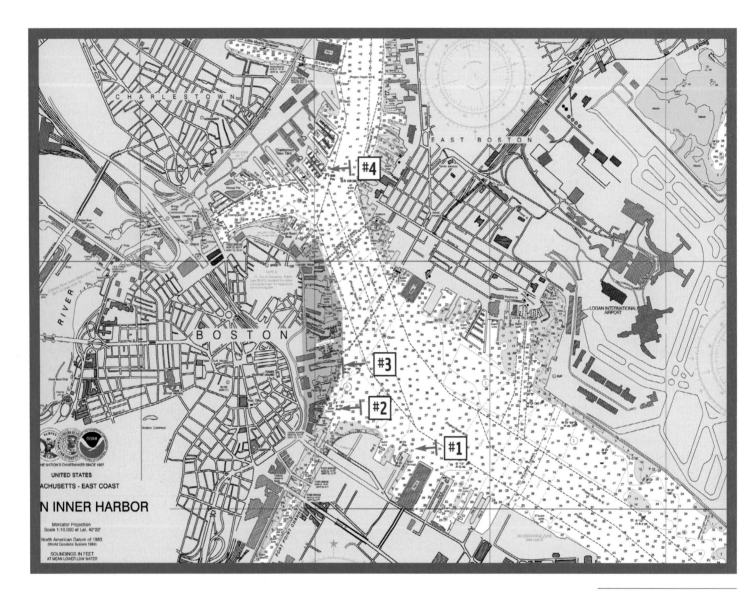

13272
50th ed., Aug. 08
NAD 83
Soundings in feet
1:10,000

#1

Institute of Contemporary Art

Federal Reserve

Rowes Wharf

North End

LONG before you've passed Fort Independence, the city of Boston looms large ahead. The welcoming arch of Rowes Wharf, home to the world-renowned Boston Harbor Hotel, will guide you to the marina on Rowes, which usually has slips available. The staff is great, and you'll be proximate to pretty much everything in this very walkable city. The other principal dockage alternatives are Constitution Marina in Charlestown or the neighboring Admiral's Hill Marina. Boston's inner harbor is subject to constant commercial and recreational vessel traffic. This is not a peaceful place, and your boat will roll constantly—but you can get your peace some other night. You're here for what Boston has to offer—endless choices of restaurants, shops, world-class museums, public gardens, Faneuil Hall, Haymarket, the Freedom Trail, the New England Aquarium, the North End, and so much more, all handy to your boat.

#2

Moakley Courthouse

Boston Harbor Hotel

Rowes Wharf

New England Aquarium

North End

#3

Faneuil Hall

North End

Long Wharf

Commercial Wharf

Lewis Wharf

#4

Zakim Bridge

Constitution Navy Yard

Bunker Hill Monument

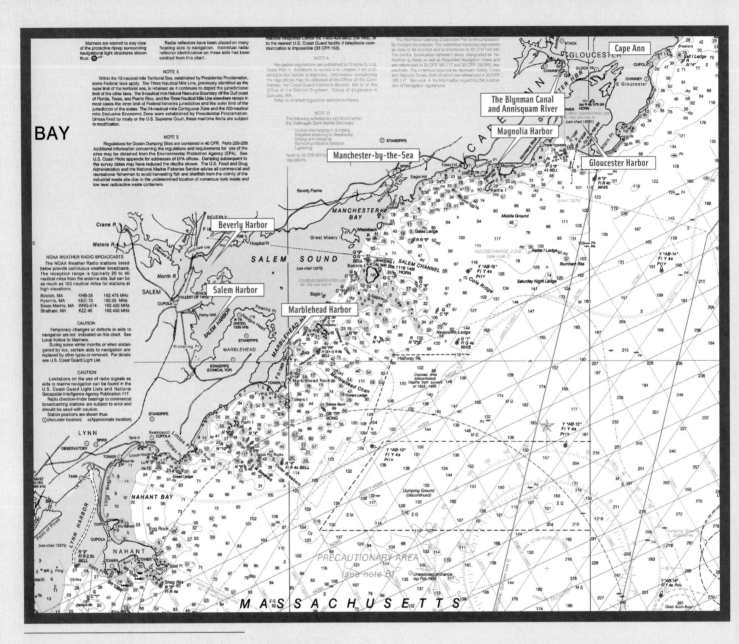

13267, 34th ed., May 07, NAD 83, Soundings in feet, 1:80,000

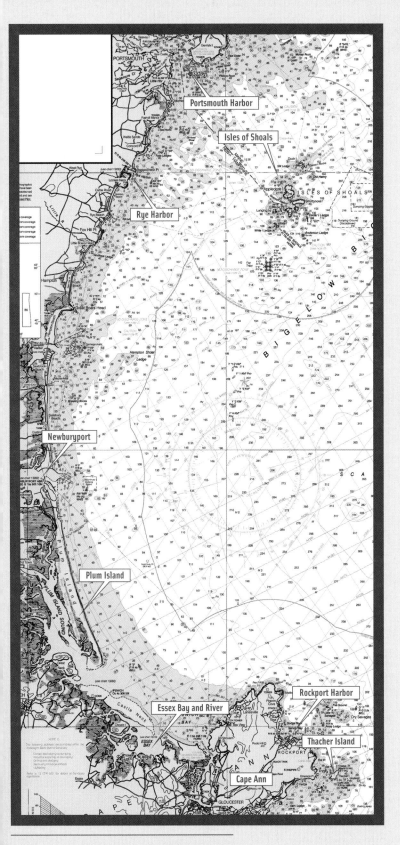

D istinctly different from Cape Cod and the Islands, the North Shore of Massachusetts is more closely reminiscent of the coast farther downeast. Colder water, rocky coasts, and classic New England villages provide cruisers with an early welcome to some of New England's best harbors.

This area includes such famous harbors as Marblehead, home to one of the country's largest sailing fleets, and lovely, picturesque Manchester-by-the-Sea, with its protected harbor surrounded by classic New England architecture and homes. We have a special fondness for this unique town, as it's our home.

This coast also includes open-ocean passages around Cape Ann and to the Isles of Shoals, inland gunkholing through the Annisquam River, the Essex River, and Plum Island Sound, and the opportunity to visit Gloucester Harbor, one of the country's premier fishing ports. With rocky headlands, long sandy beaches, salt marshes, busy ports, secluded anchorages, working towns, tourist towns, and a centuries-old maritime heritage, it offers a little of everything in a fascinating mix.

Best of all for the mariner venturing northeastward from Long Island Sound, these often overlooked harbors are days closer than their Maine neighbors to the east, and they provide the visiting boater with equally gorgeous sunsets and perfect anchorages to explore.

With apologies to Lynn Harbor, with its long and narrow access channel, and Nahant Harbor, which is open to the south, Marblehead Harbor is the first cruiser's haven north of Boston, and we'll begin there.

13278, 26th ed., June 05, NAD 83, Soundings in feet, 1:80,000

■ MARBLEHEAD HARBOR ■

ELEVEN miles north-northeast of Boston Harbor's President Roads approach is the entrance to Marblehead Harbor, one of the best-known yachting centers on the East Coast. The harbor runs straight and true from its opening in the northeast to its head in the southwest, where it is separated from Massachusetts Bay by The "Causeway," a narrow spit connecting the Marblehead "mainland"—the harbor's northwest shore—from Marblehead Neck on the southeast. In clear weather the Boston skyline is visible to the south above this narrow roadway.

Straight and nearly obstruction-free, Marblehead Harbor presents no challenge to an entering cruiser other than finding a clear path through the mass of moored and moving boats. The harbor contains more than 2,000 private moorings and is home to one of the largest sailing fleets in North America. In season, the view into the harbor from outside the entrance is a sight to behold, with a dense forest of masts standing tall in the water.

A narrow fairway, privately buoyed, gives access along the northwest shore to the Boston Yacht Club with its services and friendly staff, and to a number of marinas and restaurants. A short walk through Old Town and its Colonial-flavored residential streets from this shore takes you to stores and more restaurants in the town center. On

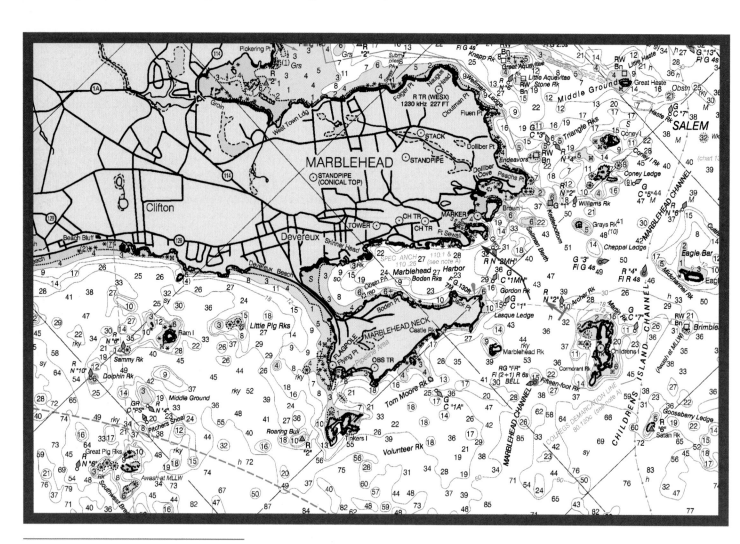

13274, 27th ed., June 07, NAD 83, Soundings in feet, 1:80,000

Marblehead Neck

C "1MH"

C "1"

the Marblehead Neck side of the harbor is the Corinthian Yacht Club with its historic gray-shingled clubhouse and its long porches, and farther in is the stately Eastern Yacht Club, with its classic New England architecture, long pier, and green lawns flowing to the water's edge.

At almost any time during the boating season, you can probably find a mooring for the night by contacting the town harbormaster or the dockmaster at one of the yacht clubs. The town also has a few transient slips available. There is no room to anchor inside the harbor in Marblehead, and the outside is exposed to the northeast.

Marblehead makes a legitimate claim to be the birthplace of the American navy. As James L. Nelson tells in his book *George Washington's Secret Navy*, it was to Colonel John Glover, a prosperous member of Marble-

head's "codfish aristocracy," that Washington turned in 1775 with his plan to outfit a half-dozen schooners and send them against the British merchant vessels that were resupplying the besieged British garrison in Boston. (Washington withheld his plan from Congress for two months because he knew Congress was not yet ready to approve naval action.) Several of the schooners were manned by Marblehead militia members, who were as comfortable on the deck of a ship as in their own homes. The schooners were outfitted in Beverly rather than Marblehead, however, because Beverly's more difficult entrance offered protection from His Majesty's ships of war, so today Beverly and Marblehead contend (not just with each other, but with several other communities as well) for the honor of being the navy's birthplace.

■ SALEM HARBOR ■

SALEM Harbor is just a mile west of Marblehead Harbor, separated from it by the intervening Marblehead peninsula. It provides alternative access to the town of Marblehead as well as the town of Salem. Like Marblehead, Salem Harbor is open to the northeast.

The approach to Salem and Beverly harbors is made through Salem Sound, which can be reached from Gloucester, Cape Ann, and points east via Salem Channel and the passage between Bakers Island, with its 111-foot lighthouse, and Great Misery Island. On a fair tide

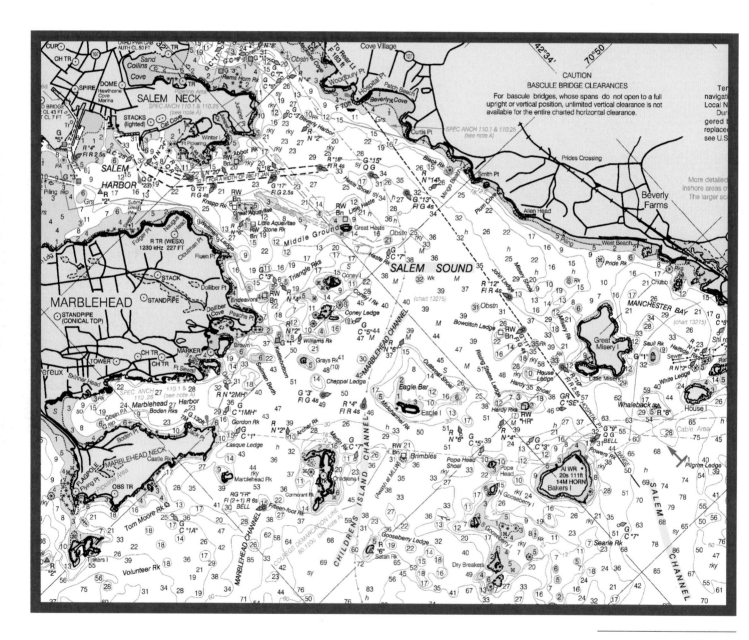

13274
27th ed., June 07
NAD 83
Soundings in feet
1:80,000

Marblehead

Salem

Beverly

Little Misery Island

Great Misery Island

Bakers Island

Salem Sound

Salem Channel

in good weather, you can choose instead to pass north of Great Misery, especially if your boat has shoal draft. Entrance into Salem Sound from the south can be made through the Marblehead Channel or the Children's Island Channel.

To proceed into Salem Harbor (see chart page 230), leave flashing green buoys "13" and "15" in Salem Sound to port, then turn to a southwesterly heading for flashing red "16" and the beginning of the dredged and clearly buoyed entrance channel that takes you into the harbor between Naugus Head and Winter Island. There is an alternative, shore-hugging route around Marblehead from Marblehead Harbor and through Salem Harbor's South Channel, but you must navigate carefully through this rock-studded approach, and local knowledge is helpful.

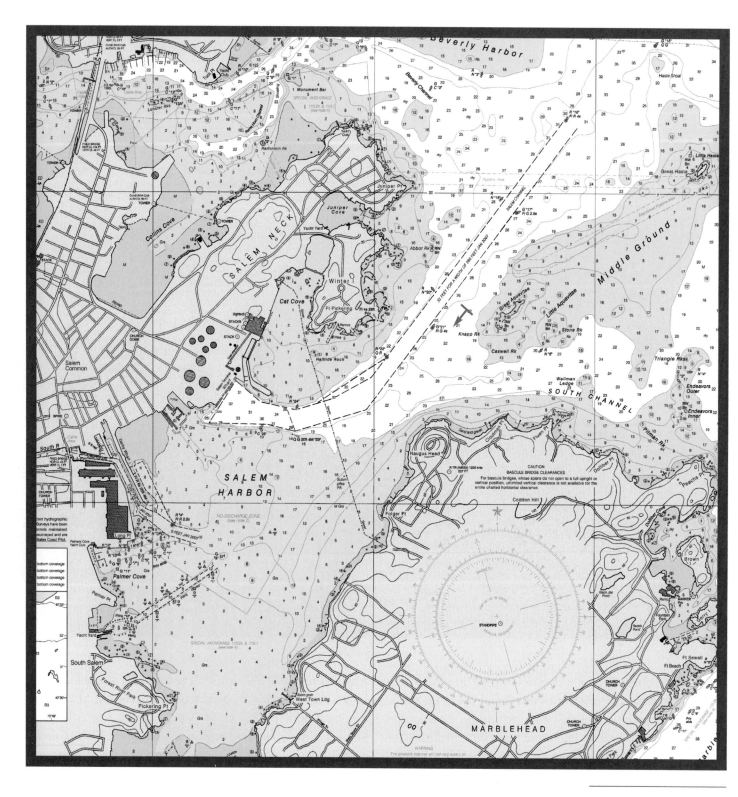

13276
22nd ed., July 03
NAD 83
Soundings in feet
1:10,000

West Town Landing

Naugus Head

Salem Harbor

Palmer Cove

Fort Pickering

Once inside the harbor, despite the dense field of private moorings, you'll find a number of places to dock, moor, or anchor for the day or night while you explore famous Salem's many tourist attractions. Perhaps the most accessible part of Salem is Pickering Wharf in the harbor's northwest corner, with its many restaurants and shops. The harbor offers the full range of marine services. Ashore you'll find the Peabody-Essex Museum with its maritime exhibits, Nathaniel Hawthorne's House of the Seven Gables, and reminders of the witch trials of the 1600s. A public dinghy dock at the West Town Landing, near the head of the harbor on the southeast shore, gives pedestrian access to the town of Marblehead.

■ BEVERLY HARBOR ■

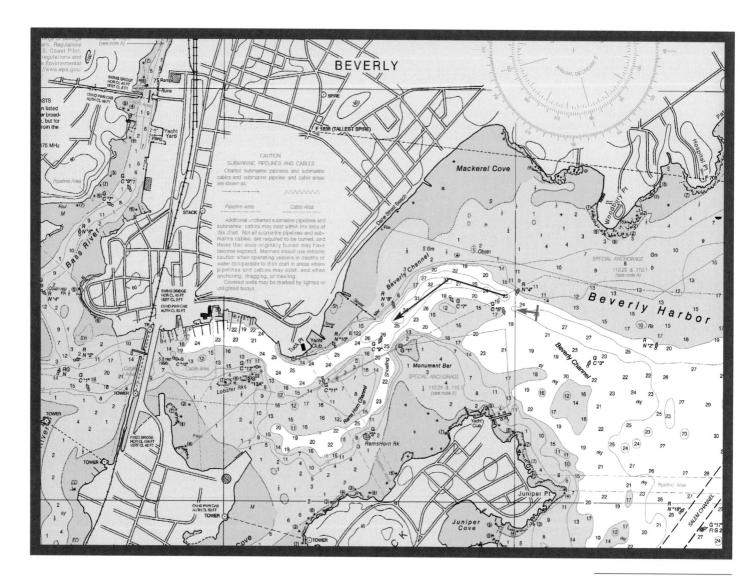

13276
22nd ed., July 03
NAD 83
Soundings in feet
1:10,000

TO enter Beverly Harbor from Salem Sound, leave flashing green "13" and "15" to port just as for the Salem Harbor approach, but keep proceeding westerly from "15." Leave nun "2" at the harbor entrance to starboard and follow the well-buoyed channel in from there. The channel hugs Tuck Point and the harbor's north shore. Mooring fields fill the harbor's southern reaches. The fixed bridge at the head of the harbor has a 49-foot clearance, and the swing bridge just beyond it opens to admit small boats to the Danvers and Bass rivers.

This is a well-marked harbor with good marine and reprovisioning services. It is busy during the summer with boats of all descriptions, and is visited by commercial vessels in all seasons.

Tuck Point

C "7"

C "5" P

N "4"

■ MANCHESTER-BY-THE-SEA ■

EAST of Salem Sound and less than a mile east of Great Misery Island, which shelters it from a westerly wind, lies snug, lovely Manchester-by-the-Sea, one of this area's most protected harbors. Bakers Island and its 111-foot lighthouse mark the approach from east or west, and green bell "9" off the north side of Bakers in

Salem Channel is hard to miss. Proceed north from the bell.

As a fair-weather alternative to Manchester Harbor, consider anchoring in the bight on the north side of Great Misery Island or in the anchorage on the south side inside Little Misery Island, as our photo shows. You

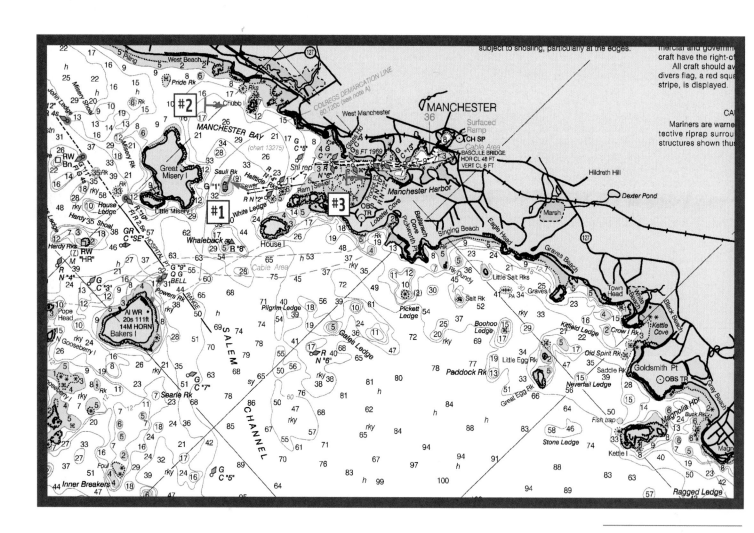

13274
27th ed., June 07
NAD 83
Soundings in feet
1:80,000

Little Misery Island

Great Misery Island

Chubb Island

Manchester Harbor

House Island

C "5"

N "4"

N "2"

#3

C "13"

N "12"

N "10"

Proctor Point

might even find an available mooring there. Maintained by the Trustees of Reservations, both islands are open for swimming, hiking, and picnicking.

To proceed north into Manchester Harbor, leave the red day marker on Whaleback rock well to starboard and the green day marker on Saull Rock, off Great Misery Island, to port. After leaving nuns "2" and "4" to starboard you'll arrive at the buoyed entrance channel that will conduct you into Manchester's inner harbor.

This is our homeport, and though we never tire of visiting the harbors downeast and in southern New England, we are always happy to return to this tucked-away

spot. There is no room to anchor, but the able and friendly staff of the Manchester Yacht Club can most often assist visitors with moorings and advice. Inside the harbor, Crocker's Boatyard and Manchester Marine can also assist travelers with fuel, dockage, and moorings.

Once your boat is safely tucked in for the night, no visit to Manchester would be complete without a walk to its most famous asset, the Singing Beach east of town. Known for the tone that the sand makes when you walk on it, this seemingly endless stretch of white sandy beach against the blue ocean provides a memory not easily forgotten.

■ MAGNOLIA HARBOR ■

THREE miles east of Manchester Harbor and just a mile west of the Gloucester Harbor entrance is an often overlooked but wonderful lunch spot, Magnolia Harbor. There are no navigation aids marking the entrances either side of Kettle Island, but the western entrance in particular is wide open (except for one reported 6-foot sounding) and easy to spot, and the boats on the east side of the harbor mark the obvious places to throw an anchor and spend the afternoon. One of the special features of this anchorage is its white sandy beach abutting a wonderful series of trails maintained by Massachusetts' Trustees of Reservations. If you are lucky enough to spend a few hours here, you'd be well advised to row ashore and take advantage of this conservation jewel.

13274
27th ed., June 07
NAD 83
Soundings in feet
1:80,000

■ CAPE ANN AND GLOUCESTER HARBOR ■

FOUNDED in 1623, Gloucester is America's oldest fishing port and remains one of the country's leading centers of commercial fishing. Big steel trawlers head for the groundfisheries on Georges Bank from here, just as the Gloucester fishing schooners did a century ago. This colorful and fascinating town, home to third-, fourth-, and fifth-generation Portuguese fishermen, also attracts artists and poets, including the late Charles Olson, who made his adopted Gloucester the focus of his *Maximus* poems.

Reminders of the town's fishing heritage and dependence are everywhere, from the fleet in the harbor to the auction and processing wharves and the statue of The Fisherman on the waterfront, built to honor and commemorate all the Gloucester sons lost at sea. The inscription on the pedestal says simply, "They that go down to the sea in ships." Gloucester was the homeport of the *Andrea Gail*, the 72-foot swordfisherman that was lost at sea with all six crew in an autumn 1991 gale, as recorded in the 1994 bestseller *The Perfect Storm*.

Approaching Gloucester Harbor is a simple task in almost any weather. From flashing red whistle "2" south of Eastern Point, an easy northwesterly approach takes you to flashing red, red-and-green buoy "RR" southwest of Round Rock Shoal. Alternatively, you can enter

Thacher Island and Cape Ann, taken from the northeast.

13279
32nd ed., Feb. 07
NAD 83
Soundings in feet
1:20,000

through Dog Bar Channel (between can "1DB" and nun "2DB"), just off the western end of Eastern Point's breakwater. From either approach, the run up into the harbor is uncluttered and simple. Cross the Western Harbor to find the opening to the Blynman Canal and Annisquam River, or turn eastward and explore the inner harbor and the commercial port of Gloucester.

For an overnight stop on a passage east or south, we like to duck into the easy anchorage behind the Eastern Point breakwater. With plenty of anchorage room and moorings to pick up, the area is well tended by the friendly Eastern Point Yacht Club, which for decades has provided traveling cruisers with warm showers, good moorings, and great food and drinks.

Anchoring is also possible northeast of Tenpound Harbor or in the Western Harbor off the Stage Fort area. There are marinas in the inner harbor and in crowded Smith Cove. The town has moorings (call the harbormaster), and the town dock is in Harbor Cove. Ashore you'll find numerous fine restaurants and historic attractions.

#1

Annisquam Canal

Tenpound Island

Cape Ann

Eastern Point

C "1DB"

N "2DB"

N "4"

#2

Inner Harbor

Tenpound Island

Rocky Neck

N "8"

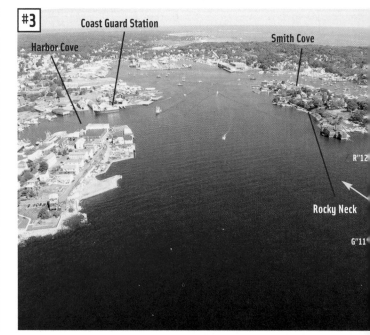

#3

Coast Guard Station

Harbor Cove

Smith Cove

R"12

Rocky Neck

G"11

THE BLYNMAN CANAL AND ANNISQUAM RIVER

TRENDING generally north and south, the Annisquam River and its southern extension, the Blynman Canal, divide Cape Ann from the mainland to the west. This passage is well marked and easily navigable from either direction in most conditions. Though some summer cruisers have compared this waterway to the Massachusetts turnpike because of its congestion and traffic, it is nevertheless well worth the trip not just for the miles it saves around Cape Ann, but for its scenic beauty and interest.

The northbound traveler is rewarded at the river's northern end with a view to port of the dazzling white sands of Wingaersheek Beach, with Ipswich Bay ahead. The southbound mariner enters Gloucester Harbor, a highlight in itself. The waterway involves a number of bridges, marinas, and turns and should only be undertaken under engine power. At about the halfway point, under the fixed 65-foot bridge, the tidal current reverses itself and runs in the opposite direction for the duration of the transit.

The southern entrance to Blynman Canal faces Gloucester's Western Harbor and is

13279
32nd ed., Feb. 07
NAD 83
Soundings in feet
1:20,000

marked by red-and-white can "BC." The Blyn-man Bridge just inside the entrance is an open-ing bascule bridge with 8 feet of clearance when closed, and is notorious for holding up traffic. On a sunny day you'll have no diffi-culty spotting the boats awaiting their turn for the bridge to open.

From the north, approach the Annisquam River entrance from red-and-white bell "AR" to its north. A southerly course from there will take you to the well-marked channel begin-ning with can "3," and you'll see the white 45-foot Annisquam Harbor light tower to your port, on Wigwam Point, as you enter. Remem-ber as you skirt the eastern end of Wingaer-sheek Beach that from this direction, you will leave nuns to starboard and cans to port.

Whether you're north- or southbound, a stop at the Annisquam Yacht Club is recom-mended. This club has long been a hospitable home to the visiting cruiser. There are also an-chorage possibilities in the Annisquam River.

13279
32nd ed., Feb. 07
NAD 83
Soundings in feet
1:20,000

Gloucester

Western Harbor

Fixed Bridge (65-foot clearance)

Fixed Bridge (65-foot clearance)

Wingaersheek Beach

Ipswich Bay

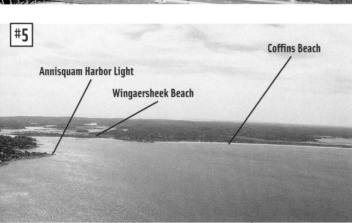

Annisquam Harbor Light

Wingaersheek Beach

Coffins Beach

243

■ THACHER ISLAND ■

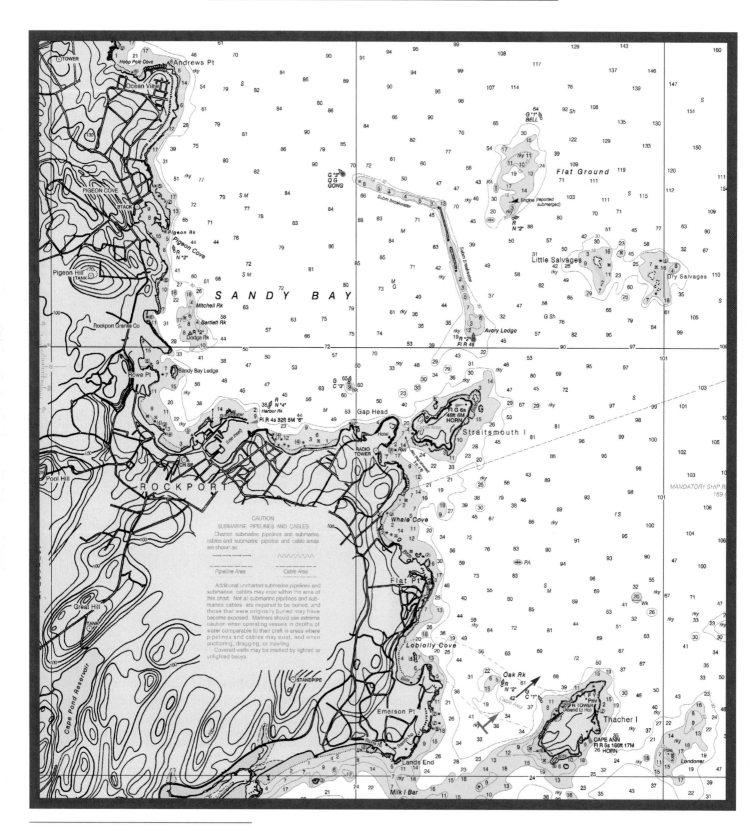

13279, 32nd ed., Feb. 07, NAD 83, Soundings in feet, 1:20,000

EAST of Gloucester Harbor and just south of the eastern-most tip of Cape Ann lies famous Thacher Island and its rare twin lighthouses. (Only the southern tower is lighted. The north tower is open to visitors.) There is no protected anchorage here, but on a summer day or night with the breeze calm or light from the south, it is possible to anchor off the island's northwest shore and enjoy the tranquility while the twin towers, standing tall, remind you of the New England coast's unique maritime heritage. Rangers ashore welcome picnickers and day tourists.

■ ROCKPORT HARBOR ■

ROCKPORT is one of the most famous harbors north of Cape Ann. Aside from being home to the original Motif #1, a red fish shack on a wharf that is one of the country's most enduring artistic subjects, Rockport is also known for its artist community and for its vibrant shops and village.

The outer harbor, Sandy Bay, is protected by the submerged seaward breakwater that prevents it from being just an open bight in the end of Cape Ann. The Dry Salvages ledges just outside the breakwater provided the title for one of the *Four Quartets*, the haunting poetic work by T.S. Eliot, who spent boyhood summers on Cape Ann. Storm surf raging against the cape's outer shores evidently made an enduring impression on the young Eliot, who wrote decades later: "And the ragged rock in the restless waters, / Waves wash over it, fogs conceal it; / On a halcyon day it is merely a monument, / In navigable weather it is always a seamark / To lay a course by: but in the sombre season / Or the sudden fury, is what it always was."

As with any navigational challenge, working your way into Rockport's inner harbor requires careful atten-tion, and prior contact with the harbormaster is a neces-sity if you're hoping for a mooring in the inner harbor. While there may appear to be no practical overnight space available in the inner harbor other than the town dock and the always-hospitable Sandy Bay Yacht Club, the very friendly harbormasters can almost always find room for one more visitor.

Sandy Bay has a southern and a northern entrance, the choice of which depends solely on your direction of approach. Either one keeps the visiting cruiser clear of the submerged breakwater—the northern end of which is marked by green flashing gong "3" and the southern end by red flashing bell "2."

Proceed across Sandy Bay to nun "4," which marks Harbor Rock just outside the entrance to Rockport's in-ner harbor—which is what most cruisers think of when they think of Rockport Harbor.

From nun "4," the flashing red 32-foot light at the end of the inner breakwater will be obvious. Give the end of the breakwater a respectful berth—there is shoal water close in—and enter the harbor midway between the breakwater and The Headlands to port. The town

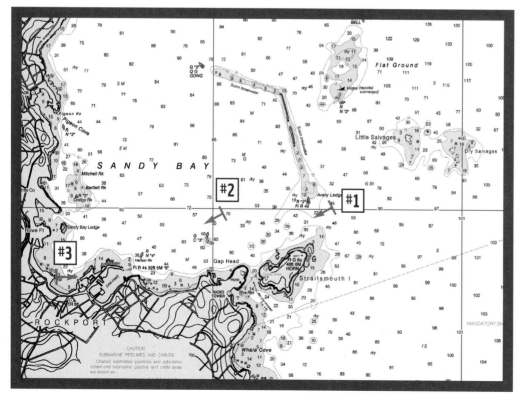

13279
32nd ed., Feb. 07
NAD 83
Soundings in feet
1:20,000

#1

Straitsmouth Island

Rockport Harbor

Sandy Bay

Gap Head

C "3"

dock is at the head of the harbor next to the yacht club. To get there you'll have to navigate around the many boats moored fore-and-aft on double moorings (because there is no room to swing). Often the harbormaster can escort you to an open mooring, but again, advance notice is required.

Once ashore, you will find no limit of things to do and see and many choices of restaurants, shops, and art galleries to explore.

Though exposed to the northeast, several good anchorages can be found outside the inner harbor in Sandy Bay. Depending on wind and weather, our favorite is the protected Sandy Bay cove immediately northwest of the harbor. In calm conditions there is plenty of deep water to go well up into this cove and still be able to take your dinghy along the breakwater and easily walk to town.

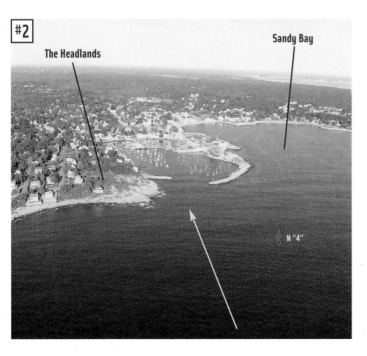

#2

The Headlands

Sandy Bay

N "4"

#3

The Headlands

Sandy Bay

■ ESSEX BAY AND RIVER ■

DATING back more than 340 years, Essex is steeped in shipbuilding and boating history. As the chart indicates and the photo suggests, the entrance from Ipswich Bay—less than 2 miles west of the Annisquam River's northern end—should be attempted only by those with up-to-date local knowledge and shoal-draft boats, and even then only at high tide in fair weather.

The approach begins from green flashing bell "1" northeast of the entrance between Coffins Beach and Castle Neck (where famous Crane Beach with its back dunes can be found). Once inside, there are precious few navigational aids, and those that are there are fre-

quently moved to follow the shifting channel and shoals. For all intents and purposes, the passage up the narrow Essex River must rely on visual sightings of the channel and sandy shoals and the handful of privately maintained stakes that mark the way. Still, the channel is said to carry 5 feet all the way to the town of Essex.

For those who navigate all the way to Essex, however, a real treat lies ahead. The town is surrounded by a number of active marinas, fresh fried clam and lobster restaurants, and the most famous local calling card, antique stores of all sizes and descriptions.

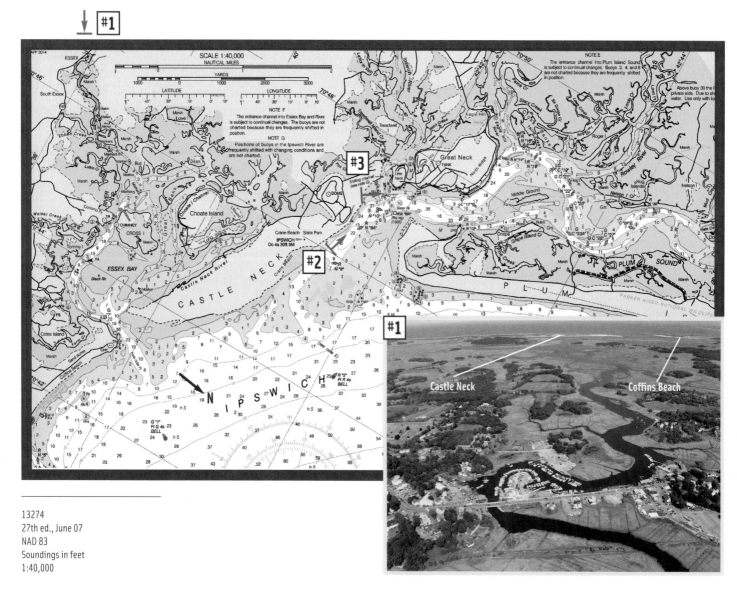

13274
27th ed., June 07
NAD 83
Soundings in feet
1:40,000

■ PLUM ISLAND ■

FROM Halibut Point, Cape Ann's northernmost projection, a passage of about 6½ miles west and a little north across Ipswich Bay will take you to the entrance to Plum Island Sound. The passage from the Annisquam River's northern end is even shorter, about 4½ miles. You'll pass the white sands of Wingaersheek Beach, Coffins Beach, and Crane Beach to the south. The entrance to Plum Island Sound is just northwest of Castle Neck. A side trip into the sound is an unparalleled opportunity to explore one of the region's most interesting gunkholes. Well protected but ever-changing because of currents and sandbars, the sound demands that you pay close attention not only to the conventional navigational aids present as you enter, but also to water color and the current.

Flashing red bell "2" marks the beginning of the entrance into the sound, and a southwesterly course from there toward the middle of Castle Neck from the bell will take you through the deepest water. Just offshore of Castle Neck, turn to starboard and carefully navigate toward nun "8." Thirty-foot Ipswich Light on Crane Beach should be on your port bow at this point and will serve as another point of reference. Observe all navigation buoys, not all of which are charted because they move frequently. After leaving nuns "8" and "8A" to starboard, you are well into the entrance. Leave can "11" off Little Neck to port, turning north into the sound and hugging the can to keep clear of the reported 4-foot spot just north of it.

While the channel continues circuitously to Parker River, it should be emphasized that the navigation aids, while providing some assistance, require significant local knowledge given the tidal currents and the frequent shoaling that take place. Nevertheless, for shoal-draft boats, this little haven surrounded by the Parker River National Wildlife Refuge is a must-see if you have the time. (Those in need of full services and amenities are best served in Newburyport to the north or Gloucester to the south.)

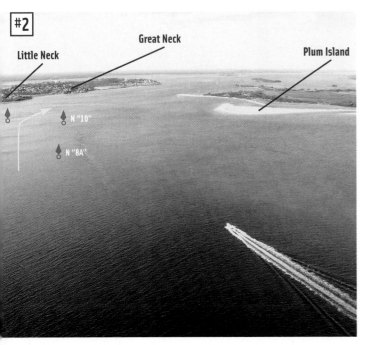

■ NEWBURYPORT AND THE MERRIMACK RIVER ■

NEWBURYPORT and its harbor host a number of facilities and some great restaurants for the visiting yachtsman. The Merrimack River entrance, 7 miles north-northwest of the Plum Island Sound entrance and only slightly farther from the northern end of the Annisquam River, is made from red-and-white whistle "MR" just outside the dredged channel. Though the channel can appear intimidating with occasional chop in windy conditions and with excessive summer boat wakes, it remains navigable in all but the most extreme conditions. Avoid entering at or near the bottom of an ebb tide, which, when confronted with a swell from the east, can create breaking surf across the entrance and render the inlet unsafe to transit. Call the Merrimack River Coast Guard for a current report on conditions at the river mouth.

From the whistle, follow a northwesterly course midway between the two entrance breakwaters. Once inside the breakwaters, local captains often favor the northern edge of the channel, where the chart shows the deeper soundings, edging toward the starboard side of the channel once we've passed the flashing red 15-foot light on the end of the northern breakwater and the 4-foot spot charted just south of it. In particular, we keep to the northern edge of the channel as we pass between flashing green "7" and quick-yellow flashing 47-foot Bar Guide Light.

Once clear of flashing red "8" off Badgers, you'll pass the northern end of Plum Island and the entrance to The Basin. From there, a westerly course will take you to the center of Newburyport with its many attractions. En route you'll pass the flashing red 22-foot North Pier light standing off the northern shore of the Merrimack River, and, immediately after that, green can "17" off Half Tide Rocks. The town docks and facilities are just beyond. You'll find several marinas offering transient services, as well as a very hospitable harbormaster. Anchoring is discouraged due to poor holding and strong currents.

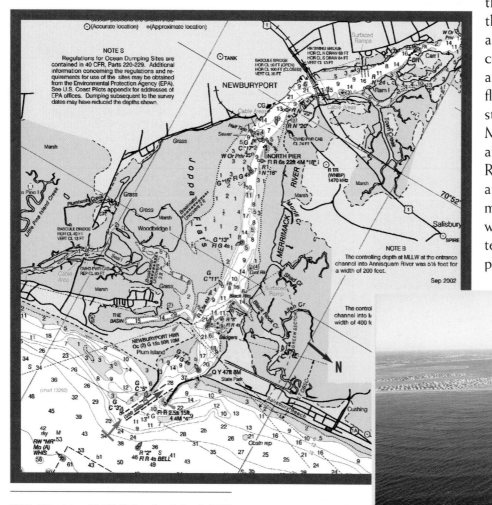

13274, 27th ed., June 07, NAD 83, Soundings in feet, 1:40,000

■ RYE HARBOR ■

HAMPTON Harbor, less than 4 miles north of New-buryport, is popular for fishing, beach-going, kayaking, and small powerboats, but its shallow depths (and its bascule opening bridge with a clearance when closed of 18 feet) limit its accessibility for cruisers. Thus, our last anchorage south of Portsmouth is Rye Harbor.

Rye Harbor is about 6 miles north of Hampton and 3 miles south of the entrance to Portsmouth. Protected by breakwaters to the northeast and southwest, Rye is easily accessed. Given the harbor's small size, mooring space is limited and room to anchor basically nonexistent, but on a quiet summer night this is a perfect place to visit. The harbor entrance is straightforward, beginning from red-and-white whistle "RH" just southeast of the entrance. A northwesterly course from there will take you midway between the breakwaters (between can "5" and flashing red 24-foot light "4" on the northern breakwater) and into the middle of the harbor.

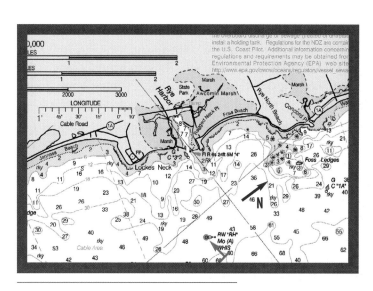

13274, 27th ed., June 07, NAD 83, Soundings in feet, 1:40,000

■ ISLES OF SHOALS ■

WHEN you approach from the south, the Isles of Shoals provide your first glimpse of Maine. This cluster of nine islands straddles the state line, with five in Maine and four in New Hampshire. As you round Cape Ann, the islands beckon from the distance, some twenty miles north. Below the horizon at first, they materialize as you draw closer in clear weather, their mysterious allure somehow in keeping with their bloody, legendary history. Though they lie just six miles off the entrance to Portsmouth Harbor, the islands impress you first with their stark remoteness. As you approach, the 82-foot lighthouse on White Island, the most southerly of the group, becomes ever more prominent, guiding you in.

On a sunny day, light may reflect off the massive structure of the old hotel, the Oceanic House, on Star Island. As you get closer, the passageway into

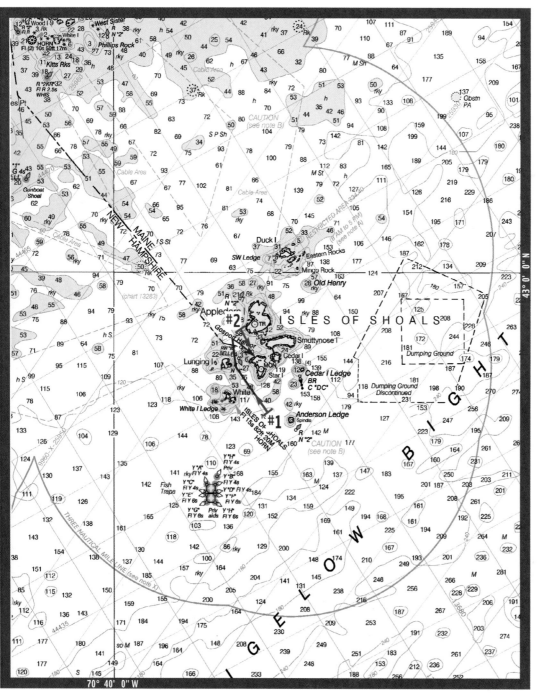

13278
26th ed., June 05
NAD 83
Soundings in feet
1:80,000

Gosport Harbor becomes more obvious, with the lighthouse still providing your clearest marking to port. The islands' distant aura of brooding remoteness will be replaced by a vision of wild beauty as you leave Anderson's Ledge to starboard and see more clearly the outlines of the Oceanic Hotel. Leaving White Island to port, you shape your approach so as to leave Lunging Island immediately to port. You have plenty of deep water on this route. As you get closer to Halfway Rocks, nun "4" comes squarely into view.

Leaving the nun to starboard, you will see immediately in front of you the channel marker bell where you turn east into the centerline fairway for Gosport Harbor.

Once in the harbor, Star, Cedar, and Smuttynose Islands surround you on the south, east, and north sides, respectively. Some moorings may be available depending on the time and day you arrive. The harbor is well protected from everything but a westerly blow. In a westerly you can make your way around Smuttynose to find shelter east of the bar between Smuttynose and Cedar. Star Island, where the hotel long ago stopped accommodating overnight guests but once again welcomes visitors to its gift shop and restrooms, is a functioning community—with restored buildings, tennis courts, gardens, recreational facilities, and an obelisk that is a dead ringer for the Washington Monument.

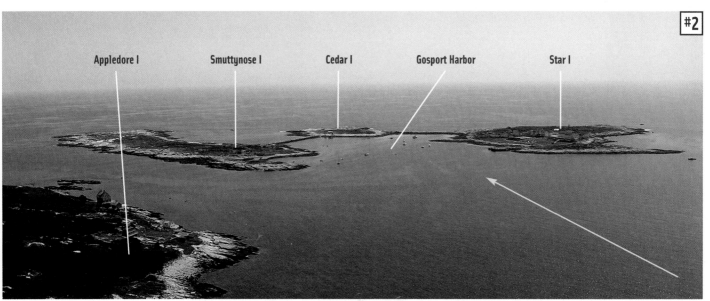

■ PISCATAQUA RIVER ■
(Approach to Portsmouth and Kittery)

AT the mouth of the Piscataqua River, which defines the boundary between New Hampshire and Maine, is a complex of inviting and well-protected anchorages. Channels and entrances are well marked; your chief navigational challenges will be the currents, which can reach as high as six knots due to the influence of the river, and commercial shipping approaching and leaving Portsmouth.

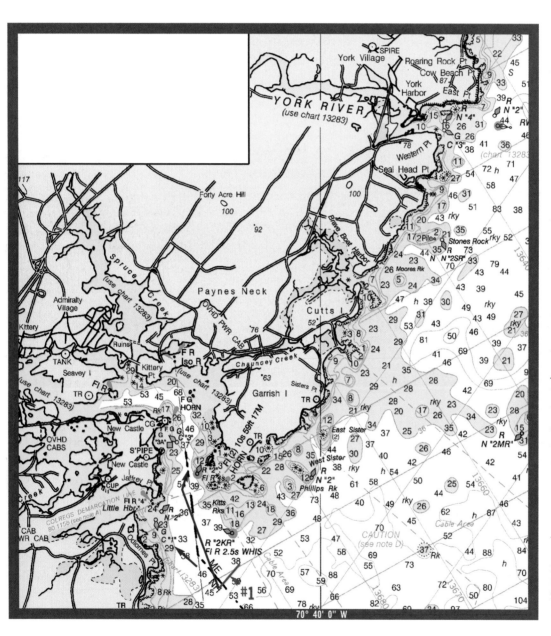

Little Harbor

LOCATED immediately west of the Portsmouth Harbor entrance, Little Harbor is the first significant mainland anchorage north of Newburyport. Green bell "1," about one nautical mile southeast of the harbor entrance, provides a good approach path when you're coming from the south or from the Isles of Shoals. The entrance channel is clearly marked with cans, nuns, and a beacon on the breakwater that juts south from Jaffrey Point. At high tide the entrance breakwaters may not be readily apparent, but stay between the navigation aids and watch for currents and small-boat

13286
30th ed., March 04
NAD 83
Soundings in feet
1:80,000

#1

Little Harbor

Portsmouth

New Castle I

Kittery

Back Channel

Fort Point

Whaleback Light

Pepperrell Cove

Wood I

C "3"

R "2"

C "1"

N "2"

Little Harbor Approach

Portsmouth Approaches
• Pepperrell Cove
• Back Channel
• Portsmouth

R"2KR"

traffic, and you'll be fine. Little Harbor is remarkably well protected, and in rough conditions it makes a wonderful place to spend the day or night. Once you leave the breakwater on Frost Point to port, turn west to follow the buoyed channel in. There is deep water on the north side almost as far as the bascule bridge that gives road access to New Castle Island. The Wentworth Marina offers full facilities and 170 slips, and overlooking the harbor from New Castle Island is a new Marriott Hotel refurbished from the historic but long-defunct Wentworth-By-The-Sea hotel. In the summer, Little Harbor becomes very crowded with yachts and all manner of small craft, and there is no room to anchor and few if any rental moorings.

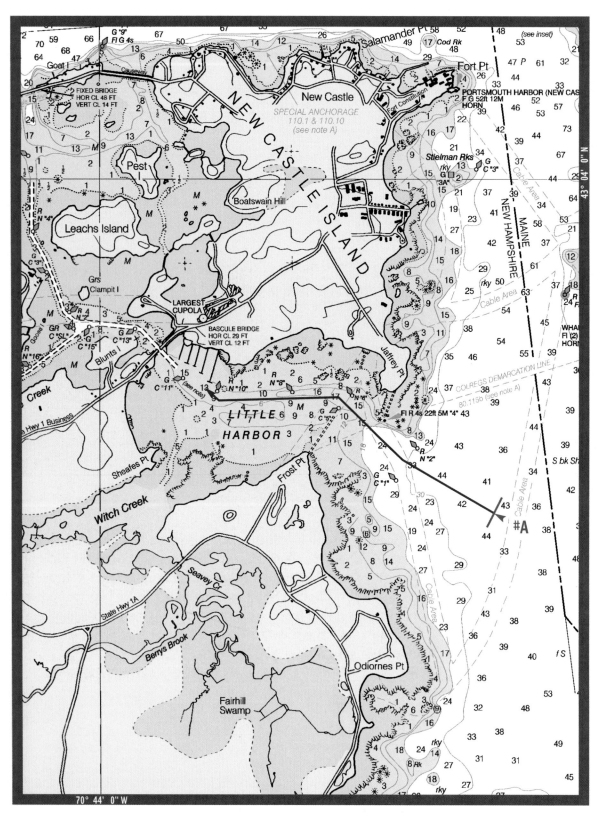

13283
19th ed., Feb. 05
NAD 83
Soundings in feet
1:20,000

■ PORTSMOUTH HARBOR

THE entrance to multibranched Portsmouth Harbor and its offshoot anchorages is marked first by flashing red whistle buoy "2KR" and then by the 59-foot lighthouse on Whaleback Reef, both of which you should leave to starboard to bypass the rocks and shoal waters bounding the east side of the entrance. The buoyed channel runs north between Wood Island to starboard, with its abandoned lifesaving station, and New Castle Island to port. Shape your course to the right of Fort Point, which juts prominently from the northeast corner of New Castle Island. This is the site of Fort Constitu-tion, a Revolutionary War-era fort, and the bright white Fort Point lighthouse should stand out in clear weather.

As you pass northward through the entrance, Garrish Island will be on your right. After leaving Fort Point to port, you'll glimpse to the west the highway bridges that span the Piscataqua River between Portsmouth and Kittery. You can either continue north into Pepperrell Cove, or turn west toward Portsmouth and Kittery or Back Channel. Along the way, you'll see many possible anchoring spots, but the swift currents make a mooring or slip preferable.

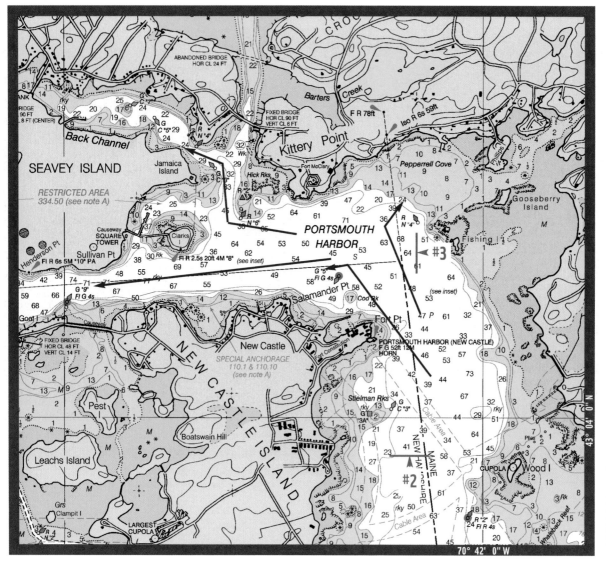

13283
19th ed., Feb. 05
NAD 83
Soundings in feet
1:20,000

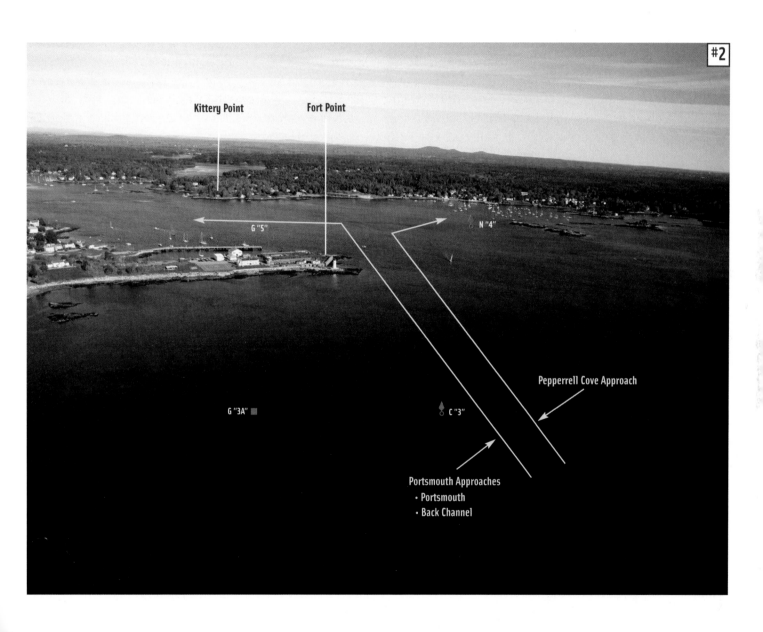

#2

Kittery Point

Fort Point

G "5"

N "4"

G "3A"

C "3"

Pepperrell Cove Approach

Portsmouth Approaches
• Portsmouth
• Back Channel

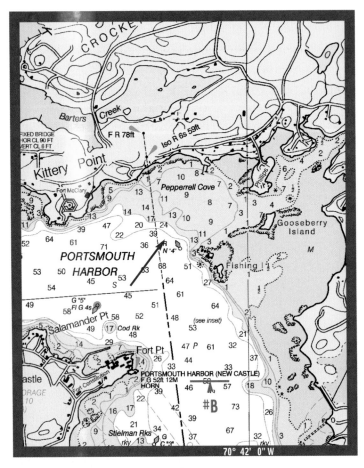

Pepperrell Cove (Kittery Point)

CONTINUE north from Fort Point to approach Pepperrell Cove. Leaving nun "4" off Fishing Island to starboard, swing slowly to starboard to enter the cove. The entrance is easy, but the cove is exposed to the south, subject to crosscurrents, and busy with commercial and recreational traffic. Moorings are available from the town of Kittery and the Portsmouth Yacht Club, and you may find room to anchor near Fort McClary.

13283
19th ed., Feb. 05
NAD 83
Soundings in feet
1:20,000

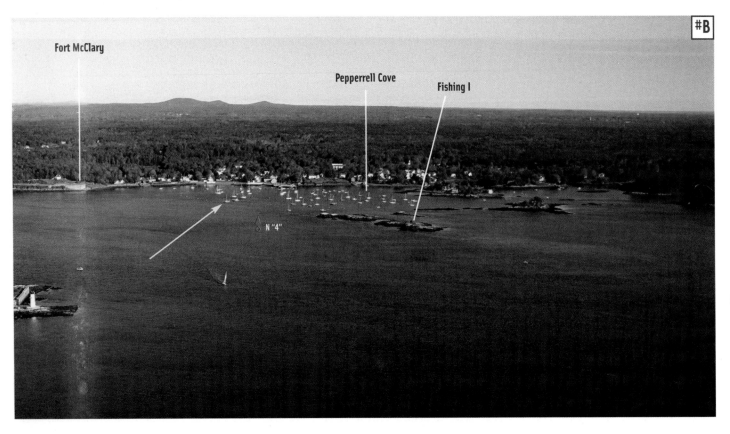

Portsmouth and Kittery

IF you elect to follow the main channel of the Piscataqua River toward Portsmouth and Kittery, you'll leave tiny Clarks Island and large Seavey Island to starboard and Kittery Point Yacht Club (which is not on Kittery Point but rather on the eastern end of Goat Island) to port. The Portsmouth Naval Shipyard occupies most of Seavey, and as you pass beyond that, the bridges across the Piscataqua River will dominate your view over the bow. The first two of these—the Route One Memorial Bridge and the Route One bypass bridge—are both lift bridges. See your cruising guide and coast pilot for instructions on communicating with the bridge tenders and coping with these bridges in the swift river currents. The fixed Interstate-95 bridge upriver provides 135 feet of vertical clearance, but navigation gets progressively trickier upriver. You may find a rental mooring or slip off Portsmouth, but the currents—equally strong on ebb and flood—complicate all maneuvers.

(See chart page 258.) #3

Goat I   New Castle I   Fort Point   Seavey I   Clarks I   Back Channel   Kittery Point

Back Channel

R "2"

N "6"

Portsmouth Approach

Back Channel Approach

G "5"

Goat I   Kittery Point Yacht Club   New Castle I   Portsmouth   Badgers I   Seavey I   Clarks I

G "9"

#4

13283
19th ed., Feb. 05
NAD 83
Soundings in feet
1:20,000

Back Channel

AS an alternative to the navigational challenges upriver or the southern exposure of Pepperrell Cove, Back Channel has much to offer. Entered between Kittery Point and Seavey Island, it provides all-weather protection and a partial respite from the currents of the main channel. Average currents here are 1.5 knots (2.5 knots maximum). Leave the daybeacon and nun marking Hick Rocks, off Kittery Point, to starboard, then follow the green-red sequence through the narrow fairway between the town of Kittery and Seavey Island. There are no places to anchor here, but moorings and slips are available in season from Dion's Yacht Yard.

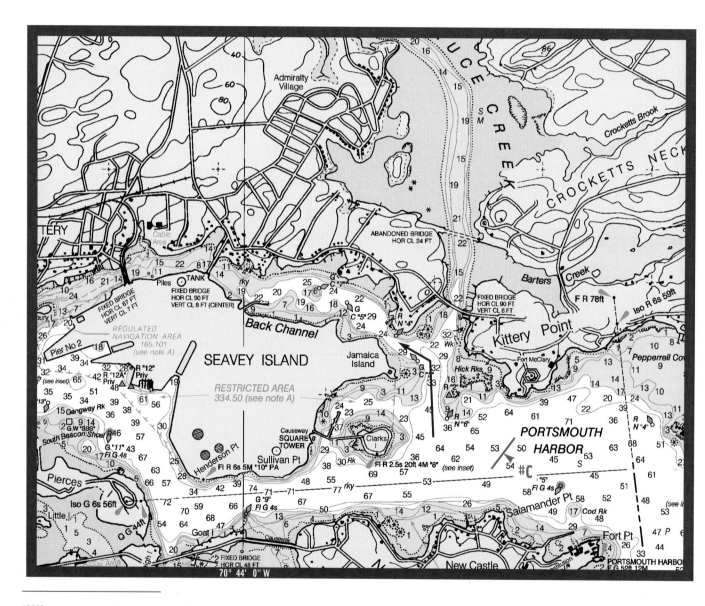

13283
19th ed., Feb. 05
NAD 83
Soundings in feet
1:20,000

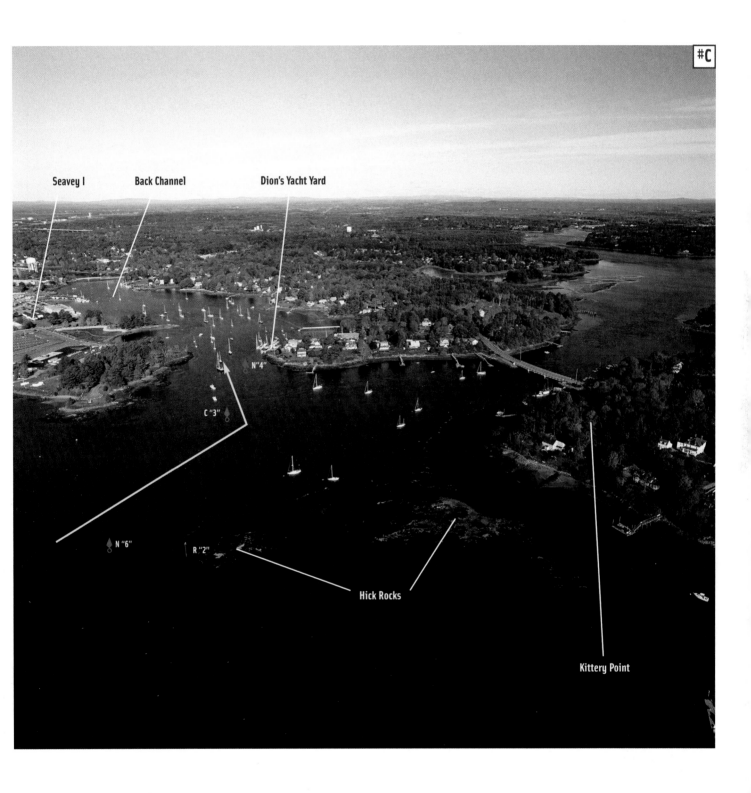

Seavey I

Back Channel

Dion's Yacht Yard

N"4"

C "3"

N "6"

R "2"

Hick Rocks

Kittery Point

#C

INDEX